THE KENNEDY CURSE

THE KENNEDY CURSE

Arthur Gatti

HENRY REGNERY COMPANY • CHICAGO

Library of Congress Cataloging in Publication Data

Gatti, Arthur, 1942-
    The Kennedy curse.

    1. Astrology.   2. Kennedy family—Miscellanea.
I. Title.
BF1728.K46G37   1976   133.5'8'973920922   76-3424
ISBN 0-8092-8213-5

Copyright © 1976 by Arthur Gatti
All rights reserved.
Published by Henry Regnery Company
180 North Michigan Avenue, Chicago, Illinois 60601
Manufactured in the United States of America
Library of Congress Catalog Card Number: 76-3424
International Standard Book Number: 0-8092-8213-5

Published simultaneously in Canada by
Beaverbooks
953 Dillingham Road
Pickering, Ontario L1W 1Z7
Canada

Contents

Introduction
1. Curses, Dooms, Prophecies, and Family Destiny   1
2. The Major Kennedy Tragedies   35
3. The Brightest Lights   39
4. What the Charts Tell Us about the Curse   99
5. The Assassins: Everyone's Questions   115
6. The Assassinations: Some Astrological Answers   131
7. The Kennedy Curse Unmasked   165
8. The Curse—Will Teddy Run Against It?   193
9. Is There a Curse on the American Presidency?   207

Appendixes
Astrological Basics   217
Planet/Sign Glossary   223
Kennedy Keywords   229
Critical Points in Suspects' Charts   241
Technical Approach to Synastry/Motive Analysis   245
Bibliography   253
Index   255

To Connie, and to my family
for all their encouragement and endurance;
and to the Hermans and Melniks
for their untiring collecting;
and to Marsha Kaplan
for her valuable professional support

Introduction

History will record that the decade from 1963 to 1973 was one of the most momentous in U.S. history.

After the McCarthyite stagnation of the fifties, the political face of this nation began to undergo great change. Civil rights activism led to the re-emergence of forces of the Left—unseen for a score of years. The two movements united to confront a war machine that had divorced itself from the sentiments of the people it was meant to serve. This New Left toppled a majority administration, it made people's hair grow, it turned them on to pot and peaceful behavior, but it also gave the nation a taste of anarchy and lawlessness which were the consequences of its general apathy.

Innovative and idealistic demands for improvements in representative government were echoed by a belligerently forthright, refreshing brand of politician. The new wave of young lawmakers saw themselves as picking up the torch shot out of the hands of the Kent State generation; eventually they were to set it to the flammable excelsior trappings of the Nixon White House, a house of cards and corruption that went up immediately under the media's cruel glare.

While the New Left may have given voice to what most Americans were beginning to feel, it was the media—television in particular—that started the whole thing rolling. Americans gradually came to invest more trust in their TV sets than in their chief executive, and there were good reasons, God knows. Watergate is only the most immediately rememberable.

John F. Kennedy's murder in Dallas was the final blow to a uniquely American sentimental optimism. The bitter war that followed somehow seems to have been our punishment for letting a president die. But, in 1963, how could we have known what plots were in the wind?

We might have known, except that those Americans who admired him chose, at some point along the way, to ignore his many limitations, chose to close their eyes to his human failings, which were also those of the Kennedys in general. Perhaps, as a consequence, we couldn't see what enemies may have been gathering to maliciously burst the bubble either. Once you have blinded yourself, you can no longer choose what to see and what not to see.

Force-fed the *Warren Commission Report*—and responding to a human impulse that is far more deeply ingrained in us than suspecting conspiracies—most people directed their hatred at the also-slain "lone assassin" of the Supreme Court chief justice's kaffee klatsch. Lee Harvey Oswald's guilt was easy to accept in a culture reared to do battle against a single human enemy embodied in Satan. It was, in the long run, far simpler to ignore the telltale clues that now seem to scream "frame or conspiracy,"—simpler to put all blame on one man who had already been dispatched by what appeared to be the quick hand of Providence, in a tight-fitting glove called Jack Ruby.

After his death I found myself, as though in a dream, answering Jack Kennedy's call to arms, wanting to take the torch "passed to a new generation" and to make a mark for America. I had given up the simplistic dream of my early youth that such service lies in surrendering to a grim military, in allying myself with The Bomb. There had to be other ways.

First, there was civil rights, the great cause that spread across the late sixties and early seventies. The movement was an affirmation of human cooperation, coexistence, and dedication to social ideals, as well as a denial of the inhuman institutions of isolation and ignorance. But before I could leave college, the war in Vietnam had caught fire. Teach-ins, organized marches took up all the spaces of my life and of the lives of hundreds of thousands like me who might have been dedicated to more self-serving—at least more peaceful—undertakings.

Although Jack Kennedy had been dead less than a year, my classmates and friends and I had gone a long way down the road of radical politics. Andy Goodman didn't come with me to work in Mexican barrios in the summer of 1964; instead, he went to keep a date with two brother civil rights workers named Schwerner and Chaney. Mario Savio didn't return to the place south of Mexico City where we had both worked the previous year; instead he went to get his beating along with all the rest in the Deep South of Freedom Summer. That fall he moved with his people to Berkeley, where the Free Speech Movement introduced student strikes as a means of holding up a mirror to the society it was striving to change.

After helping to set up the Queens College chapter of Students for a Democratic Society (SDS), in Flushing, New York, getting the antiwar machine rolling, and leaving it ready for the next wave of freshmen recruits, some of us went across the bay to Newark to work with Tom Hayden and others in community organizing. The Newark Community Union Project helped to politicize the black population, giving it the initial impetus to eventually topple a corrupt city regime—after which many other bailiwicks of corruption crumbled before a federal onslaught that swept the state of New Jersey like the plagues of Pharaoh.

For the white organizers like myself, the positive results of these years of involvement were harder to pinpoint. Many stayed in related areas, working in social services or teaching school. Some went the way of the fugitive and some dissolved to drugs or alcohol, while others took even stranger pathways.

Rennie Davis, the organizer of another urban project and a codefendant, along with Hayden, in the Chicago Seven trial, decided that the Guru Maharaj Ji was God and, apparently, the ultimate organizer. I turned astrologer.

To put it simply, in astrology I found structures to be analyzed that I could find nowhere else. When faith in religion goes, when social institutions become transparent and government becomes suspect, when national ideals are questioned wherever you turn, astrology is a way of seeing things clearly. I'm not a fatalist; when I'm analyzing my own future trends, I tend to be overly daring in my conclusions—simply to defy the concepts of predestination that fly in the face of personal freedom and evolution. I recognize such concepts to be tyrannical traps built into astrology by ancient metaphysics. But I'm a practical man, and I find that I must use what works best.

I approached astrology with all the sneering disrespect sixties radicals were caricatured for. Cocksure that over the centuries near-sighted men of science had missed their chance, I meant to discover the fatal flaw in this mystifying superstition that had survived for so long. If I couldn't demolish other targets in my gallery of dead minds, at least I would add astrology's scalp to my war belt.

Mine was a classic case of youthful hubris; events, and an unavoidably expanded consciousness, soon led me to stand in awe of all that astrology could tell someone who would take the trouble to develop and wield a proper sensitivity.

I spent a year in almost total isolation, emerging from my tiny Greenwich Village apartment only to attend classes or lectures in astrology at New York University (NYU), or to pick up the latest publication in the field. Astrology was my sustenance. Driving a cab part-time paid my rent and kept rice and beans in the pot.

In 1971 I became feature editor of *Sybil Leek's Astrology Magazine.* In the next two years more than a hundred of my own articles were published in its pages. Late in 1973 I accepted the managing editorship of a group of Warner Communications astrology publications, chief among them the monthly *Astrology Guide.* I wrote dozens of articles for those magazines in the group, as well as Dell's *Horoscope* and Llewellyn's *Astrology Now!* For the last chapter of her biography of Elton John (Popular Library/*Circus* magazine), Cathi Stein interviewed me about the superstar's natal horoscope.

For the photo-news monthly *In the Know,* I wrote a column

titled "Tomorrow's News," which created quite a stir for its accuracy. Some would call it "uncanny accuracy," but anyone knowledgeable about astrology would have expected that. "Tomorrow's News" was not a horoscope column based on the twelve signs, but one in which mini-readings were given to public figures, from politicians to entertainers. The approach was simple enough: constructing birth charts for celebrities, I scanned the future planetary factors and suggested probable trends that would be affecting their lives in the months ahead. There is nothing psychic or earth-shattering about this, such as one expects from the ESP people who predict earthquakes or tidal waves. My successful predictions have been low-key in comparison. I warned about Elvis Presley's glaucoma; a radical change in Liz Taylor's life at the close of the summer of 1975 (she remarried Richard Burton); vast changes in the life of Princess Grace of Monaco (her separation from the prince); Haile Selassie's midsummer crisis (preceding his death in August); and Patty Hearst's critical days early in September (when she was caught). In every instance, my writings have sought not so much to *prove* anything or to give someone an *answer*—prefabricated, custom-fitted, and effort-free—but to demonstrate astrology's efficacy.

I recognize that for every good astrologer there are two or three downright novices in the counseling game, several competent power-trippers and mesmerizing fatalists, and half a dozen "madams," "sisters," and "brothers" who play on people's fear, ignorance, and superstition and sometimes spell what they do "astrolegy." For this reason I have associated myself with professional organizations, many of which—like the American Federation of Astrologers (AFA)—are seeking to set standards in the field. This may be a good time to suggest that certification for astrologers who counsel others should include psychological testing, not just of novices but of long-established professionals as well.

I've been a member of the AFA for five years and for the past three have held the silver card of an Accredited Advanced Astrologer. I am also a charter member of the New York chapter of the National Council for Geocosmic Research, a group seeking to reopen the jammed doors of academia to astrology through a blending of disciplines: astrology, psychiatry, medicine, biology, statistics, and mathematics.

While this effort may take many lifetimes to accomplish, it seems worth it. We see extremes everywhere we look, and paradoxes are the human expressions of those extremes: Babe Ruth held the record for both hitting home runs and striking out, and scientists can be among the most and least objective of people. Recent attacks by scientists on astrology convince me that we've got a long way to go to place in perspective the last of the great sacred cows, the Scientific Method. Of course it's all a matter of political influence. Scientists may be the "professionals" but we astrologers are better at prediction, and that's what strikes the raw nerve.

Astrologers, in fact, are among the oldest known class of political advisors. Ancient kings never moved in the affairs of state without consulting with the chief stargazer. Someone, after all, was required to predict the outcome of a proposed action—be it war or treaty—and possibly incur the wrath of the gods (or the king) should his bold revelations fail to come to pass. I have no interest in guiding kings; rather, I prefer to use the machinery of wisdom and preparedness they have discarded to weigh the balance on the side of the lesser-armed.

We, the people, are the lesser armed in case of real conflict. Once, in our youthful innocence, some of us spoke hopefully of "when the Revolution comes." What is much more likely is that the revolution will arrive in the form of an armed-forces coup d'etat overthrowing an unwieldy popular government. Who will be on the side of us, the people?

Is astrology outdated? Is the future with statistical analysis computers? Perhaps, but you don't have to *plug in* astrologers. They hold the keys to mysteries that, without astrology, we could not even investigate.

Top-secret areas are not immune. Nothing is immune if only a few things are known about the events or people involved: the date of inception or birth, the exact time, and the place. Carl Jung said, "That which is begun this moment of time bears the markings of this moment of time," and I'll have to say that my experience as an astrologer and astrological journalist has borne this out. I hope that this book, this retrospective and foreshadowing of a fateful part of our lives, will be just as convincing to you, the reader.

While the original intent of this study of the Kennedys was to determine the family's destiny, indicated from composite family charts over the generations, the recent snowballing public concern over the assassinations of the Kennedy brothers has directed my interest to other areas. In the chapter on the assassinations, I have sought to show, using the sensitive tools of the astrologer, that others may bear more guilt than Lee Harvey Oswald in the first of recent assassinations, in Dallas, November 22, 1963.

Robert Kennedy's murder five years later is receiving closer scrutiny too. While Oswald is *said* to have committed the crime he was charged with, RFK's assassin, Sirhan B. Sirhan, was caught in the very act, smoking pistol in his hand. It would be foolish to look as closely into his chart as I have into Oswald's, for there is little question that Sirhan was indeed in Los Angeles doing what he was convicted of.

Yet the conspiratorial mysteries become compounded. New and long-suppressed evidence has prompted private researchers to call for a reopening of the investigation into the RFK assassination. More bullets than Sirhan's gun held in its chambers were recovered on the scene, they say; bullets from two different guns were found; and, according to some reports, the paths of certain bullets—notably the one that entered the senator's brain—came from locations *none* of the many witnesses have been able to place Sirhan in at that fatal moment.

Meanwhile, the public sits and waits, but it is seething these days. Bread and circuses do not lull us in these times of great political and economic uncertainty. Caught in one of the most urgent periods of our recent history, we are demanding better answers.

Those who felt strongly attracted to the murdered men may be motivated by a strong sense of justice or a simple need for vengeance. The more fervent hope should be that what guides us is an enlightened self-interest that demands not only that justice be done but also that the institutions of our young democracy be preserved at all costs. One of those costs may mean the rooting out of otherwise ancillary groups who have, quite simply, come into too much power. The American people must be sure that those they elect will be obeyed by paramilitary and police branches of our national services, that lives of these representatives will be as sacrosanct as the will of the people they (imperfectly) represent, and that rights to individual privacy take precedence over policies devised by groups who have been charged solely with protecting these rights. This is little enough to ask of our government—yet the task taken on by private researchers may already be far more than it's possible to ask of so small a group. There are no more than a hundred full-time unofficial investigators looking into the shadier operations of an intelligence community that numbers close to a quarter of a million, that is armed with the latest technology, and whose excessive budget comes from our tax dollars.

The phenomenon we have all learned to think of as the "Kennedy Curse" has substance, indeed, in the history of this family. It is *not* a curse as we have come to think of the term. What it *is* will be revealed in this book. But so, I hope, will be the roles of those conspirators who helped activate the curse. If this effort to undo our blindness is of any value, then it will have served its highest purpose: to show that astrology can, indeed, assist responsibly in guiding the public destiny.

THE
KENNEDY
CURSE

1

Curses, Dooms, Prophecies, and Family Destiny

The best known augury in history was that shouted at Julius Caesar from the crowds:

"Beware the Ides of March," thus spake Vestricius Spurinna.

The rest is not just history and drama, but a turning point in the glories of the ancient empires. Would it have been different—would the world now be some unimaginably different place had Caesar heeded the seer? All we know for sure is that Caesar had not just stubbornness on his side when he proceeded against all pleading to the senate that fateful afternoon; he had chosen another prophet, one that suited his fantasies better.

Augury had its heyday in Rome at that time, but Caesar resisted its spell. Yet he was not without respect for all prognostication. His boundless ego found metaphysical significance in the Sibylline Books, in one of which was written his favorite prophecy, that of a great king ascending to power in the East who was destined to conquer and unite all the peoples of the world and whose reign would usher in an age of splendor. Well-informed along these lines, Caesar was aware that "his" prophesied coming had also been foretold among the Gauls, Druids, Greeks, Jews, Egyptians, Indians, and Chinese, all of whom—chiefly through astrological reckoning—did in fact predict the coming of a Messiah.

Thus was Caesar able to shake the warning of Vestricius Spurinna as well as that of Calpurnia, his own wife, who, in a dream the night before her husband was to address the senate, saw her house crumbling about her and her husband stabbed and dying in her arms. This is classic hubris, which precedes classic tragedy. Choosing which auguries one will follow can indeed be dangerous; a life spent pursuing a personal interpretation of those auguries can be disastrous. So did Caesar err.

See how far he went in ignoring all the signs that might have warned him that he was, in fact on the wrong track:

> The impending death of Caesar was announced by the most patent of omens. A few months earlier, the colonists of Capua, who had emigrated thither in consequence of the Julian laws, came in the course of their building operations upon prehistoric graves. These they opened with all the more alacrity owing to the fact that they found in them many vessels of ancient craftsmanship. In the monument that served as a tomb for Capys, the founder of Capua, they discovered a bronze tablet bearing the inscription in Greek, with the content: "When once the houses of Capys are brought to light, then a branch of the Julian house will be slain by the hand of one of his kindred; his death, however, will soon be avenged by terrible occurrences in Italy."

This, according to its author, the historian Suetonius, had been related to Caesar months before the seer's warning. Yet did Caesar prevail against friend, wife, seer, and all common sense.

Classic tragedy, as I have pointed out, is preceded by classic hubris—the failure to recognize one's mortal limitations. Oedipus thought he could out-travel his fate, Achilles did not know every inch of his invulnerability well enough, and Caesar, as it might well be said, thought he was Jesus Christ.

Upon the birth of his son, Augustus (Octavian), Octavius was told by Nigidius Figulus, "You have given us a master." Nigidius was a renowned astrologer; however, Octavius was more a lover of democratic ideals than he was a father to his newborn, and so he asked Nigidius whether it would not be better if he killed his son, where-

Curses, Dooms, Prophecies, and Family Destiny 3

upon the astrologer convinced him that nothing could be done to the child. Fearing, one would suppose, to test the gods—who spoke, for all he knew, through Nigidius—Octavius let it be, and in so doing delivered to the world the first of the Roman emperors.

All of the oracles who were consulted—each augury made to decipher the young Augustus' future—foretold the greatness he would achieve; however, when the time came for him to accept the laurels of the emperor-god, he first consulted the most favored of his oracles, the Tiburtine Sibyl. For Augustus this was indeed an auspicious moment, and he was not unprepared for it. His consultation of the Sibyl was an action born of propriety by one who owed much to prophesy. He did not expect discouragement from the soothsayer. Seriously concerned with his image and role in the development of the Roman empire, he asked the Sibyl to consult her sacred books to see if the time was ripe to accept the great elevation. This priestess was not just a skilled augurer and magician but also an adept astrologer. She was, as were the most educated among the readers of the orbits of the planets, aware of what had first been discovered years earlier in the East: a backslipping of the relationship of planet Earth at its vernal equinox to the constellations and signs of the siderial zodiac.

Knowledge of the precession of the equinoxes was a basis for her augury, though certainly far too epochal to have immediately apparent personal meaning even for one so forceful upon the history of the world as Augustus Caesar. She did not, in fact, think at first to consider the question on a very grand scale, but—as do astrologers at all times—sought the relationships between the planets and lights in their current courses in the skies and those positions at the time of the querist's birth.

So she set about her task. Yet, before she could decipher many of the symbols, through the vast portals of her observatory flashed the bright white light of a meteor that cut a burning path across the night sky. This was the answer. Closing her book, she turned to Augustus and declared: "One world is ending and another is beginning." In this, she hinted at the change from the Age of Aries to the Age of Pisces, but went on to say: "A child born at this time, a king of the ages to come, is the true god of this world, yet he is humble of race and of birth. As yet, there is no hint of his divinity. When he reveals this, he will be persecuted. He will be a worker of miracles, he will be accused of dealings with unclean spirits, yet I see him triumphant in the end over death itself, rising from where his assassins have buried him. He will bring all nations together once again."

The transition from one great empire of the ancient world to the next seems particularly magical in the case of the transitional person between the splendor that was Egypt and the glory that was Greece. Nectanebo was the last of the Egyptian kings of the old dynasty's vast influence and unchallenged might. He was also renowned as an astrologer of the highest order, as he is said to have averted a planned assassination and was known to employ astrology and ritual magic to assure victory on the battlefield.

History tells us that Nectanebo was indeed a successful campaigner, and that his reign was blessed. It is said that he felt compelled to leave Egypt because of omens. The gods, men said of his sudden disappearance, were no longer favorable toward him in the exercise of his magic. Omens? Perhaps, yet there would certainly have been evidence enough, in his reading of his own planets and lights, to urge him on to other lands to give witness to history. Were they angry gods scolding him from Egypt, or *directives*—signs that told him "get thee hither" to where he would find that destiny—in Macedonia.

On the Thracian peninsula, in the foreign climes that had beckoned him, he found the love and appreciation befitting his office. Actually, he didn't let on that he was a self-exiled king of Egypt; instead, he claimed he was an incarnation of the god Amon. This ploy paid off by earning him the post of royal astrologer to King Philip of Macedonia.

Philip's wife was about to give birth, and Nectanebo/Amon was at her side, calculating away so as to astrologically read the moment. Firm in his words to Olympias, he urged her to hold the child within her until a most auspicious moment—the one he had seen in his charts.

The moment came, as did the phenomena accompanying it: Earth tremors startled the countryside, as thunder bellowed and lightning flashed the arrival of the child.

Curses, Dooms, Prophecies, and Family Destiny 5

"O Queen," beamed Nectanebo, as Alexander the Great bleated his arrival cry, "now thou hast given birth to a governor of the world."

Among earlier records of the service of astrologer priests to their lords is that of the princes Hi and Ho, court astrologers to Emperor Yao, three thousand years before the birth of Christ. In those days in China, the position of court astologer was an inherited office, and it is likely that in many instances unfavorable records were attached to these ministries for reasons that were traceable to the policy of heredity. Assured of such a fine position, few young nobles were willing to ruin their eyes in study, as did astrologers in many lands who had first to vie with an entire priesthood before attracting the attention of the ruler. In all but the case of the Chinese in the third millennium B.C., astrologer-priests to the nobility needed first to prove themselves through the accuracy of their predictions.

With Hi and Ho, none of this study effort was called for, and apparently little was given. Finally—blunder of blunders!—they failed to predict a solar eclipse (something the most novice Chaldean would have flunked third grade for). Emperor Yao charged them with "having done violence to the five fundamental forces and having idly abandoned the three fundamental regulations," for which the penalty was, of course, death.

As the power of absolute monarchs gradually declined throughout the world, prophesiers of every variety came to depend less and less upon the good will of the king for their continued well-being. Prominent families—always the source of monarchs' power, as well as the chief threats to the continuance of it—became major establishments within those societies. History swells with more or less supernatural accounts of the destinies of great families, how they fulfilled a certain great promise, how their heroism immortalized them, how they were elevated to eternally honored positions by the king (or through their opposition to the king), how they were supported by luck or local wizardry, and, on occasion, how they went without effective resistance to a preordained doom.

Chief among these latter legends are those of men, or lineages of men and women alike, who were on the receiving end of great and dire *curses*.

This book endeavors to ask what, exactly, a curse could be. Rather than believe what we are told—that someone cast a curse on someone else by saying what evil or painful manner of ending they or their families would come to—I take the initial position, at least, that we must believe only what we see: a negative prophesy of doom. When someone says: "May a giant camel trounce upon your pup tent," I take it to mean simply "A great camel shall trounce upon your pup tent." When and if this great camel comes along to my pup tent, I will take it to mean that the prophecy has come true. I have many historical precedents to draw from: prophesies of this sort have been verified by their coming to pass. But for the benevolent miracles of the great prophets, I have no evidence that the claim is true, simply because the (usually egomaniacal) curser/prophet *says* he or she is making a certain doom befall someone. On the other hand, I have every reason in the world to believe that they are displaying clairvoyance in seeing correctly into future events.

As for simple matters of faith, it would seem to me that such powers to effect events are reserved for those who put them to good, rather than spiteful, purposes.

The curse of the House of Cowdray is well known in English folklore. It stands as an example of the difficulty inherent in timing—and thus being in some way prepared for—the culmination of a curse.

Cowdray was once owned by a family named Browne, of which line one, Sir Anthony Browne, succeeded to the property in 1543 at the death of his half brother. Sir Anthony was a favorite among Henry VIII's retainers and was elevated to the honorable positions of Master of the Horse and Chief Standard Bearer. At that time, Henry, branded by Rome a damned renegade, busied himself dissolving the papal spheres of influence in England by confiscating and giving as gifts to his loyal followers the vast and opulent estates of the monasteries.

To Anthony fell a ripe plum in the estate and all buildings of Battle Abbey. Since he was not so ardent an ex-Catholic as Henry, by any means, his friends suspected Anthony might be a bit too squeamish to be involved in so heretical an undertaking. Nothing of

Curses, Dooms, Prophecies, and Family Destiny 7

the sort. He went about with great enthusiasm remodeling one of the larger buildings on the estate to create less ascetic, more creature-comfortable surroundings.

When the reconstruction was complete, Anthony hosted a great bash that had them coming in from all over the countryside to tilt a few and warm the house. (In those days, when you had a lot of people over for a house warming, that was exactly the point: they were there to help you, with their natural radiations—aided by flagons of ale and wine—to *warm the house!*) In the midst of the revelry, an uninvited monk muscled his way to the lord's table and, grim with his contained pious fury, cursed the man and his entire lineage for his desecration of the holy temple.

It must have been quite a party. Either the exact words of the dire prediction were recorded and then lost, or the liquor and morning-after blahs obscured all but the intent of the curse in the memory of those who heard it. It is sufficient to say that the monk pronounced the following as punishment for Anthony's transgressions: that by fire and water would the House of Cowdray and the line of Anthony Browne be destroyed.

Well, as hangover memories mercifully fade, so too did all but the dimmest of recollections among neighbors and kin of the words of the understandably distraught cleric. Had someone made a point of seeing to it that the fate of the Brownes be watched closely, he or she would have had to pass the task down as far as their great-great grandchildren until, that far removed from a busy descendant's schedule, it would have doubtless been dropped simply because absolutely nothing of great interest happened to the Brownes in 250 years.

They had their high moments at court before—like so many others far less blessed with longevity of royal favor—eventually slipping into royal oblivion. What about the monk's pronouncement?

The answer to our question lies in the year 1793, and in a generation of Brownes both unmoved by, or simply unaware of, the fascinatingly terrifying doom that was *supposed* to befall the line. So unwary—so unprepared!

The main character had been elevated in the English nobility by this time, for Queen Elizabeth had conferred the title of Viscount Montague on an heir of Anthony Browne's. By the fateful year of 1793, the line had progressed as far as the eighth Viscount Montague. This young rake was the imprudent descendent foolish enough to go in for water sports and, while on vacation along the Rhine, insisted on shooting the rapids at Schaffhausen Falls.

"By water" died the foremost male of the lineage—but what of the fire? Had modern communications been available to the young viscount, an old retainer might have been on the phone, the words of the centuries-old curse suddenly recalled, warning the young man: Cowdray Castle had burned to the ground (a scullery maid clumsy with her bucket of coals?) a week earlier. Surely, for anyone concerned who had ever heard of the curse on this family, the fact that the centuries-old castle had been destroyed by fire would have caused a moment's pause to recollect where the owner of the family jewels had gone off to. Off to the *shore,* you say?

Thus did the Curse of Cowdray become fulfilled. The lands went to the young viscount's sister. A distant cousin, a *monk,* was made the ninth Viscount Montague. Since it was his duty to maintain the line, he received dispensation to marry. But the curse was a relentless one, the marriage was fruitless, and he died leaving no heir. The final spadeful was thrown on the genealogical records of a cursed family named Browne.

The gloomy moors of Scotland provide us with the setting of still another Gaelic curse, that of the House of Seaforth, in the 1660s.

Kenneth McKenzie, the third Earl of Seaforth, had the singular misfortune to wed a shrewish commoner whose indomitable temper and carping ways soon drove him to travel extensively on whatever business he could drum up. However, the woman, being even more incensed by his response to her demonstrated concerns, only grew more shrewish.

Coincidently, in nearby Strathpeffer there lived, in a cave, a prominent seer, also by the name of Kenneth McKenzie. This renowned personage, known to most as the Warlock of the Glen, was summoned before the wife and friends of the powerful Earl of Seaforth. "Gaze into the whereabouts of the Laird," she de-

Curses, Dooms, Prophecies, and Family Destiny   9

manded of him. He was initially reluctant, noting her hysterical demeanor; however, once he sighted in on the Laird he was overcome by a most mischievous bout of mirth, causing the livid lady to hurl angry threats against his life unless he revealed what he saw. Finally, he admitted to her that her husband was indeed in Paris, as she had suspected. This, though galling, pleased her, as those gathered about looked at her in awe, recognizing her *own* very keen senses; however, the fully revealed vision had quite another effect. For it turned out that the seer had perceived the laird in the presence of two very young ladies, one of whom was sitting on his lap whilst the other toyed with his locks.

Adding great insult to great injury, the seer had unwittingly humiliated the powerful lady of the manor before her every friend and supporter. Bitch that she was—her reaction shocked even the most merciless of the landlords present. She harkened back to some barbarian divine right of nobility to put to death the poor, miserable messenger chosen to deliver the bad news, and in her impious fury ordered her guard to execute the Warlock of the Glen. Those with the slightest sense knew it was much too daring to tamper with the supernatural in so severe a way. Ah, but she was enraptured by her own urgent passions and hatreds and was willing to play even such a game. But, as in all games, there is something at stake, some token to be purchased, some dues to pay somewhere. In her case however, the only thing of value she played with was her husband's very fate, and that of all who followed him in his line.

Before he died, Kenneth McKenzie, the seer, foresaw and with great relish related to a slack-jawed gathering the coming destiny of Kenneth McKenzie, Earl of Seaforth. The following is quoted from *The Prophecies of the Brahan Seer,* by someone named McKenzie:

"I see into the future," the seer is reported to have said, "and I read the doom of the race of my oppressor. This long-descended line of Seaforth will, 'ere many generations have passed, end in extinction and in sorrow. I see a chief, the last of his house, both deaf and dumb. He will be the father of four fair sons, all of whom he will follow to the tomb. He will live careworn and die mourning, knowing that the honours of his line are to be extinguished forever, and that no future chief of the McKenzies shall bear rule at Brahan or in Kintail. After lamenting over the last and most promising of his sons, he himself shall sink into the grave and the remnants of his possessions shall be inherited by a white-coifed lassie from the east, and she is to kill her sister. And as a sign by which it may be known that these things are coming to pass, there shall be four great lairds in the days of the last deaf and dumb Seaforth—Gairloch, Chisholm, Grant and Raasay—of whom one shall be buck-toothed, and another harelipped, another half-witted and the fourth a stammerer. Chiefs distinguished by these personal marks shall be the allies and neighbors of Seaforth; and when he looks around him and sees them, he may know that his sons are doomed to death, that his broad lands shall pass away to the stranger, and that his race shall come to an end." (See also: Burke, *Vicissitudes of Families*.)

Over a hundred years elapsed before anything happened. It was 1770. War and politics caused the title of Earl of Seaforth to change hands several times. And then it came to pass. . . .

His name was Francis Humbertson McKenzie, and he became earl by stroke of luck and of the enemy swords that slew both his brother and his second cousin. Since age twelve, Francis Humbertson McKenzie had been deaf and dumb from scarlet fever. He had managed to cure his dumbness but remained deaf all his days. Little hindered, he advanced the glories of his line, as well as his family's status, by becoming invested as Earl of Seaforth and, not at all secondarily, by sireing three (not four) sons and six daughters.

I imagine that by this time neighbors and tenants would have begun to sit up and take notice. The infamy of the seer's execution would live forever, and there were few who doubted that the McKenzies of Seaforth would meet a fate with all the gloomy weight that had been prophesied. Once the old family tomes had been dug out for the exact reference, and perhaps some of the forgotten details, the worry would have quickly turned to panic, for had they but looked around it would have suddenly dawned upon them that the moment of the elaborate curse was at hand.

There lived at the time, as neighbors and allies of Seaforth, four rather powerful lairds, all suffering from the afflictions that were predicted to be the signs of impending doom: MacLeod of Raasay stammered, Sir Hector McKenzie of Gairloch was bucktoothed, Chisholm of Chisholm was harelipped, and Grant of Grant was half-witted (by whatever scale wits might have been measured in those days). It was understandable that the tenants who depended on Seaforth were half-witless with fright and foreboding.

At that time, the earl—as yet, one would suppose him ignorant of the part he was to play in the grim tableau—fell under severe financial distress. To extricate himself, he decided to sell some of the family's gift lands. These were the "broad lands" referred to in the prophecy, and naturally the tenants took desperate steps to prevent this fulfillment. Poor as they may have been, they raised a great sum and sent it to the earl with the expressed hope that he would not let go of his land.

But the earl's gambling debts were always hounding his heels, and he eventually disposed of his property, great portions of which were "sold to the stranger."

One after another, McKenzie's sons died. By now all too aware of the prophecy, the lord watched as the last of them perished; embittered and forlorn by his powerlessness against the prophesy, he himself gave up the ghost, leaving no male heir. The estate reverted to a distant collateral, and so died the noble lineage of the McKenzies.

And to prove that the dying prophet's words were the true expressions of an unrelenting Providence, the unfulfilled parts of the prophecy fell neatly into place shortly after the laird's death.

A daughter of the earl, widowed only a week, received the sad news of her father's passing. Returning to claim the estate as her inheritance, she arrived at Seaforth from the east—where her husband had been serving with his majesty's fleet—dressed in a widow's cap and weeds: "a white-coifed lassie." Shortly thereafter, while she was driving in a pony cart with her younger sister, Caroline, one of the horses bolted, throwing both women and fatally injuring the younger.

It happened—or so they say—as I have told it. Who can explain such precise and fearful accuracy? And who ventures a guess as to the mechanism?

Are we to assume that, because Mr. or Ms. X, a wronged party, has a valid complaint, that any dire pronouncement he or she makes must then come true? If that were so, then this world would be more cussed (pun intended) than it actually seems to be.

I prefer to think of cursers as psycho-sadists of sorts—those who bring all the power of the curse to bear on their victim (oppressors, whatever) through their own resources. Cursers reach an emotion-induced trance state at the moment of the prophetic vision, for that is precisely what the curse is—simply the pronouncement of the prophetic vision. The curser no more *causes* the elements to fall into place than does the doctor who, through his diagnosis and subsequent revelation to his patient, causes the patient to have the disease described. Right? Not exactly. While there may seem to be no possibility of a causative relationship (because the vision, or the diagnosis, is supposedly an external and future reality, only a glimpse of which has been granted the observer), *both seer and doctor can help the patient or client along the grim path to full realization of the particular affliction by pronouncing it.* Simply by pronouncing it. A doctor can do a patient severe psychological and, ergo, psychosomatic damage by fully describing a particular condition rather than concentrating on the cure. The curser, of course, *intends* to enhance the fate by pronouncing it. This added element of premature revelation not only enlivens the sadistic glee of the vengeful pronouncer but also creates an atmosphere that further predestines the situation. (I say "further" precisely because I can never accept the absolute inevitability of *anything*. There's always room for change. There's a lot more to be said for enlightened free will and the part it plays in our seemingly empatterned lives.)

Such vengeful curses we might better classify as "pronouncements of doom." The *Bhagavad-Gita* says that the only sin is giving advice that is not wanted. Under that admirable code of ethics, the curser's offense is seen as a greater abomination than any injustice that may have been done him or her. It is against the law in New York State—as it is in many states—to offer a dire prediction, and well it should be. We've all heard of the psychological phenomenon called "self-fulfilling prophecies." It is

Curses, Dooms, Prophecies, and Family Destiny 13

real. Astrologers must treat it more severely than the Christians do their devil, for it is a real demon because it literally destroys the will. Such is my catechism. Tell a person that he will fail a college course because it's in the stars and, unless he possesses uncommon will or stubbornness, he is likely to become so depressed at the news that he will actually be unable to study.

Yet, in one of the cases mentioned above, the main character knew nothing whatsoever of his impending doom. Did the seer's doomsaying miss affecting *his* psychological environment? Not likely. Looming over the recognized psychological phenomenon just mentioned, is the parapsychological. And this, too, must be reckoned with, as we shall see in the case of cursed objects.

Some modern parapsychologists would contend that, although a man had no experiential knowledge of a grave pronouncement that has threatened his existence, the fact that his ancestors did know might be enough to instill somewhere within him the same realization. That somewhere, contend this radical few, is in the chromosomes. Thus, a grave psychological disturbance, induced by the pronouncement of a "curse," could be so implanted in the memory and so afflict the vitality as to be passed on as familial, sub- or supra-level of a more long-term racial consciousness. The implications of this reach far into realms dreamt of by the biology-is-destinyists.

The analysis of more staid parapsychology researchers, themselves nurtured by an age of spiritualism, would be more in keeping with modern theories regarding extrasensory perception. The power of prayer has been *verified* in the laboratories. Prayer is, like any other impassioned communication, an activity fed by the emotions. The stronger the emotions, the more trancelike the prayer meeting becomes; it has been shown that, when in a trancelike state, most subjects register increases in ESP.

Well, that's prayer—but what about those neighbors of the laird? I don't know if they prayed very hard, but they certainly lived in a cloud of gloom and dread—worried, thinking, thinking, constantly thinking *at* the man who sat at the head of the manor table. Who knows how many thousands of times tipplers at the alehouse recounted each word of the curse? How many children had nightmares about the doom, related to frighten them by sneering older brothers and sisters?

What then, is a curse? Are we to take it at face value, decide that any given mortal may take it upon him- or herself to alter the destiny of another—and succeed? We must surely know better by now. I believe there is truth in the findings of ESP specialists who claim that, while wishing another ill can make one equally ill, such concentration upon the more negative aspects of another—an enemy's life, for example—cannot help but cause him or her to receive, to some extent, your intentions on one or another level of manifestation. However, it would take a lot of such negative praying to seriously affect the matter. While we can say that a lot of negative prayers were sent Hitler's way, and we can see what it did to him, what about the other dictators and tyrants who survive? Even if the ministers or pronouncers of curses had thought such dark thoughts at their enemies all their lives, certainly at their deaths one would expect the gloom to dissipate. But it isn't so.

That mortals should not be able to lay such transgenerational heavy trips on people seems the metaphysically logical—or, at least, the just—thing to expect. But no, the essence of a curse is in something else. Take away all the satanic, liturgical trappings, take away the rituals, the fact of the dire moment of the pronouncement, the seemingly malevolent powers of the speaker, and you are left with one thing: the pronouncement. This is the sentence, as it were, the divine verdict thrown into the mud by grimy mortal hands, its syllables spittled out by a grotesque face red with rage. As a gesture, the curse is the supreme insult, for it says to its object person: "I know something very sensitive about your life or about something you hold quite dear—it's quite a lousy piece of information— and here, for all your enemies to gloat over and your children's children to lose sleep over, it is: . . . " (Cursers, fill in the blanks.)

The curse is traditionally the pronouncement of what will soon—or eventually—come to pass. It is the very private vision of a very twisted clairvoyance. It is brought on by unusual stress caused the visionary by the person or persons who are objects of the pronouncement. Very often, the vision is a complete one, even down to the very last detail, as in the case of the Seaforth curse, wherein the pronouncer went so far as to describe the characteristics and tell the names of neighbors, *witnesses* to the last moments of the curse.

But various forms of derangement have been known to accompany the pronouncer's visionary powers and render them unable to communicate on normal human levels. Thus, the history of great curses contains many whose wording is deceptive and vague, often falling from tongues in the form of apocalyptic verse.

I do not intend to go into other areas in which curses seem to operate. My belief, and all my observations regarding curses pronounced by human beings, tell me two basic things: first, that very often, in an incensed trance, one can see and announce to the one who has caused injury what dire fate may await them. Since I do not believe in an unalterable fate, the second observation—gleaned from what we know from modern psychology—is most significant: that any pronouncement can act both psychologically and parapsychologically to *help the event predicted to actually occur.*

This general conclusion would then suggest a few things about the seer who pronounces the curse: He or she may actually be having a clairvoyant experience; the seer may simply sense a doom hovering over a person or family and, with demagogic force, fabricate a scenario for that doom that those cursed may help bring about on their own; and there is also the very strong possibility that many curses that come to pass are pronounced by egomaniacal super-demagogues with very little in the way of supernatural inspiration backing up his or her imagery. In this instance, the personality of the pronouncer will usually be found to be electric, and the manner of presentation may approach the hypnotic. This will often be accompanied by a subconscious acceptance of that doom by the accused. Very often, there will also be widespread local awareness of the curse, and it may even have become a part of local folklore.

Both the acceptance by the community and fatalistic expectation on the part of the accursed contribute heavily to the curse's manifestation. Not only are there psychological implants bringing about the common phenomenon of the "self-fulfilling prophecy," but there are, as well, probabilities of parapsychological influences equal to, if not stronger than, the psychological. I'm referring here, again, to "the power of prayer" and what can simply be thought of as general mind power, or thought power. That any being is conscious of a thing or event not yet experienced seems to add to the abstract bank account of that reality; and eventually a withdrawal is made and something happens on the material plane. When an entire community waits for something drastic to happen, whether the person to whom it's supposed to happen is aware of the doom or not, in the "second state" (or parapsychological plane, in which all souls are supposedly one) the person cannot escape the myth that has been imposed upon him.

Curses, then, are not so much a matter of holy visions and privileged communications that come to often questionable messengers, but are very often only the perverse personal power of an individual that may or may not survive his or her death.

Curses seem to exist in things and places, too. We have all heard of the curse of the Hope Diamond and of the Mummy's (Tutankhamen's) Tomb. In rare instances we may attribute certain elements of the self-fulfilling prophecy to a curse. If, shall we say, an archeologist unearths the tomb of a powerful ancient potentate and discovers an inscription, which when translated turns out to be a curse, it is equally possible for even so academic a person to react as would the ancient noblemen. In moments of depression, as one waits for a subway train, if it is "written" that the person will die in a horrible way, and he or she cannot dismiss that possibility, the chances of an "accidental slip" increase immensely.

Why believe such things? Everyone has a reason. Archeologists dig in tombs and look for bones. They must have more than their share of grimness in life, seeing always how fleeting life is.

In the case of owners of the incredibly valuable Hope Diamond, might we suggest that, glutted by their own materialism, they may have been prime candidates to "buy" the fatality of that fabulous rock?

This last idea may, in the long run, prove too easy. People who were never told that opals are unlucky for all but those born with the Moon, Sun, or Ascendant in Libra, have reported afterward that troubles began to plague them soon after coming into the possession of an opal. Now, of course, serious error awaits in such retrospective judgment—in the reporting of normal vicissitudes but putting the blame on some irresistable supernatural force. Yet, I don't think we can so easily dismiss the possibility that there are untoward energies in the gems themselves.

No one, for example, has yet offered a satisfactory explanation of why astrology works, why energies interrelate how and when the astrologers say they will. Few are able to offer explanations satisfactory to modern physics as to why various ESP or second state phenomena occur. With this great scientific canyon facing the student of the energies available to man, we can expect to discover far, far more than we already know about the various kinds of energies and their vehicles. Only very special gems can conduct the energies drawn from light that scientists call laser. It is not going too far out on a limb, then, to postulate a time when science will discover that, say, opals—or diamonds *faceted* in a certain way—conduct certain energies that may be related to depressed psychological and parapsychological states.

In a final look at the tombs of ancient kings, it must be pointed out that recent findings tend to prove that *pyramids* can be power generators of sorts. Besides being protective of the god-kings housed within, the power was supposed to send their souls' energy streaming to a distant star and to preserve their bodies for millennia. That power, then, may have been so controlled that it would activate like a karmic klaymore mine at the moment someone vaulted a key barrier.

There are few hints as to how this might occur, yet we must remain open to the possibilities and explore as many as come our way. There is a strong likelihood that pyramids act as generators albeit the energies they utilize are unknown to us. They may also serve as storehouses: Legions of priests—even 5,000 years dead—may have saturated a particular area with fatally negative emanations (prayers, "bad vibes," etc.) to assault any who violate the area. Tombs within pyramids, then, may be inhabited by the corporate spirits of such priests—super-Harpie spirits that follow transgressors to the ends of the earth and beyond.

While this may seem a bit much, consider the very probable psychological and parapsychological explanation offered for the phenomenon of prayer chain-letters that seem to work. There are scores of reasons why an individual might "get lucky" after getting and passing on one of those prayer chains, chief among them probably being connected to all the expectation that permeates the mindless, almost trancelike ritual of preparing twenty copies of anything. What fascinates even more are the accounts that come along with such prayer chain letters warning of what may happen if you *break* the chain. This suggestion—that, as in the case of Harry Smith of Salt Lake City (who broke his back in two places and totaled his brand new Fleetwood after tearing up and throwing away his letter), bad fortune will plague *you* too, if you don't keep the chain—*is a curse.*

Rather than helping a friend by sending along one of those chain letters, you increase the person's accident potential should they choose not to honor the communication. Not only does not keeping the chain implant the possibility of doom psychologically, but, parapsychologically, the belief built up in the power of the letter contains not just the positive elements of every participant, but also their deeper negative hopes that all the doom suggested will afflict someone else—in the context of the letter, the s.o.b. who doesn't take the time to grind out his or her twenty copies.

Following this logic of negative implants, we must come to recognize a curse when we see one: Next time you watch a commercial on television (itself quite a hypnotic medium) notice not so much what is *said,* but what is *implied.* Very often, a simple TV ad will show a "beautiful person" who is beautiful only by virtue of the sponsor's product; there may be an unattractive person compared to the beautiful one—unattractive because he or she does *not* use the sponsor's product. Or else, we are shown a totally idyllic state that few of us ever reach and are told that that state is reachable only through the sponsor's product. In either case, the implication is not only that we need something that we may not want, but also that if we *refuse* to get it we are doomed to lead a wretchedly ordinary life. The head of J. Walter Thompson may not wear sackcloth and carry a dimly glowing staff, but you can be sure that he's got his spectral fingers in parts of our psyches we don't even know we have yet.

Of course, if itinerant prophets capable of sudden doomsaying were the only means people had by which to read their own destinies, we would be in a sad and fatalistic state. Most of the cave-dwelling seers throughout ancient history were, to say the least, disenchanted with the societies they found themselves in. They were ascetics, for the most part, eschewing the comforts of the wealthy who often came to them for great enlightenment and were sent away with as much chastisement. At times, this chastisement cost the seer his life, as in the case of the Seaforth prophecy and in the most famous of such cases—that of John the Baptist. Seers who get carried away have been known to lose their heads and vice versa.

Mavericks in every sense, such prophets were set upon for their visions. Had they been the solitary representatives of occult arts and sciences, they would have been banished forever from all but the most libertarian of nations. In the authoritarian theocracy of Salem, Massachusetts, in the late 1600s, such a banishment and eternal damnation almost succeeded.

Seers who were known to pour favorable prophecies over the troubled brows of their lords and employers to salve their spirits were always in demand, especially if their prophecies were in the habit of coming true; this latter consideration was less important, though, than one might assume. People of wealth simply didn't want to know about bad times awaiting them. Unlike the educated of our own time, the more learning one had then, the more one believed in the inevitability of fate.

As the nobility grew more educated, however, scientific methodology, such as it was, became a fascination. If an occult method could be both applied to reading the future *and* analyzed or understood in its actual workings (unlike the clairvoyant vision), it grew in appeal. Numerology, astrology, palmistry, and myriad other methods developed or were revived as the rich grew more sophisticated. Yet when almost anyone could learn methods of reading his or her own destiny, consulting the *experts* retained its glamor and certainly its respectability.

Of course, as we have seen, in the case of those laying a curse on the unlucky victim, the act of foreseeing was not at all carried out in a selfless, hoping-for-the-best attitude of cosmic community service, but in a spirit of fiendish glee—the more horrible the fate perceived, the more fiendish the glee. But only an injured seer was *dangerous;* the others were the voices of the Fates, to be consulted only when one was certain that one could deal with the information and, if need be, remake one's entire life according to prescribed moral guidelines or any other trip plan.

Generally, the pronouncements of the most famous seers were curiously metaphoric. What did it mean to young Oedipus that such a gifted emissary of the gods as Tireseus should tell him that he would kill his father and marry his mother? He didn't know that he didn't know his true parents. The safest move for anyone consulting such oracles would have been for the questioner—once given such an answer as the above, so seemingly clear a reply—to ask once more what does the *answer* mean? Had Oedipus followed this vital guideline he might never have had a play written about him.

In ancient times, priests were summoned by the rich to read the prevalent omens at the moment of the birth of the heirs. Today one goes to visit the psychic usually in a large auditorium. In the United States, the role of the psychic revealer was forever sanctified by the gentle personality and charitable works of a man named Edgar Cayce.

Edgar Cayce is a more vivid—if less widely known—figure in American folklore than all of its Paul Bunyons and Johnny Appleseeds put together. His amazing contacts with the astral plane have given him a reputation that goes far, far beyond the domain of the common soothsayer, and perhaps this was so because of his inspired notion of love and service to his fellow man. Cayce did not simply say, "And this shall be." When he *read* a person, it was more as though he had written an encyclopedia.

When Cayce spoke during a "life reading," he spoke from the great distances of a deep trance. He said not only what was to be, but what once was. What of those past earthly incarnations? If blood relationship is so karmic, tying us so closely together on all planes, then it would stand to reason that there are connections on the other planes of existence Cayce peered into, as well as in the flesh of past existences. The readings bear this out. Throughout the records of the years of life readings given by this amazing man can be found numerous accounts of the relationships in past lives between parents and offspring. In many of these, while the parents and child may still have been related by family, it was often the case that the child was parent to the mother or father, or that some other familial relationship was in effect. In some cases the relationships were more spiritual: parents were inspirations or goads to their children in other lives.

Cayce did not, however, trace an entire lineage, nor was he interested in the worldly, continual destiny of a particular family. And so, his tie-ins were of a nongenealogical, person-to-person nature.

His readings do tell us, though, that destiny ties those of us sharing lineage in a clearly evident way. His readings were a means of guiding parents in the upbringing of their children through understanding and trying to recall or realize the lessons of past experiences, which were, if not the same in terms of relationships, at least closely analogous. Thus, if a father was once a serious goad, or rival, to his son in a past life, it would be best to watch for conflicts arising again in this lifetime. Cayce's predictive record was usually preserved in these deductions; the study institute he began, the Association for Research and Enlightenment, has followed his words over the decades and has done follow-up reports on a good number of the lives read for.

But then, there are few Edgar Cayces born. The rest of us, determined to lift the veil of the future and urged on by meddlesome-social-worker motivations, must first learn well the skills of the veil-lift operator. One of those skills is knowledge of the secrets of numbers.

The implications of the occult science of numerology to the reading of a family's destiny seem the most obvious of all. The basic mechanics of numerology show that each letter of one's name has a numerical value. Added together these values give a numerical total for one's name—always reduced by being added together until the result is a number from one to nine, or eleven, or twenty-two. Thus, if the letters in your name add up to sixty-nine, this would be reduced to fifteen by adding six and nine; then one would be added to five to get six, the final reduction. Readings for each number describe the individual's basic character, talents, propensities, and probable course in life.

There are several other ways of arriving at significant numbers. One is to take readings for the individual parts of our names. In such readings, the family name will reveal the similarity of numerical character that we inherit from our forebears. Did you ever notice how similar the lives of the men in a family are when they are named John Smith, John Smith II, John Smith III, etc.? The numbers II or III at the end of a name are not totalled in, so we essentially get a carbon copy of the same individual. Of course nothing is that precise—no one is ever *exactly* the same as someone else, and in a good number of instances, an offspring's own decision-making prowess will make him stand out among the rest. Still, the very clay matter of his life is likely to be quite unchanged for several generations.

Destiny heredity in numerology is everywhere apparent. Ancestors in the dark and distant past have given us all the karmic implications of our family names; down to the wire of the present generation, our parents have called from the depths of their own psyches an image that is to be a name and thus a piece of a fate that each of us must carry for a lifetime.

The basic link between biology, character, and destiny grows more and more convincing; in the case of the biology we call heredity, that heredity always has a name, and even those names themselves speak to us of things that are and things that are to be. Archetypes, too, are transmitted to us by the meanings of our names. What do you think, Mr. Listener, Mrs. or Ms. Reader, Stone, de Jesus, Ember, Hope, Fiorello, Frank, Goldman, Grimm, or Merry?

The links between biology and character and destiny manifest themselves in unexpected places. Who, after all, would look for the meaning of life in the palm of one's hand? Who indeed?

The left hand in palmistry represents the character and destiny we were biologically endowed with. If you study both your hands, you will discover a slight dissimilarity. The right hand represents to the palm reader what you've *done* with your potential, as seen in the left.

Curses, Dooms, Prophecies, and Family Destiny   23

Reading your hands over a period of time will reveal even more amazing things. As you study harder, the head line on your right hand will become deeper, broader; if you put a strain on your heart, you may find the heart line growing thin, or perhaps developing wavy crosslines. Sudden occurrences appear as sudden markings: a mole on your line of Saturn might indicate a career setback; an island on your line of life (an island is an enclosed grouping of two or more lines forming an ellipse, oval, diamond, or circle) might mean a recovery from a near-serious illness or a close call of some other sort.

The length of lines, obstructions, cross-running lines, and so on, are the signs by which palmists read the future and time events. Yet can a common family destiny be found herein? The answer—again, yes—serves to further the idea that what is true in one discipline of the occult is generally true in the others. (Palmistry and astrology are closely related. Both Nostradamus and Cayce translated visions into astrological symbolism, even though Cayce knew nothing of the ancient art.)

Family destiny gets passed down in hands in hundreds of different ways; there are that many markings to assimilate or be on the alert for. Common physical traits are the most likely to be inherited. Deep, long, broad lines of life indicate a hearty physical type who has a good chance to live a long time; conversely, a thin line of life crossed several times by horizontal lines indicates a life of low vitality and illness.

Marked tendencies show: two artists may have a child with a conical hand, thus indicating his natal propensity to follow creative urges. The gnarled or knotty knuckles of the philosophical hand may combine in a child with a strong line of Neptune, one who ardently pursues his parents' religious or metaphysical beliefs.

This method of destiny reading is, unfortunately, useless to my study of the Kennedy family. No palm prints of the dead Kennedys exist, to my knowledge, and I'm reasonably sure that the average Kennedy would be just as reluctant to be photographed in the nude as to expose him- or herself to further analysis of any kind. Anyway, historically, palm reading proves useless to the study of transgenerational propensities or fate. The data simply does not exist.

Some elements of fated behavior might be seen in the immediate generations of Kennedys by using palmistry, yet it is difficult to clearly define this behavior. *Some* elements of familial destiny can be understood in each of the methods outlined, yet never quite enough. In searching for the perfect language of symbols, through which the knowledge of one is the knowledge of the many, most occultists come to rest at the mother of the sciences, astrology.

Astrology is the tool I will use in this study of the Kennedys. Its appeal has remained great throughout the ages for several reasons: It is far less hard to swallow than most other methods and it depends less on the powers or talents of an intermediary, as nearly every person who applies him- or herself can become proficient.

While it was chief among the fatalistic pseudosciences throughout most of its history, we must recognize that fatalism was the paramount characteristic of much of the religion that existed during astrology's earliest development. Today it needs to be neither pseudoscientific nor fatalistic. Computers across the entire world are assisting astrologers by compiling verifiable findings. Astrology's main connection with scientific methodology remains in gathering *empirical evidence* and not in reasoning techniques. And people feel it to be a controllable factor in judging the future and not a mystical voice that will tell them what *must* be.

The healthiest perspective seems to be of astrology as *cosmic ecology*—part of an earthly, political, economic, and psychological universe we all live in. The warnings we glean from astrological readings may be used to convince us to "stay in bed," or to forearm ourselves so as to maintain our places or advance them, as the case may be, within our own particular scheme of things. We may use the stars, in other words, to excuse our slavish behavior, or we may be *their* masters. "The fault, dear Brutus, lies not in our stars, but in ourselves, that we are their underlings."

Not at all an absolute in terms of what an astrologer sees in the future, astrology is instead a storehouse of affinities, the knowledge of which can help each and every one of us *transcend* the destinies read for us. So, when something seems dangerous to a family's development, an astrologer might simply see what *alternatives* are

Curses, Dooms, Prophecies, and Family Destiny

present in the same celestial configuration that symbolizes that danger, then advise his client accordingly. This is what I have done at the close of my study on the doom that seems to hang over the Kennedys.

In analyzing a family's destiny, astrologers go first of all to the symbols or configurations that repeat themselves in charts spanning generations. Within these symbols lie the keys to the common destiny each individual shares.

What follows are a few examples of how this works in simple parent/child or sibling relationships, those spanning only two generations, sometimes within just one. As you will see later, the number of generations that can be studied, so as to arrive at the most accurate analysis of their common destiny, is limited only by the availability of birth information.

Father and Daughter: John and Hayley Mills

To begin with, in this parent-child relationship we find a personal closeness and what we might call a complementary similarity. At best there is a mild complementary quality to people born under adjacent signs; in this case, however, there is a *conjunction* of both natal Suns.

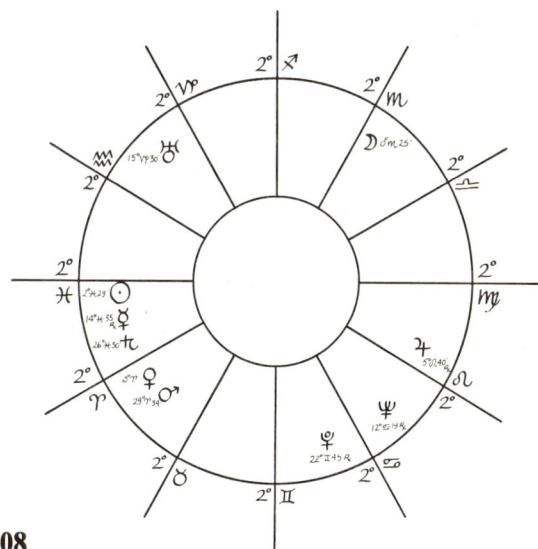

John Mills
February 22, 1908

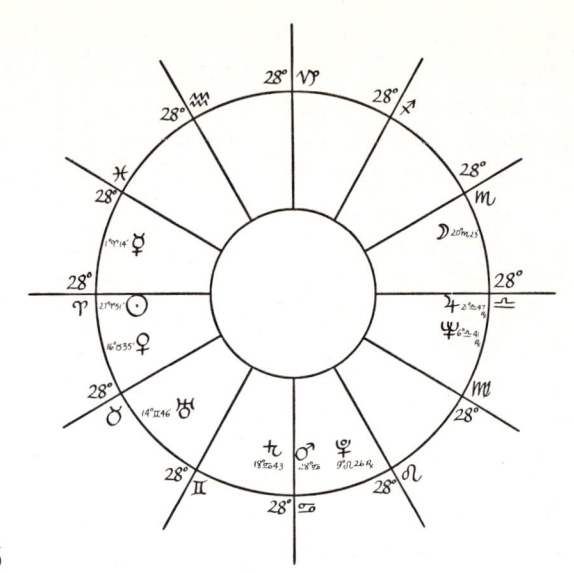

Hayley Mills
April 18, 1946

Such a close aspect between these vital lights indicates not just the possibility of close interacting, but of similarity of selfhood and purpose. One might say that this was a tip-off that Hayley would follow in her father's footsteps. Moreover, while this combination makes them personally very similar, the marked differences that do exist never seem to clash but always to operate in mutually helpful ways.

The depth of personal as well as karmic connection is expanded twofold when we note that both have Moon in Scorpio, in or near the eighth house, last over a sixth-house Jupiter and both *elevated*. The statistical improbability of these compound similarities occurring between both sets of lights is *enormous*. The Millses are, therefore, a most destined father-and-daughter team and an excellent example of the passing on of biology and destiny from one generation to the next.

The Moon is many things. It is the body. The Moon is responsiveness—the sensitivities of an artist and actor, the ability to take in all that is sent your way—and it is the public. The more highlighted the Moon in a chart, the more that person's body goes before the public. Scorpio is overintense for the emotional Moon, and is thus considered detrimental to it. It is, however, well placed for strong dramatic content in all the native's reactions to life, as well as in the native's art or performance. Being last over Jupiter ensures widespread acceptance and professional success, or great involvement with children. This has been true in the case of John Mills's attentions to his daughter's career, and time will yet tell if this gift of careful teaching is passed on to Hayley's children. The fact that both Jupiters are in the solar sixth house shows the two to be happiest when hard at work in their profession. No one has to tell either of them to observe shooting schedules or curtain calls; if anything, each may tend to take on too much responsibility. That both Moons are in or near the cusp of the eighth further emphasizes the importance of the teacher or teaching in both actors' lives, as well as strengthening receptive sensitivities and giving them a sense of drama and conflict that may be described as universal.

Personally, both inherit a very changeable tradition and lifestyle. For the Moon in Scorpio—the natural eighth house sign as well—is at its most changeable, and the sign Scorpio and the eighth house bring heritage before us: what we get from others in teaching, for instance, or as inherited fortunes. The Millses pass on to at least three generations a strong dramatic tradition of a land credited with the birth of modern drama.

The dedication to home and tradition shared by both these actors is further symbolized by the powerful, dark force of Pluto in the solar fourth house, that of one's home, roots, and homeland. In its most benevolent manifestations, Pluto is one of the most tenaciously protective motherly symbols in astrology and often shows the areas we seek to protect at all costs.

Both father and daughter share a similarity in the planet Mars, the planet that is, with Pluto, co-ruler of Scorpio. John's Mars is at twenty-nine degrees of Aries, while Hayley's is at twenty-eight degrees Cancer. The significance of the degree numbers indicates a highly developed Mars faculty. The further along in numbers of degrees in a sign, the more developed the faculty therein described should be. Also, the angle formed by these sets of degrees is a *square* and foretells, by its nature, that there should be many conflicts between them. And so there may have been, but only at times.

Hayley's Mars is at its weakest in Cancer, while her father's Mars is in its home sign, Aries—strong and dominant. This combination is basic for a rather traditional male-female polarity—the feminine, negative Mars of Cancer submitting meekly before the insistence of the masculine postures of Mars and Aries. It's likely that John bullied Hayley at times, but it is equally likely that this forcefulness inspired her to the full use of Mars' potential in her own life, albeit she was born with this faculty at a disadvantage.

And what is the essence of that faculty? Doing, simply doing: the verb of career. Thus, he directed her doing, took pains to direct and shape her acting talents, to bring out the aggressive element of Mars. Thus, together in many ways (as great a benefit for teacher as for student), they perfected the *doing* in their lives—the element so critical to the actor's art.

Father and Son: Ed and Keenan Wynn

Here there are only a few similarities, but they show the close relationship between these tragi-comic performers. In Ed's chart, there is an out-of-sign conjunction (similar to that between the Suns in the

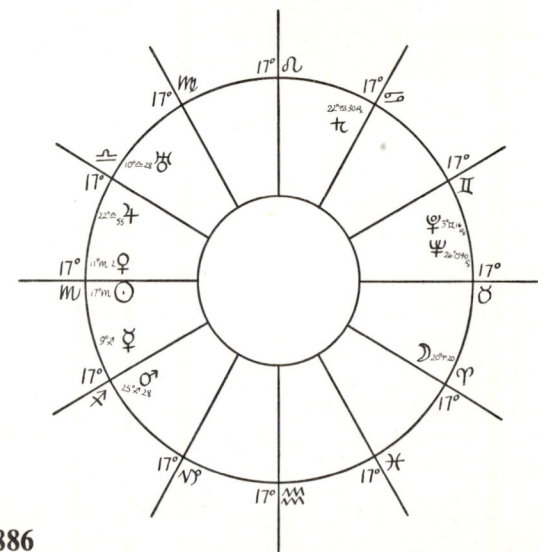

Ed Wynn
November 9, 1886

Curses, Dooms, Prophecies, and Family Destiny   29

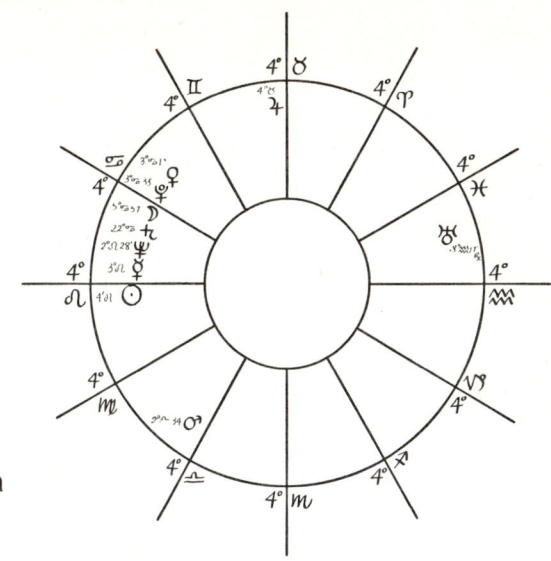

**Keenan Wynn
July 27, 1916**

Millses' charts) between Neptune and Pluto, while in his son Keenan's chart there is a semisextile closely formed by the same two planets. This may not really point to much, as these aspects of outer planets span generations, but their closeness of aspect in both charts brings the greater significance of the combined symbols into play in both lives. One meaning is the awareness at deep psychological, as well as conscious, professional levels, of the prevailing artistic mythos, a sense of the ruling dramatics, or artistic aesthetics of an age. This is a valuable asset for any artist, but even more so for one involved in the extremes of the actor's art.

The remaining similarity has application not only on a deep, personal, karmic level, but on a vital level of each man's profession. This is the exact conjunction of the planet Saturn between both charts; both men have Saturn at twenty-two degrees Cancer. On a personal level, this means that Ed Wynn became father to Keenan at a most critical and fated period of his life—at the very completion of his first Saturn cycle. Saturn, the serious ruler of time and the bringer of just rewards, brought a child to the great comic's life in many ways as a test of his strength of character. For Ed Wynn, his son Keenan often proved a bearer of trial and tribulation. And yet he was tied inextricably to him.

30   THE KENNEDY CURSE

This Saturn, at this degree, makes both men typically American talents, as the degree comes into close contact with planets in Cancer at the time of the birth of the United States, July 4, 1776. The greater significance to the two brought by this shared planet and degree is in the professional artistry of the planet Saturn. Many insist that, while Uranus rules ready wit and Venus pleasurable ideas, Saturn represents the truest core of humor, for it is a mirth that full well knows its term and is ever aware of the stretches of ennui or sorrow or trial that lie between.

Thus, Saturn is two-sided, for it is also the consciousness of endings, separations—ergo, tragedy. So it was that son followed in father's footsteps, to try his hand at both comedic and serious acting. Both men achieved many well-deserved honors.

The Wright Brothers

The exact trine between Wilbur's Sun in Aries and Orville's Sun in Leo made them a natural team, even though Wilbur was four years older. Both signs are of the element Fire, making them strongly

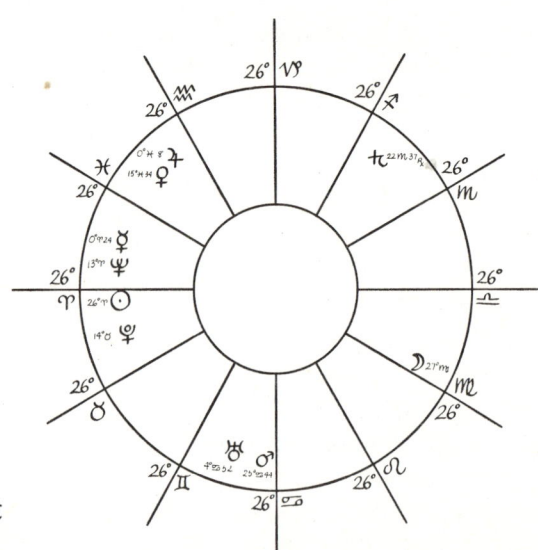

**Wilbur Wright
April 16, 1867**

Curses, Dooms, Prophecies, and Family Destiny   31

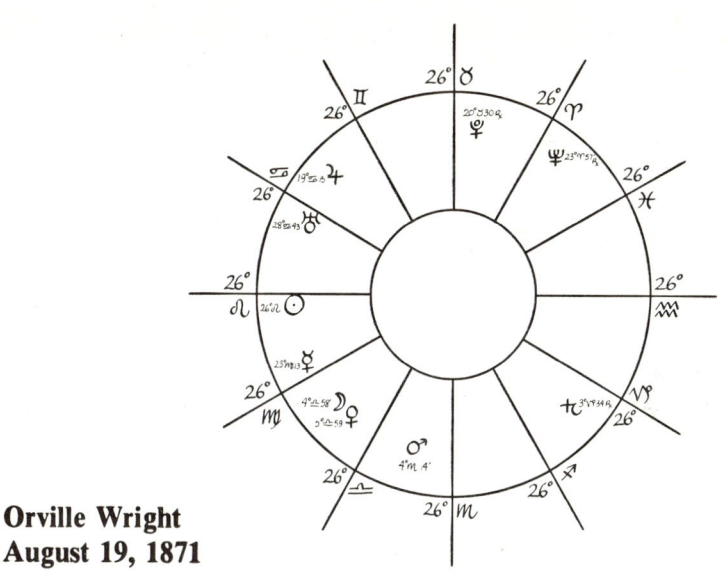

Orville Wright
August 19, 1871

creative and driven by incessant pioneering urges. Both men had Jupiter in a Water sign in the solar eleventh house, indicating that they would find the resources and the backing to realize their dreams—dreams that were indeed far-ranging and prophetic, due to the placements in Water, a very psychic and intuitive element.

Jupiter is also the planet of long-distance communications, so it was natural that they shared dreams of air travel to far-off lands, laboring long and hard to realize them. To add to their deep personal ties, as well as to their teamwork, the Moons of both were conjunct. They shared almost the same responses to life's situations. In many ways their childhood must have been quite similar. Their conditioning, as it were, was to dream and realize dreams via the same routes.

The direction their teamwork took was further defined by the similarities between charts that were forty-five months apart. Uranus, the planet of motors, electricity, genius, and invention, as well as other break-with-the-past matters, the planet of all revolutionary things, occupied mutable sign houses in both charts. These are the areas of thought preceding action, and both men were inspired at their better moments by sheer mechanical genius. These same houses are those of transportation, so of course this is where their genius was directed and where their imaginations brought them the most success.

But didn't Edison once say that inventions are 10 percent inspiration and 90 percent perspiration? Could they have worked together so long and hard with just the aforementioned intellectual and personal similarities? It wouldn't seem likely, unless another strong physical planet had been brought into play—that of work and expended energy: Mars. When Mars is found at the top of the chart, on or near the career point that is the zenith, one might read that the person's work or energy expenditure itself would be his fame. Very often, in such cases, a physical career is indicated, such as sports.

In the case of the Wright brothers, hardworking Mars is found close to the nadir, or point exactly opposite the career point. Here, it may be said that the natives' fame comes as a result of very hard work—work that may never be fully understood, for all its mundane demands, and perhaps never really appreciated. Those of us who have watched clouds from the window of a Boeing 707 are grateful. Both men had this same Mars not just in approximate opposition with the career focus of the Midheaven, but in the third house as well. Among the four mutable houses, the third is specifically "mode of transport," and so we have found the missing element of an unbeatable team—that of travel-inventive hard work toward a goal that it would take years to realize. Both Mars are in Water—perhaps they *knew* they would get there all along.

The Brothers Grimm

I should tell you whom I am describing here. I see the fascinating fairy tales of these eighteenth-century German children's literature pioneers as the unexpurgated notebooks of somewhat deranged neurotics, and I think that their fame comes from their being very much in touch with some of the greatest of childhood dreads—a period of growth far more brutal then than now. I view their work with awe, for a good number of their tales, altered for exporting through genteel translation, were integral to my own, as I'm sure they were to your upbringing.

Curses, Dooms, Prophecies, and Family Destiny

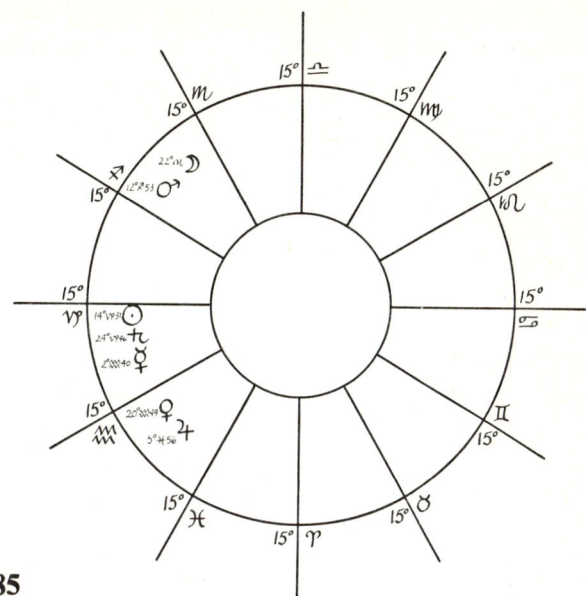

Jacob Grimm
January 4, 1785

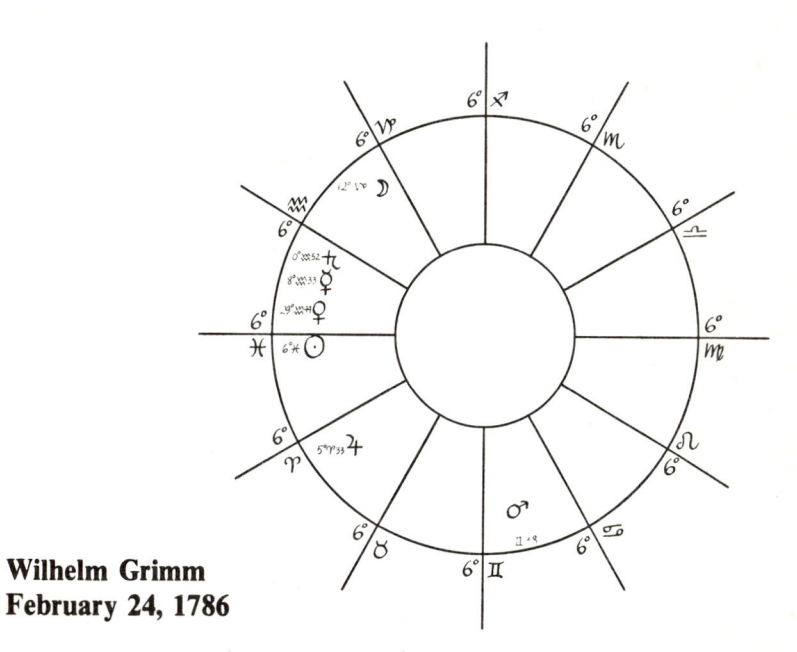

Wilhelm Grimm
February 24, 1786

Yet, I am forever dumbstruck at what parents read to their children just before bedtime. Like my parents, at the time of the comics-code fiasco in America in the fifties, "What'll it do to their minds?" becomes my chief concern. I find myself, civil libertarian and potential kids' libber though I may be, almost willing to ban such thoughts. Imagine! ". . . and along came a blackbird and snipped off her nose."

But to get to their two charts—the men were born a year apart and obviously there was instant antipathy between the two. Natal Mars in one opposes natal Mars in the other. Brutality may have been a shared trait from the first ear pulling in the crib. Maybe they had a thing about going for the nose, as Aries' Mars rules that part of the face. Both were born with strong imaginations that stayed wrapped up in childhood things. The Moon in the eleventh brought keen mental interests in something connected to children and development. The eleventh is a house of the realization of wishes, and, with both Moons squaring Jupiter, perhaps too much of childhood imagination was realized in print (Jupiter rules publishing) or too deep a level was related to. Both Moons are in distress, with one overintense in Scorpio, the other at its lonely "fall" in Capricorn. Neither placement bodes well for the child each man was, nor for the child ever within each man, nor for the children in their lives.

The square to Jupiter is excessive mothering. The Sun signs of the Grimms were themselves somewhat grim: Pisces, a sign of sorrow and endings, and Capricorn, another endings sign, known to be the coldest (loftiest) of all the signs. The three darkest signs were represented in the lights of both men: Capricorn, Scorpio, and Pisces.

Fortunately for them—I don't know about us—there was some way to translate this all onto some other plane. Both have Mercury and Venus in Aquarius. This very logical, objective sign communicates (Mercury) what must be said in or through artistic means (Venus), and so they took the horrors and fears of their childhood, added their own excellent imaginations, a strong element of Aquarian detachment, close analysis, and aberration/perversion, and, as we say these days, laid their trip on the rest of us. Well—thanks, I guess.

2

The Major Kennedy Tragedies

Ever since its forebears landed on these shores, the Kennedy family has taken more than full advantage of every opportunity to advance its status. In a few short generations the Kennedys went from keeping saloons to the highest elected offices in the land, from hustling ignorant immigrants to hobnobbing with the wealthiest and most cultured of the world's citizens. Is this a curse? *Anyone* reading these words would be tickled to be so cursed. It's the "catch" that would put us off: striving for too high a position seems fatal.

The Kennedys just might have survived *intact* the years since World War II began had they not sought the presidency. But three of the brothers thus far sought that office, and all three have died quite suddenly. Joe, Jr. had been, as Kennedy-watchers know, "primed" for the presidency by Poppa Joe Kennedy ever since he was a stripling. The oldest, he bore all the old man's dreams—went to the finest schools, was raised in the most influential strata of society; it was for this holy goal that Joe, Sr. amassed as much power as he had wealth in those years prior to the outbreak of the war.

Then came the tragic plane crash, and all eyes shifted to Jack, the next in line to bring to life Joe Kennedy's vision. Although he sustained back injuries in the war, he succeeded in eventually wresting the presidency from its heir-apparent, the Republican fair-haired boy of 1960, Richard Milhous Nixon.

John Fitzgerald Kennedy then became the fourth president in American history to be assassinated. His younger brother Bobby, in 1968 the Democratic junior senator from New York State, announced that he would try for the nomination thrown wide open by President Lyndon Johnson's decision not to be on the ballot in November. As he won a crucial primary in California—on his way to making his victory speech—he was gunned down in a crowded hotel pantry.

Is vast power their worst enemy, and if so, why? Maybe Jack Kennedy was right—knew what he was doing when he first sought a more academic and sheltered life and began making his mark as a writer.

The elements that seem to prevail in the Kennedy skein are manifold: there're the undeniably strong charisma and equally effective persuasive powers and mannerisms. There's a strong—and legendary—degree of ruthlessness; certain members of the family, like Joe, Sr., can be properly accused of quite often allowing ends to justify shoddy means. On the other hand, there's an excitingly illicit side to their mystique that seems to fly dangerously in the face of morality and convention and even safety. Reputations have marked each of the males as romantic addicts, escapists who often have become reckless at the cost of their very lives. Most of their small plane accidents have been brought on in this way: Joe, Jr., feeling perhaps that he had to outdo his younger brother Jack's heroism in saving the crew of the PT-109, volunteered to go out on "one last mission"—the most dangerous he could find—which, in fact, was his last. Teddy's accidents seem to have occurred under similarly questionable conditions—especially the one that took the life of Mary Jo Kopechne.

Like attracts like. Those not related to the Kennedys by blood have added to the scenario of tragedies. Living dangerously may have entered into the assassinations: both Kennedy brothers took on some of the darkest forces in the land when JFK took office. People who take on such forces often die unexplainable deaths, as do the witnesses—as have some thus far 100 or more of the witnesses to the assassination in Dallas.

Everyone loves the Kennedys; everyone is out to *get* the

Kennedys. Which is true? It often seems that both are true: When one runs for office, supporters flock to his side; yet, once in office, it is naturally expected that someone will be out to get him if he gets too powerful. It seems, in this land of often extreme contrasts, that if someone is strongly loved, we just assume that there will be those who will sneer at that love with bullets. Love, to some, still seems a detestable human weakness.

Travel seems dangerous, too. It was on a trip, that Jack was killed; Bobby was killed in a state he had never spent much time in, except to win a vital primary election. Joe, Jr., Kathleen, and Ethel Kennedy's parents and brother—Mr. and Mrs. George Skakel and their son George—were killed in airplanes.

Common elements such as these may *seem* coincidental, but astrology teaches that behind such apparentness lie hidden valuable lessons or guides to future action. Travel, air travel, fatal reckless attraction to a public that arms with great regularity, ruthlessness, lawless means to achieve what are thought of as desirable ends, the willingness to allow behind-the-scenes turpitude, so long as it's *their* brand—all of these have bearing on the total picture of a family accursed by a seemingly irreversible common destiny. Retardation occurs occassionally in any large family, as might a stroke afflicting a patriarch. But so many chances to do great things snatched away? How many of us would be still plugging along if our family history looked as ominous as the Kennedys'?

Chronology of Major Kennedy Tragedies

Rosemary Kennedy, daughter of Rose and Joe, Sr.: born retarded, September 13, 1918;

Joseph P. Kennedy, Jr.: killed in a World War II plane explosion, August 12, 1944;

Kathleen Kennedy Hartington, daughter of Rose and Joe, Sr.: killed in a plane crash, May 14, 1948;

Mr. and Mrs. George Skakel, RFK's in-laws: killed in a plane crash in 1955;

President John Fitzgerald Kennedy: assassinated, November 22, 1963;

Edward Moore Kennedy: severely injured in a plane crash, June 19, 1964;

George Skakel, RFK's brother-in-law, and Dean Markham, RFK's closest friend: die in plane crash, September, 1966;

Joseph P. Kennedy, Sr.: partially paralyzed from a series of strokes, fall, 1966;

Robert F. Kennedy: assassinated en route to announce victory in the California Democratic Primary in Los Angeles, June 5, 1968;

Ted Kennedy: involved in the controversial and tragic drowning of Mary Jo Kopechne, at Chappaquiddick, July 18, 1969;

Edward Kennedy, Jr., Ted's son: diagnosed as a victim of bone cancer, resulting in a below-the-knee amputation, Spring, 1974.

3

The Brightest Lights

Horoscope means, simply, to watch the hour. A horoscopic chart is a celestial picture of any given moment in time, whether the birth of a child, the initiation of an important action, or the inception of a plan or idea. Consequently, unless given the accurate time of an occurrence, an astrologer encounters very real obstacles to interpretation and prediction.

There are many who, not knowing the exact time of their birth, must settle for what is called a solarscope, or solar chart, based on the longitudinal degree of the sun at sunrise—in some solarscopes, at noon—on the day of birth. While such a makeshift method is not precise, and the Moon's exact degree, the rising sign, and house cusps cannot be known, there is much to read in the aspects formed between the planets and lights (Sun and Moon).

In compiling data on the Kennedys, I have tried in every way to come up with accurate birth times. On March 13, 1974, I wrote a lengthy letter to Rose Kennedy, sent to her home in West Palm Beach, requesting this information. While I tried to show that astrology poses no real threat to the dogma of the Roman Catholicism she holds dear, a matter that I, born and raised in that faith, feel secure in, I suppose my arguments and pleas weren't convincing enough.

It's all understandable. On one hand, I'm sure the Kennedys are by now fed up with the nonsense written about them by fan and "pop" magazines. Also, if I were Rose Kennedy, I would think twice before allowing someone who, for all I knew, would turn out to be a doomsaying fortune teller to take it upon himself to judge the overall destiny of my family. Another consideration is that Rose Kennedy actually may live in dread of an unending string of bad luck, something dubbed by an insensitive multitude as "the Kennedy Curse," attaching itself to her brood.

It will seem strange to hear an astrologer say that he feels obliged to dispel such supernatural nonsense; but this must first be attempted before an honest person can devote his energies to the lost art of astrology, fouled by centuries of ignorance, superstition, and fatalism. It is clear, however, that no angered, uninvited witch crashed the christenings of Joe, Jr., John, and Robert, that no curse was ever pronounced that could never be lifted, only ameliorated by a higher power of good. Yet even the most sensible must admit that the "bad luck" of the Kennedys goes far beyond the normal share and that there might even be something to the curse nonsense people bandy about. If not an actual curse, then—what?

My research has identified various elements of this bad luck, this curse, karma, what you will. Had I been able to obtain accurate times of birth for the more than thirty charts included in this survey, no doubt many factors could have been eliminated.

In the end, I consulted existing sources, some of which have proved of great value. Chief credit must be given the single-most-borrowed-from of my reference pieces, *Astrology in Action* by Marcia Moore and Mark Douglas, published in 1970 by Arcane Publications. My other sources are listed in the bibliography, and I am grateful to each of them.

Five of the charts appearing in this chapter are, I hope, accurately timed birth charts and therefore precise horoscopes. With few exceptions, all other charts are solarscopes.

> Edward Moore Kennedy
> Born: February 22, 1932; 4 A.M., EST
> Dorchester, Massachusetts

The Brightest Lights 41

Ted Kennedy is a Pisces Sun, with a Virgo Moon and Capricorn rising. The Lord of the Horoscope, which is the planet that rules the rising sign, is the serious, responsibility-bound Saturn, itself rising in its home sign, Capricorn.

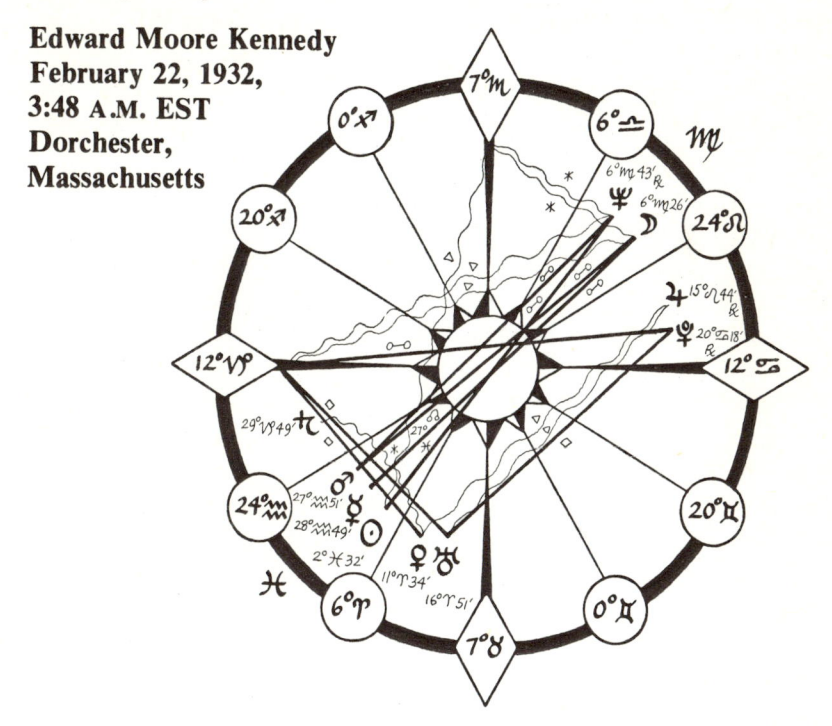

**Edward Moore Kennedy
February 22, 1932,
3:48 A.M. EST
Dorchester,
Massachusetts**

The first and most worthy of notice among the configurations in this chart is the bunching of the planets and lights at opposite poles. Five planets and the Sun are in the lower left quadrant of the chart, while the Moon and remaining three planets occupy the upper right quadrant; some of these opposites form afflicting aspects with one another, while a few work together in harmony. Always facing a profound need to effect balance between opposites and extremes, Ted Kennedy's life will, even under the most desirable of circumstances, remain a turbulent one.

A characteristic in keeping with this seesaw arrangement of planets and lights will often find him intensely involved in one direction, until finally being alerted to unmet needs that lie in the opposite direction. He will turn full-tilt to those neglected areas, only to eventually need reawakening to those shelved and unresolved matters he was pulled away from.

Many elements of what is known of the man bear this out. Most telling of this configuration is the call of public life, vis-à-vis the needs of a family tragically full of his orphaned nieces and nephews. This tendency is enlarged upon by another set of planetary placements. Capricorn and the rising planet, Saturn—*in* Capricorn, its home sign—when rising, give enormous personal dedication. Since Saturn receives no afflicting aspect, an otherwise grim tone to Ted's life is spared the additional prospect of tragedies hounding him into his old age. Nevertheless, heavy responsibilities and tragic burdens have not been spared him. The opposite side of this astrological paradox is Jupiter, in the confident sign, Leo, setting. When Saturn rises, there is caution and a rather stern introspection, often bordering on an outright lack of confidence: yet, as Jupiter sets, a person reserves a good deal of optimism about other people. The two can also be seen as a need to deal firmly with males, balanced off against a certainty of female support, since the astrological sex of the planet Saturn is male and of the planet Jupiter, female. It might also be concluded that he is often overly hard on himself without a practical political need to be, since a good deal of support is always guaranteed him. Typically, he may drive on too hard once he's made his point.

The domestic/career dichotomy is again evident: Saturn rising in Capricorn is the ultimate ambitious achiever, while Jupiter setting in Leo brings great joy from large families, as well as a maternal/paternal need to protect them.

The third way this tug-of-war is symbolized, and thus driven home as a certain indicator of life conditions, is in the opposition of the Sun and Moon. Representing will and initiative, the Sun drives ahead toward goals, here with the aid of an active and progressive Aquarian combination of Mercury and Mars. The Sun is the path through life, along which the combined faculties of an individual shine. It is a strong career factor. The Moon, on the other hand, represents equally strong, yet less-controlled, deep urges. It guides one's response to others. The Sun is authority, while the Moon is children, growth, and all things domestic.

It is said that if the Sun and Moon are thus afflicted at birth, the individual's parents themselves were not "getting along" at that time. This is probably a well-guarded or long forgotten memory, if true. It promises some internal conflict from male-female, mother-father crises, affecting Ted's role-conditioning. It is likely that he is concerned by the movement for women's liberation, as the same aspect promises a good deal of personal growth from involvement in these matters.

Politics or family, leadership or support, heightened consciousness or *macho,* the choices such a chart presents are many and urgent. The Sun opposition Moon reassures that, even in retirement, Ted will remain in the public eye. Sun opposition Moon means that he was born on the day of a Full Moon, thus light and visibility characterize this life.

The second greatest factor in the chart is what we might label *confusion.* The term itself, from an astrological point of view, is misleading. Astrology, among other things, is a language of affinities; therefore, when an astrologer says *confusion,* he also means: disorder, deception, self-deception, delusion, self-delusion, disarray, escape, escapism, mysticism, abnormal behavior, absence, absentmindedness, alienation, that which is totally alien, ambiguities, visions, visionaries, unknown diseases, dissolution, dreams, mystery, et cetera, through experience.

Several factors promise this in Ted Kennedy's chart. The sign Pisces is chiefly associated with both positive and negative refinements of this quality, and, of course, this is the sign of the senator's sun. Pisces is co-ruled by Neptune, co-rule contributing confusion to Pisces, and this planet is in the *exact degree* of his Moon *and* in opposition to his Sun. And as if the three repeats of this symbol weren't enough, there is also an opposition from the mind planet, Mercury, to Neptune of cosmic confusion. The same is true of Mars, slightly affecting his energies, but this latter opposition is weak.

The mind (Mercury), the emotions and both physical and mental reactive capacities (the Moon), and the will (the Sun) are all touched by the Great Confuser, Neptune. Pisces is Neptune-ruled. The first factor we looked at, that of the seesaw configuration, with, for example, Jupiter-Saturn, Sun-Moon polarities, caused *division,* itself a contributor to confusion.

Neptune, ancient god of the waters, also represents water. The Moon is the other body symbolic of water. As it was pointed out earlier, these two, of the 360 places they *might* be, occupy the same degree. The Moon is also women (Neptune is also of the feminine astrological gender); in fact, three of the prime indicators, or keywords of this combination, are: *water, women,* and *confusion.*

Thus, the Mary Jo Kopechne episode: The combination is in the eighth house, the death house. The opposition of Moon/Neptune in the eighth to Sun/Mercury in the second confers bad press and generally poor information, as well as a lack of trust. The lunar combination is in favorable aspect to his rising degree, however, promising that he can overcome any bad image he may have gotten. Since the Moon is also family—and Mercury, brothers and sisters—the death mysteries forewarned in the eighth house have been even more pronounced in the senator's own family.

So far, we've been concerned chiefly with the more foreboding matters in this chart. Since the search is for an astrological cause of a family's tragic misfortunes, this is warranted. Yet mention should be made of the more positive sides of these manifestations. Senator Kennedy is, after all, prime presidential material for 1976, and it is only fair to point to the strengths conferred by these trial aspects.

The seesaw division of planets and lights enables him to concentrate his energies with admirable zeal. Practical matters, especially financial ones, have been problematic; therefore he has developed an appreciation of and talent in dealing with such affairs.

The confusion factor has a broader reach. To begin with, it makes Ted Kennedy a natural politician. A positive manifestation of Neptune is an ability to convince others and to project and sell an idea or image. He has also been forced to face various weakening conditions in his life, so he has an understanding of strengthening factors. It should be pointed out here, however, that the fact that the Lord of the Horoscope, Saturn, is at home and rising well aspected, goes a long way toward explaining his uncanny grip on seemingly impossible, confused situations.

Combining the strengths of the aforementioned two factors, we have a person who might be the ideal American president for this point in history: The bolstering of major weaknesses in financial areas is what current economic conditions call for. This strength is also significant to those who are concerned about the critical state of the world's environment. Substitute the word dissipation for confusion, and Ted Kennedy's talents are clearly valuable in the protection and administration of natural resources.

Many other points of this chart might give us a better picture of Ted Kennedy, but my purpose is otherwise. There is exuberance in the Venus/Uranus combination in his third house, an exuberance that can't help but rub off on others and win him support and votes. Pluto and Jupiter in the seventh house bring about strange dichotomies in marriage or partnership; there are intense and emotional moments stimulated either by loving pride and magnanimity or by petulant secretiveness. The Scorpio midheaven gives added dedication to goals, if not a somewhat compulsive approach to achievement.

All that remains to be discussed about this chart is a multiple aspect called a T-square—where two points in geometric opposition (180 degrees) are *squared* (square=90 degrees) by a third point. In Ted Kennedy's chart, Pluto in Cancer in the seventh opposes the ascendant, 12 degrees Capricorn, and is, at the same time, squared by the Venus/Uranus combination in Aries in the third. Pluto is symbolic of great power, but a power that often operates unseen, almost as a force of inevitability. To be sure, it's his own fears of the oft-suggested fate this book searches out, of the unseen forces that guide the assassin's hand. But it is also every other malevolent power that holds this nation in its grip—we are a nation born under the sign Cancer, where Pluto is, in this case—and, because he is a dedicated politician, a power he must struggle against.

The T-square is a dynamic, in that it forces growth in certain directions. In this case, the action resolves through the

Venus/Uranus combination; there are ingenious solutions not yet arrived or even guessed at, that he may be capable of. If he can overcome the somewhat negative image he's gotten, he can muster great support for programs that confront power dealers acting against the public's interest. Above all, he can drag these dark forces into the spotlight's glare.

True insight demands extensive evaluation of this chart. Predominant factors, however, suffice to shape the puzzle piece, and we examine Ted Kennedy first because his life may prove more important to us than any that has gone before. The year of our bicentennial includes a presidential election. Ted Kennedy's chances, should he choose to run, will be assessed in detail in closing chapters. However, should fear of further tragedy cause him to decline to run it is expected that what light this study sheds will be no contributing factor.

> Robert Francis Kennedy
> Born: November 20, 1925, 3:15 P.M., EST
> Brookline, Massachusetts

Robert Kennedy was born with the Sun in Scorpio, the Moon in Capricorn, and Taurus rising. The Lord of the Horoscope—the planet ruling the rising sign, or ascendant—Venus, is close to the midheaven, or zenith, of the chart. That the Lord of the Horoscope should be a fortunate planet, as Venus is, and close to not just the top of the chart but to Jupiter and the Moon as well, ensures a successful public career. But success is not the foremost factor in this difficult chart.

As is the case with Ted's chart, Robert's shows a strong element of *confusion*. The planet responsible, Neptune, is in difficult aspect with the Sun, and it also receives an easy aspect from Mercury. However, since both of these "mind" planets differ so sharply in nature, it would be better if they were in no aspect at all.

To begin examining Neptune's influence, the house it falls in should be looked at: The fifth house is that of youth and one's

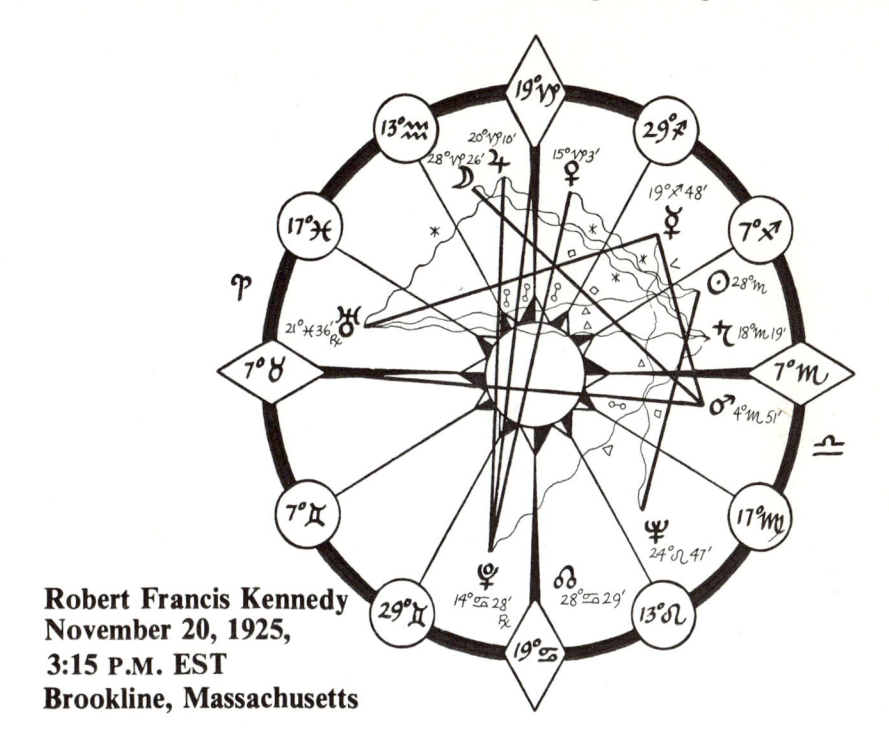

Robert Francis Kennedy
November 20, 1925,
3:15 P.M. EST
Brookline, Massachusetts

children. What possible confusion could afflict this area of Robert Kennedy's life? For one thing, it is possible to conjecture without much chance of contradiction that his family of eleven children (the eleventh born soon after the senator's death) was, in itself, an unavoidable, organic kind of confusion. That good aspect to Neptune from Mercury in the eighth probably represented, to a great extent, the joys Robert Kennedy got from that kind of living and *sympathetic* (another Neptune word) brand of confusion. Many of the ideals to which he later shaped his political programs might be traced to his experiences with not just his own children, but youth in general.

Much of this chart is stern and self-disciplining. Neptune's rays softened some of the more grim characteristics, led him to dream beyond immediate, practical necessities, opened him up to the plight of the downtrodden throughout the world. In many ways, however, its disarming faculties proved a hindrance. Since

Neptune is best off not aspecting a rational mind planet like Mercury, its effects can be seen in a lack of objectivity in areas of ideas and communications.

The signs of the zodiac can be broken down into four basic *elements,* each representing a group of human faculties; thus: Water (Cancer, Scorpio, and Pisces) is *intuition* and *responsive emotions;* Earth (Taurus, Virgo, and Capricorn) is *sensation;* Fire (Aries, Leo, and Sagittarius) is *feeling* and *impulse;* and Air (Gemini, Libra, and Aquarius) is *intellect* and *communicative capacity.* It is rare for one of these elements to be missing (one in twenty charts, or so); when it is, it often drives the subject to go overboard to compensate for its lack. Robert Kennedy had no Air whatsoever in his chart; therefore, an expressive, active, and rational mind was so important to him that it often left him literally at a loss for words.

Mercury, being the main astrological symbol of the mind, is also the chief vehicle of its communicative faculties. The chart is already heavily weighted toward the element Water—yet, the Neptune aspect quadruples the influences from the subjective, emotionally responsive, intuitive nature. Robert Kennedy was, therefore, ineffective as a speaker unless he was feeling strongly about the subject matter. Once this was satisfied, the fact that the Mercury/Neptune aspect is in Fire meant that expressive, convincing oratory would issue forth. Otherwise, and this is so broad an otherwise as to seriously injure his political effectiveness, he was an unsuccessful, uncertain, and unconvincing public speaker.

To fully appreciate Neptune's influence, I should now acknowledge the still-remaining adversities of the planet within this chart. The Sun in the seventh is conjunct Saturn, a serious, firming influence. The Sun and, in a wide orb, Saturn square Neptune (90 degrees adverse).

Among its many talents, Saturn knows *time* inside and out. In many ways, this particular combination in Robert Kennedy's chart, casting some very benevolent aspects throughout the chart, was a useful and building complex of astrological relationships, capable of catapulting him to critical leadership positions at important episodes in our national life. However, the square from this very practical, political duo to formless Neptune, as he responded more and more to the cries of youth, brought him to very emotional positions on issues later in his life, so that many distrusted him for his public changes of heart, and there were few who could decide daily whether his newest positions came from rational political analyses or something more akin to blind faith.

Neptune's is a generally *sapping* influence, so it is regarded by many as a compound tragedy that, before his assassination, RFK's presidential campaign seemed doomed by an earlier loss of faith. Antiwar activists, a majority on many campuses throughout the nation in the late sixties, loudly condemned his candidacy at first. Regular party politicians were loathe to follow in his footsteps.

Few could identify with his metamorphosis. How, they reasoned, could a no-holds-barred politician expect people to swallow an abrupt, overnight pacifist line?

Neptune afflicted the timing talents of Sun/Saturn and, in doing so, flung the senator from New York headlong into a frantic campaign that ended just as suddenly as it began. One's beginning and end flash, milliseconds apart, in Neptune's dim rays. Like a megacrystal ball, a globe of oceans no imagination can pierce, astrologers can dwell upon its meanings and, when it is so integral to the native's life, need see no other planet to read that life.

Many indications remain: the fact that the child-raising and interrelating called for in his unusually large family demanded, and still does demand, a major expenditure of energy. Certainly it was not Robert Kennedy's energy that was spent in this, but his wife, Ethel's. She is always described as energetic—she must be! Although a generally fine relationship between husband and wife is indicated in the senator's chart, there is a certain aloneness of the wife, indicated by Saturn conjunct the Sun in the seventh, the house of marriage.

The sapping influence of Neptune comes from an area of children, as indicated earlier; but, in a more esoteric sense, it also afflicted Ethel from an area of her social involvements and political chores or commitments. Between being mother of his children and distaff representative of his every campaign and policy barnstorm, this chart shows that Ethel became more and more confused and alienated by the distinction between Robert F. Kennedy, the man, and RFK, the presidential contender. Neptune seems almost innocent in this chart, receiving, as it does, only two tight aspects and one weak one. Perhaps some of the weakening influence it brings can be blamed on the preponderance of the element Water, where Air was needed.

Neptune is nearly always prominent in a politician's chart, assuring selling talents. Robert Kennedy took good advantage of his image. He was a hard-driving salesman. The image he could *not* successfully project—hindered as he was by Neptune—was that of a determination coupled with a *consistency* that could be counted on. His influence over American politics did not grow gradually but waxed and waned instead.

Robert Kennedy's chart is basically the chart of a conservative. In American politics during the sixties, a common mistake was to label reactionaries conservative. Yet, while reactionaries tend to resist change that has already occurred, conservatives are wary of impending change. This characterizes anyone with five planets in Water and three in Earth. Taurus rising also confers this kind of political approach. Robert Francis Kennedy a *conservative?* Those who find it hard to believe need to be reminded that he was one of Sen. Joe McCarthy's pet prosecuting attorneys.

The Neptunian affliction from the Sun gives identity crises, and this chart amplifies that propensity. The Sun sets, and, in doing so, made the senator pliable to the other people in his life. While, on one hand, conservatism holds something fast, his watery nature and setting Sun soften and compromise foundations and identity structures. The picture presents an inconsistent yet severe man. His struggle in life was to soften both extremes. Great familial involvement, as in his brother Ted's chart, was a concession to the fluid part of his nature, while a political ambition others characterized as ruthless exemplified the more unchanging side of the man.

Ambition characterizes the greatest of the planetary complexes in this chart: Jupiter is in Capricorn, right *on* the Capricorn midheaven; the Moon is in Capricorn, with both Jupiter and the midheaven; Venus is in Capricorn, also with the Capricorn points (Venus is also Lord of the Horoscope). Mars opposes the ascendant; there are three planets in Scorpio. But the list needn't go

The Brightest Lights   51

on. All will agree to this life trait. Let it suffice to say that this was a masculine balance to the more effusive and often otherworldly, feminine (Water and Earth) side of his nature.

Earlier, it was pointed out that Mercury, an essential mind planet, might be the channel through which someone dealing with a total lack of the astrological element Air might attempt to compensate. Mercury is in the eighth house in this chart and is recipient of some of the most significant aspects in the chart.

The eighth house is called the death house and, from that placement, was participant in volatile aspects with the two most violent planets in the chart, Mars, which Mercury semisquares, and Uranus, squared from the eighth to the twelfth house field, which represents, among other things, hidden enemies. Mars in Scorpio in the sixth represents workers and the common ground on which one meets the public. The two planets symbolically reconstruct the conditions under which an unguarded moment resulted in an assassin's fame.

This is the first of the two Kennedy assassinations this book examines. Any opinion I may have had about the death of either Robert or John is indefinitely switched to hold; my evaluation of what I see in a chart is and must be only astrological. Thus must I introduce one final consideration of this chart for a true evaluation of what seems to be a tragedy factor within the common charts of the entire family. While the chart shows, as I have said, a set of violent aspects connected with the planet Mercury in the eighth, sometimes called "death" house, one such set of indicators is rarely enough to assure so violent an end. Others must be present to bear out such a conclusion, and this chart is no exception.

The signs Mercury traditionally rules are on the cusps of the third and the sixth houses. In the sixth, as I have shown, Mercury and violent, Scorpionic Mars conflict. However, in the third, seemingly divorced from the matters of the eighth, sits the dark and barely visible planet Pluto. Pluto is co-ruler of Scorpio with Mars; Scorpio is not only the sign of Robert Kennedy's Sun, Mars, and Saturn, but it is the traditional ruler of the eighth house, the aforementioned death area. In this chart it receives no less than three oppositions from the career area at the top of the chart.

Pluto is known to some as the Great Destroyer, yet all students of astrology recognize in it a power so self-assured as to bide its time, like the Fates themselves, before overpowering what stands foolishly in its way. The change it brings can be good or bad for you. As a burrowing force, it represents the detective or the investigator, and this latter role was as closely tied as Pluto itself to the area of the senator's earliest reputation. From the McCarthy witchhunt, young Kennedy continued his Capricornian (Moon) climb to sensational fame in the Senate Rackets Committee. This doubtlessly irked *some* manifestation of Pluto, also the underworld.

One of the most general ways astrologers characterize Pluto is as an unseen or unrecognized force, which, by virtue of its going undetected for so long, brings gradual changes that cannot be altered. Death, most certainly, is one of those changes. Pollution, a Pluto word, is another. But power (criminal, political, police—all the kinds of *power* one can wield over others) is one of the most innocuous of these forces. Cancer, the disease, not the sign, is Plutonian. Power, of the underhanded, unseen, or criminal nature, is also cancerous and as impossible to be rid of.

Robert Francis Kennedy was abundantly aware of these forces that bent the world toward destruction—aware, yet wary. For a long while he sat on a fence as a relative independent. He was adaptable enough to recognize that the deadliness and all-pervasiveness of this dark power was inimical to him, yet he remained wedded to a power structure to which he owed a very real allegiance. When he finally reconciled his ideological tendencies with these unspoken alliances, he broke his traditional political trusts and stuck his neck out to a point where fellow congressmen came close to accusing him of treason.

Shortly after declaring open war on what he considered to be power cliques no longer worthy of faith or allegiance, shortly after announcing that he would buck the party and oppose what Eisenhower called the "military/industrial complex," he was dead.

There was a trial, and Sirhan B. Sirhan, was found guilty of assassination. Most of the nation was convinced that justice had been served by the trial. The only question I, as an astrologer, have to reserve concerns that triple Plutonian opposition. A conspiracy cannot be ruled out in Robert Kennedy's assassination, but I do not offer it as an explanation. It is possible, but not very probable, chiefly because Pluto is in so out-front a house as the

The Brightest Lights 53

third, where words, mostly, can be accused as major conspirators. Scorpio assures it, and the senator's career reflected it. People loved him or hated him and, by the time his distrusted public stand on the war in Vietnam took the form of a full-fledged presidential campaign, hatred was strong and was reflected nationwide in the press, itself a third house matter.

Hatred is one of the most destructive of the human Plutonic forces. It allows a zealot like Sirhan B. Sirhan—and so many like him, in his native Palestine and elsewhere—to believe that the lives of some men are expendable in the struggle to realize a blinding idea.

>John Fitzgerald Kennedy
>Born: May 29, 1917, 3 P.M., EST
>Brookline, Massachusetts

John Kennedy was born with the Sun in Gemini, the Moon in Virgo, his Ascendant in Libra. The Lord of the Horoscope, as in the case of his younger brother Robert, is Venus, a planet

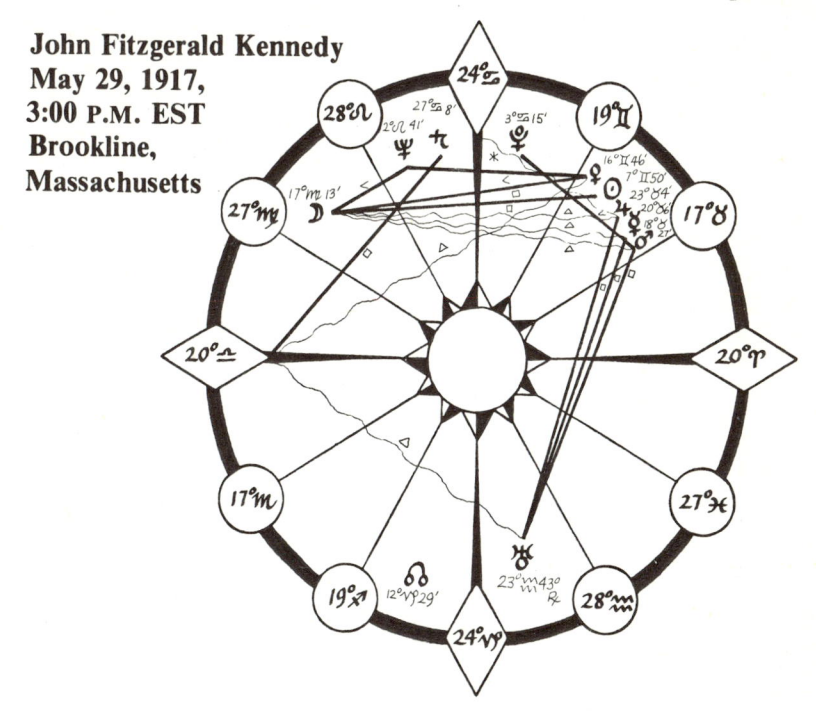

Jacqueline Kennedy Onassis
July 28, 1929

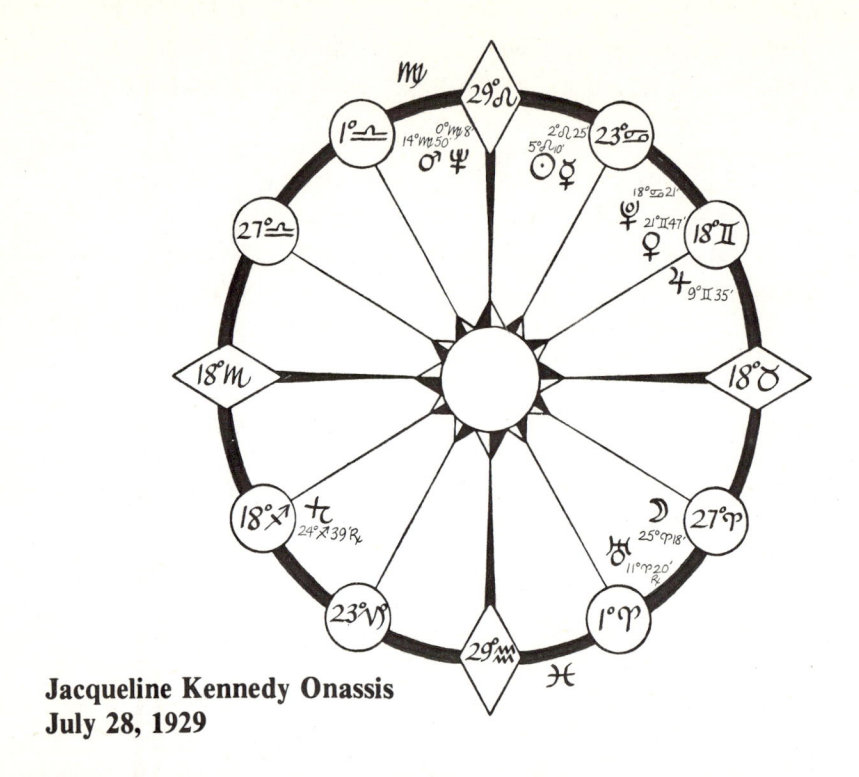

whose benevolent rays assure a person of good opportunities and winning ways. Widely conjunct the Sun, it promised John Kennedy popularity. Venus is close to the cusp of the ninth house, indicating not just pleasure connected with travel and foreign matters, but the love of millions throughout the world.

Yet, Venus is *in* the eighth house. Fame and the death house are here tragically combined, and it is his death that each of us remembers most about him.

However, before dwelling on endings, the ways this chart reflected his life should be pinpointed for a fuller evaluation of a Kennedy family mystery, perhaps best exemplified in our thirty-fifth president. Much is mysterious about the chart, as it was about both life and death of the man it represents. Although Gemini usually can never be accused of mysteriousness, all of JFK's Gemini, as well as two Taurus planets, are in the eighth house, natural place of the sign Scorpio. With Pisces, this is one of the most mysterious and magnetic of all the signs of the zodiac. Saturn in the tenth house promises great achievements in career, yet, with Neptune, ruler of Pisces conjunct, more mystery attaches.

So much is known about the man that, doubtless, by applying the astrologers' skills to a reading of the chart, a good deal of new light could be shed on JFK's life. Again, this is not my intention.

But we must return, at this point, to a further discussion of confusion, mystery and weakening factors this study has thus far brought to light. Since lighthearted and cordial Libra rose at the late president's birth, these traits attached in a very individual way to his personality. The fact that the Lord of the Horoscope, Venus, was in communicative Gemini and conjunct the Sun assured him of a ready and charming wit, and of being established as a writer at an early age. Gemini rules early adulthood and, near the cusp of the ninth house, augers success in publications. When he was twenty-three he published what began as a scholarly dissertation and ended up a best-seller, *Why England Slept.* While still quite young, he wrote *Profiles in Courage,* which won him a Pulitzer Prize.

The eighth house—which by now may seem somewhat ominous—also is a house of advisors, counselors, and teachers. Many planets in this part of the chart promise great intellectual talents that are best used in evaluating the problems or needs of others.

Had Joe, Jr., not died, this first-born of the sons of Joseph P. Kennedy would have been groomed for a political career, and Jack would have been free to pursue the academic life he wanted in the first place. Scorpio (the eighth house), Gemini (Sun), and Virgo (Moon) confer not only a keen intellect and sharp analytical abilities, but a need to be in constant interplay with others. Thus, teaching in the intellectually stimulating atmosphere of an Ivy League college was John Kennedy's dream at one point in his life. Instead, he became President of the United States. It's sort of like the joke about the artist who wanted to drop out and become a shoemaker. It may have been funny even to John Kennedy. However, if he laughed it was only briefly, for once politics had been forced upon him by what were very strong family obligations, he earnestly involved himself in it.

John Kennedy may have been the most brilliant man to occupy the presidency in modern times; he was certainly one of the most intelligent. The extent to which that intelligence translated to political expertise, however, may be indicative of a tragic failing. With Saturn elevated in the tenth, Libra rising, and Libra's ruler, Venus, on the Sun, a strong element of honesty prevailed; and with so many analytical skills at work for him, he would often barge ahead, calling a spade a spade, unwilling to compromise on critical issues and thus earning more enemies than he could, it seems, adequately handle.

Do not misjudge the signs though, for he *was,* in every respect, diplomatic and willing to give ground where it seemed necessary. He was, in fact, noted for legislative and behind-the-scenes compromises. However, when the ultimate power in the land rested on him, the truth he lived by was essentially his own.

Enemies are a seventh-house matter. In John Kennedy's chart, the seventh appears vacant, yet its ruler, Mars, rests on the very cusp of the eighth, pointing to the heavy planetary involvements within and promising an accumulation of hatred that would eventually set the scene for Dallas. (The eighth house is said to be indicative of how seventh-house matters "pay off.")

While heavy family involvement shows up very clearly in the charts examined thus far of the late president's two younger brothers, family matters become significantly different in this chart. We see early plans to be a college professor shattered suddenly by aspects between the eighth house and the fourth, the latter being the traditional house field of one's family. Jack's brother Joe Jr.'s death (eighth) brought great family pressures on him to enter politics. Uranus, violent planet of sudden events (Joe Jr.'s fatal airplane crash) is in Aquarius, an Air sign. Yet, the aspects to John's chart are to the house not only symbolic of death, but of the intuitive talents of the teacher or counselor. That phase of his life had suddenly ended.

Saturn, squaring his ascendant, caused his eventual fame to be of some discomfort to Libran personableness and graceful response to life. Saturn is in Cancer, showing that career is a family (Cancer) responsibility (Saturn). The Moon (family)) is widely square the Sun (self) from the eleventh to the eighth houses. The Virgo Moon of public service, which is only a few degrees from the place of his father's Sun, was the call to politics, and the eleventh house is the place of the congress. Its drain, once again, is from the eighth, the analytical and academic arena that was John Kennedy's first career choice.

The eighth is also called the House of Legacies. JFK inherited from his dead brother the family's political legacy, by that time a half-century old, and while he held it, he had the trust of an entire nation.

Eighth-house types are always well aware of any trust they have been given. A great metamorphosis accompanied John Kennedy's ascendancy to leadership. New interests possessed him; he read constantly to understand the nation's problems and needs. He was *responsible*. Like any good president, he did all he could legally do to see to it that his solutions and programs were implemented. The tenth house Saturn of career is also a hindrance. Since it is conjunct the sapping influence of Neptune, the slim plurality by which he won the 1960 election over Richard M. Nixon prevented him from amassing a broad enough base of support in the legislature to insure the passage of the bills he sent to Capitol Hill. This meant further bulldozing by him personally and by his brother Bobby, then Attorney General (already a few years into his newest crusading public image, summed up by the label "ruthless"). JFK continued to win friends, as he continued to earn some very dangerous enemies.

He was a dedicated man and a good son. In the final analysis, he respected and obeyed his father's wishes. In a traditional, European family the father's influence is felt through the tenth house and its ruler. We have seen how its ruler, the Moon, is right on the degree of Joseph P. Kennedy's Sun and represented the political arena. Saturn, *natural* ruler of the tenth, is also the father, and is, in this case, also in the tenth. Yet it is conjunct Neptune.

Saturn and Neptune together are the symbol of the strongest of self-sacrificing urges. When the two are together in such major houses as the tenth, we may well have a martyr. The political career of JFK began and ended in self-sacrifice. Yet, initial impulses may have been to follow other paths. (One of the late president's last impulses was said to be a foreboding about a motorcade through an unfriendly southwest town.)

On the day of the assassination, where were *you* when you heard the news? How many times have you heard that question? Another bunch of questions that still go around about that day a dozen long years ago has to do with the specific whereabouts of others. Fingers have been pointed. Mysteries abound. I, and millions like me, cannot buy the official story of JFK's assassination. Much has been held back. Too many pieces of evidence demand further investigation.

It's agreed that John Kennedy took on very powerful foes, but all of them—if you could identify them all—couldn't have killed him or had him killed. In subsequent chapters I will attempt to shed more light on the *nature* of those who, it seems, *may* have conspired to murder the thirty-fifth president of the United States.

Compounded astrological factors spell out boldly the word *enemy*. The eighth house has already been emphasized by the position of the seventh house of enemies' ruler, the angry and violent Mars on its cusp. Widespread hatred builds up quite a tab, and this is further represented by the crowded condition of the eighth, house of payment from or to enemies. Violent, inimical aspects between the planets also prevail, and they were manifested earlier in his life as ill health and being prone to accident. All of the six highly violent or tragic aspects concerned operate in or on the eighth house. Mars, ruling the enemy house and on the cusp of the eighth, exactly semisquares Pluto in the ninth. This adversity is between two of the three most deadly of the planets of astrology, which are also the two co-rulers of the eighth house sign, Scorpio. Mars is in Taurus, a sign of the Fixed quality, Pluto is in Cancer, of the Water element; Scorpio is Fixed Water, the only such sign in the zodiac. This pairing grimly sets the stage, but, still, it is only the first.

Five adverse aspects reflect from the planet Uranus, which is in the sign it co-rules, Aquarius, sign of reformers and revolutionaries alike. Terms like reformer and revolutionary were often applied to JFK's style and higher purposes. Yet, in its more characteristically destructive ways, Uranus is a destroyer of the past and challenger of all authority. It receives afflictions from Mars, Mercury, and Jupiter in the eighth. I have pointed out that this is an area of legacy. The fourth, in which Uranus sits, is the area of one's roots and family. Seen in this far more violent light, it may be suggested that not only did family obligations drive John Kennedy to a career that was essentially against his will, but Uranus may have triggered an opposite reaction in him to the extent that many of his political struggles were against what he inherited from his father.

Political bossism typified Massachusetts politics, and, while JFK was noted for his top-notch campaign machinery, his career was always an uphill struggle against long-entrenched municipal, state, federal, and party fortifications that stood against the changes his involuntary political career eventually came to demand.

Who—if it wasn't Oswald alone—were the hidden enemies that might suggest a conspiracy? An astrologer seeks out hidden enemies in a person's twelfth house, but this one is empty. At such an impasse, a more powerful lens is used by examining the ruler of the empty house. The traditional ruler of Virgo, John F. Kennedy's twelfth house sign, is Mercury—one of the planets squared by suddenly violent Uranus. Yet this only says that there is potential for violence from these hidden sources. What ensures some kind of tragedy is the fact that Mercury and Venus, Lord of the Horoscope, combine in a unique aspect.

Astrologers rarely use the fixed stars in their interpretations these days, but when they do the Pleaides are the ones most frequently looked at. This group of stars, also known as the Seven Sisters, are cited in ancient manuscripts as certain portents of sorrow. They can be found in the twenty-ninth degree of Taurus. Even though no planet in this chart occupies this particular degree, an important barometer of human affairs, a *calculation* called a *midpoint* becomes involved. The midpoint of Mercury and Venus is at twenty-nine degrees of Taurus. The planetary picture is of hidden enemies (Mercury) bringing tragedy (twenty-nine degrees Taurus) directly to the person (Venus, ruling the Ascendant). For an astrologer, such a double confirmation of the violence of hidden enemies is enough to throw major weight behind a theory that a conspiracy was responsible for the assassination of John Fitzgerald Kennedy.

There are many new-wave astrologers out there who no longer respect the traditional rulership of Mercury over Virgo, preferring to reserve that planet as sole ruler of Gemini. The rulership of Virgo, they claim with convincing, albeit technical arguments, lies in the Asteroids. If this is so, I am wrong to look at Mercury. Thus, to be doubly sure, I've also employed the Asteroid rulers—chunks of rock that, as it turns out, shed even more light on the picture.

Juno is at thirteen degrees Aquarius, in rather good aspect to eighth house positions. Vesta, however, sits in wide opposition to the Moon; at the same time, Pallas, at twenty-two degrees Leo, forms a tight opposition to destructive Uranus, and Ceres, high deity of the Asteroids, is conjunct with the Moon. Not only is this latter prime indicator on John Kennedy's Moon, but it is also at the *exact* degree of his father's birth Sun! As a prime indicator of *choice,* one of Virgo's chief functions, Ceres again emphasizes Joe Kennedy's role in his son's career direction. But what does this say about his illustrious father's part in his tragic ending? Could it be that many of those who could have been involved in a conspiracy were once sworn enemies of Joseph P. Kennedy, Sr.? This latter set of considerations can only suggest, but the suggestion they make shouts out at us: was the debt of hatred, of unpaid political wheeling and dealing forgotten by most, the legacy inherited by John Kennedy? Were the instruments of a "curse" in reality men of flesh and long, unforgiving memories?

Having briefly examined the three most critical charts of the Kennedy family tragedies, it's time we gazed deeper into the roots. Astrological sources strangely provide two birth dates for Rose Kennedy, but standard reference sources all seem to agree on July 22, 1890. I've decided to work with this date, rather than July 3, given in *Astrology in Action.*

The Brightest Lights 61

Like his wife's, Joe Kennedy's is a timed chart; the last three charts appearing in this chapter, those of Patrick J. Kennedy, John F. "Honey Fitz" Fitzgerald, and Joseph P. Kennedy, Jr.,—are solarscopes, calculated for sunrise.

>Rose Fitzgerald Kennedy
>Born: July 22, 1890; time (approximately): 11:00 A.M., EST
>Boston, Massachusetts

The Grand Dame of the Kennedy family is of the maternal Sun sign, Cancer, with both the Moon and ascendant in Libra. The Moon, ruling Cancer, is within a few degrees of the ascendant, balancing strong Libran-Cancerian traits, but fluctuating most often to the maternal nature.

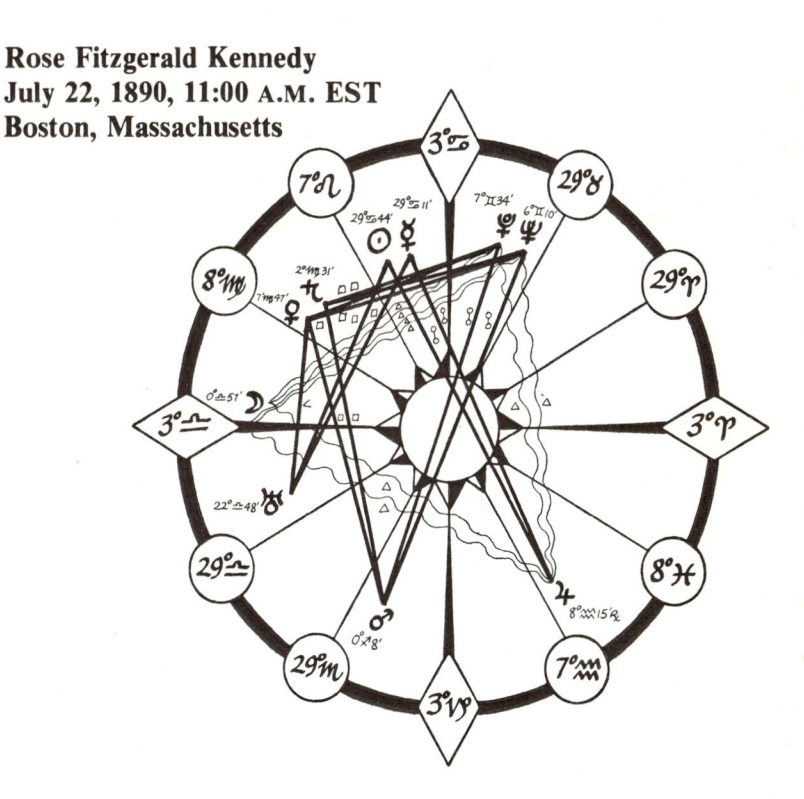

Rose Fitzgerald Kennedy
July 22, 1890, 11:00 A.M. EST
Boston, Massachusetts

62   THE KENNEDY CURSE

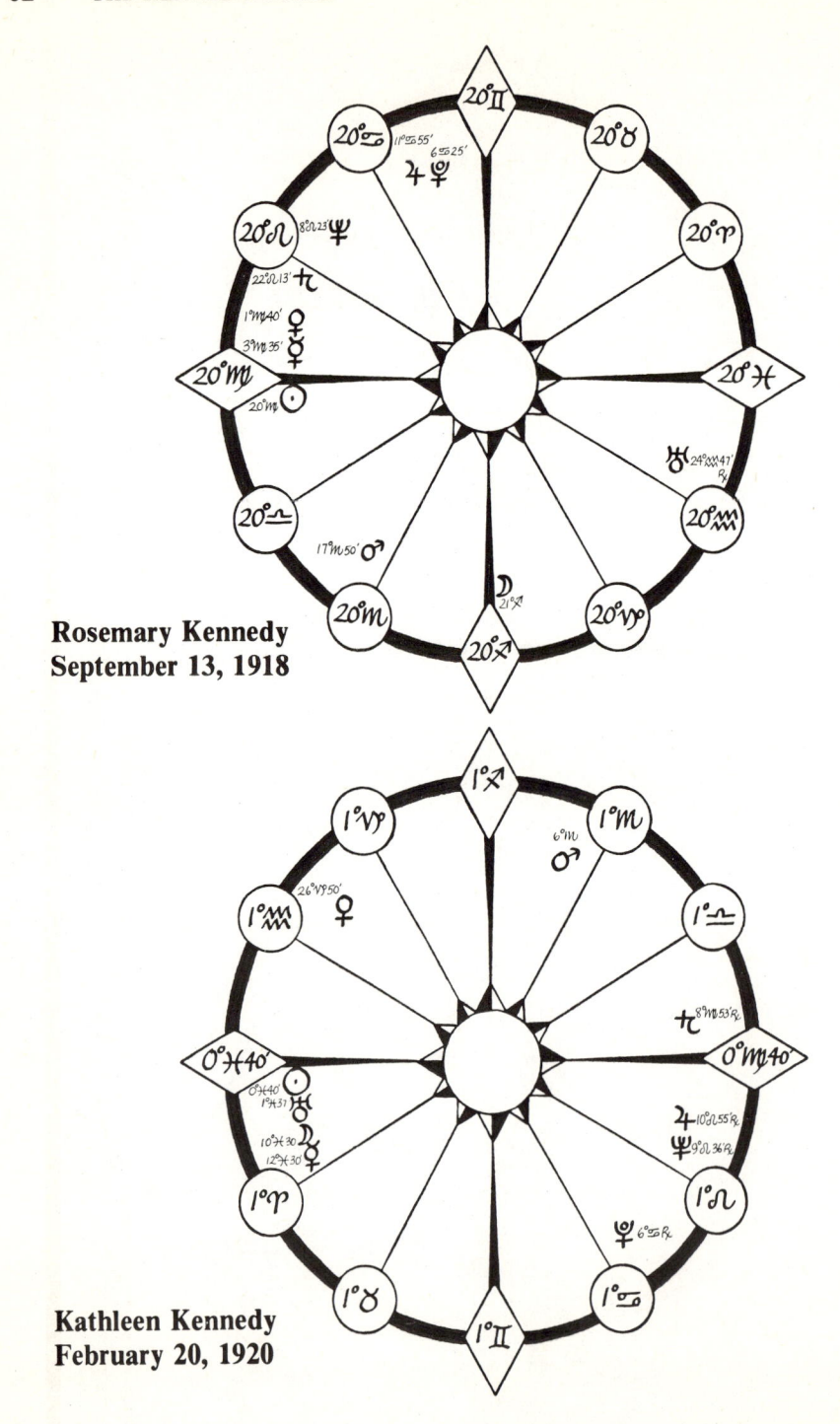

Rosemary Kennedy
September 13, 1918

Kathleen Kennedy
February 20, 1920

The Brightest Lights

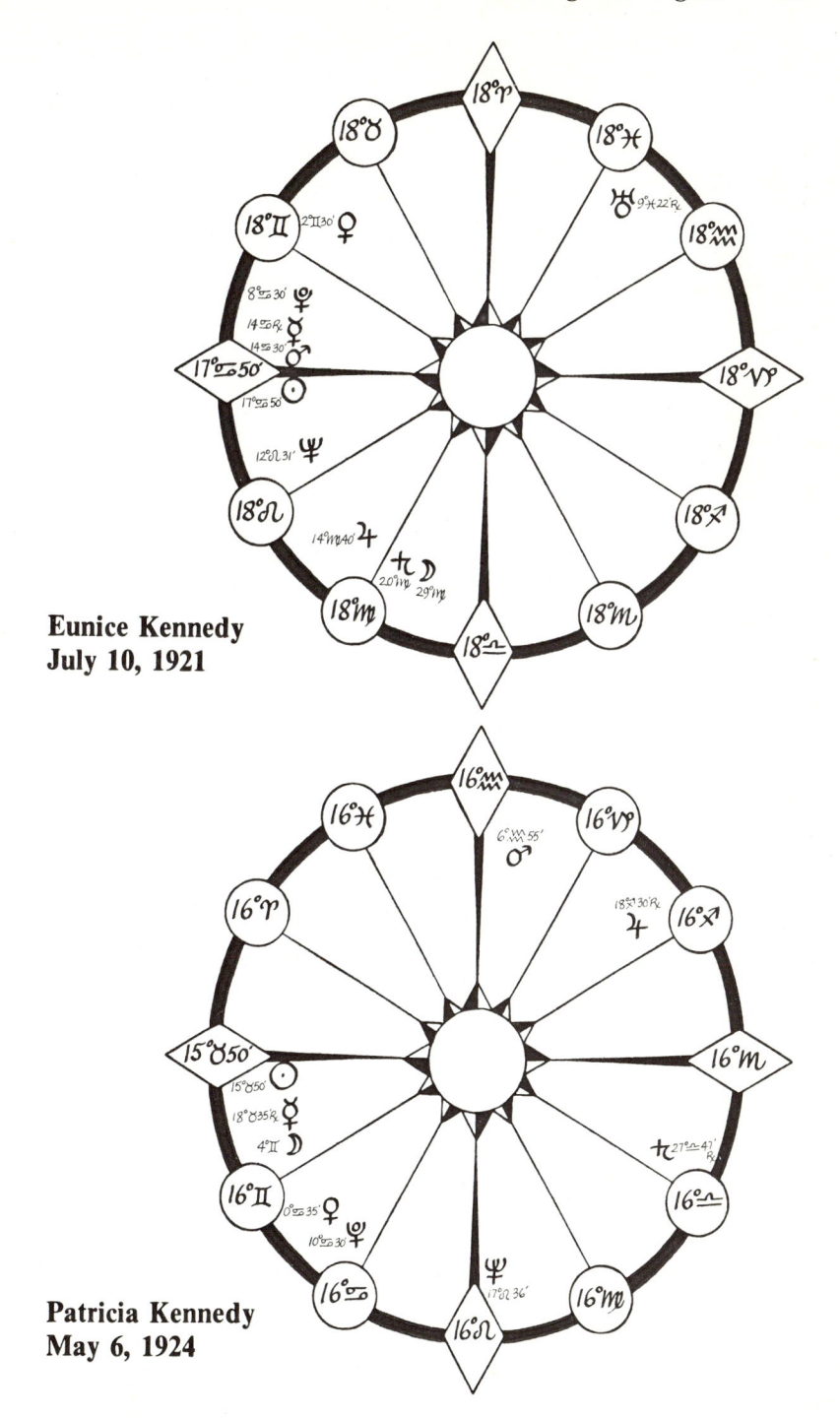

Eunice Kennedy
July 10, 1921

Patricia Kennedy
May 6, 1924

64   THE KENNEDY CURSE

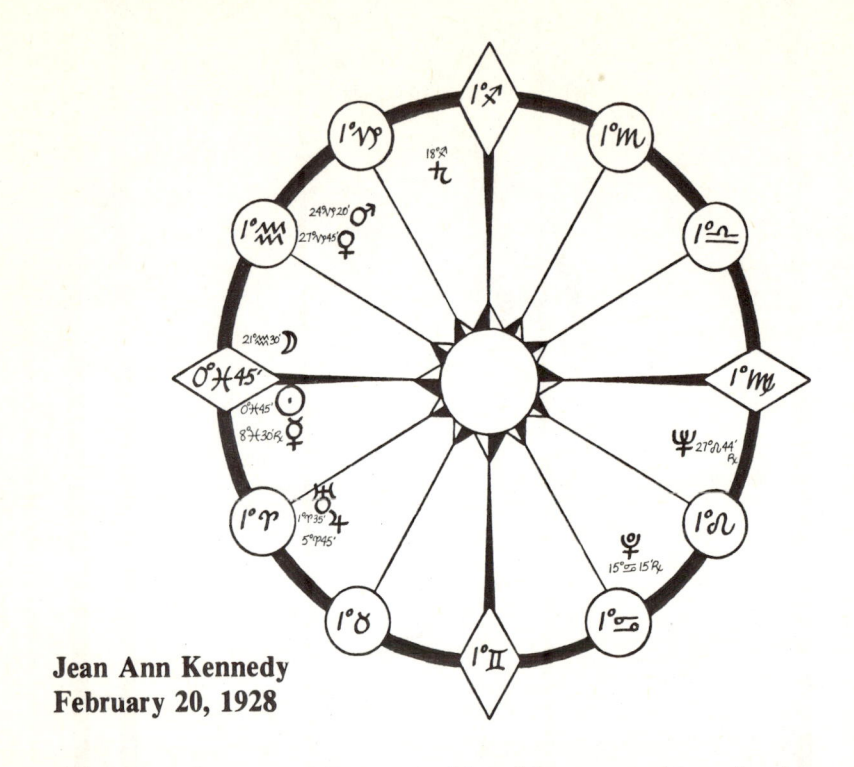

Jean Ann Kennedy
February 20, 1928

The two signs are often at odds with one another, in that energies are aimed in divergent directions. Cancer is emotional and often petulant, while Libra is logical and personable, sometimes gracefully diplomatic, sometimes embarrassingly ingratiating, yet never so self-involved or moody to be discourteous. Cancer dives into family and domestic matters; Libra trips lightly through social affairs. The former seeks survival and the latter justice, two often incompatible absolutes. The arena in which these concepts *do* combine, however, seems to be that of domestic politics.

The glory of this woman has been in her roles as the wife of Joseph P. Kennedy, the mother of successful men and women (Libra relates to one's mate, Cancer to one's children), as well as having originally entered society as daughter of the most powerful politician in New England, John F. "Honey Fitz" Fitzgerald. This is mirrored in the benevolently aspected degree of Jupiter in her fifth house, area of youth and early pleasures. Jupiter is a factor of broad growth and personal development. It is creative, optimistic, and conventional in religion, and it offers great opportunities.

Besides being the house of one's youth and early pleasures in life, the fifth also is the house of one's children. From its critical position just inside the cusp of the fifth, Jupiter receives four benevolent trines (120 degree aspect) and is focal to the four Grand Trines in Air. This indicates a very full and productive youth, joyful throughout—and Rose Fitzgerald was the Belle of Boston as a young woman.

The wide, yet excessive opposition of the birth Sun and Jupiter may have been the earliest indicator of the size of the family she brought into the world. It is ominous in that it promises some difficulties beginning in her middle years. Another adverse aspect to Jupiter comes from the Lord of the Horoscope, Venus, ruler of Libra in the eleventh house. Venus is usually rather ineffective as a hard times indicator, especially in connection with Jupiter. Venus opposite or square Jupiter always indicates some excess, perhaps oversensuality and probably luck that sours. In this chart, however, this important chart-ruling Venus is with Saturn, promising self-control and grim realities, especially in more advanced years.

Although her chart abounds in helpful aspects, Rose Kennedy's tragedy is there, too. There are not only significant benevolent aspects between the planets, but also benevolent *formations* (geometric) between three or more points in the chart. However, formations of stressful aspects are there as well. Time has been the factor responsible for the dichotomies being so sharply drawn: The helpful aspects and formations involve all the indicators of her youth, so they prevailed until her middle age; destructive elements are tied to more advanced years, elements which seem to be having their way with her life now.

Terms like *brilliance, grace, young fortune, perseverence, balance,* and *inspired individualism* characterize both the chart and the woman. Articulate, imaginative, indomitable might also be added, and so much can be seen about her life through this most singular chart that volumes might be written about her.

With so much going for her, where did things start to go wrong? I have already shown how the planets of youth are sharply divided from the planets of age and how, as she gets older, her burden of grief seems to grow. But she is hardly a prime mover of these mysterious forces, they only reflect themselves in her life. For her, it "was written" that she should confront them now.

Rose Kennedy has always been a devout Roman Catholic, and she strives to instill this faith in her children and grandchildren. Her religious guidance showed in her three political sons, men whose approaches to the usually mundane arena of politics seem elevated by a sense of mission and by an urge to lead a purposeful existence. However, the planetary aspects that signify a deep religious sense are themselves pivotal aspects that reveal themselves to be two-sided as her life progresses.

The house of traditional religion, as well as of the unconscious mind, is the ninth, the cusp of which is twenty-nine degrees Taurus, the place of the fixed star group the Pleaides, already noted as a place signifying sorrows. The ominous conjunction of Neptune and Pluto occurs in this house. Alone, they would signify conditions that weaken the matters of that house over a long period of time.

There are several other ways to look at this grouping. Judgment, of the religious, afterlife variety, is one of them. Judgment is a concept rooted deeply in Rose Kennedy's subconscious mind.

These two planets aren't the only villains in the ninth house. Two oppositions and four squares also afflict that area, the former from Mars in the third and the latter from the unhappy combination of Venus and Saturn in the eleventh, turning the promising indicators on their heads and introducing new religious elements that are dark and ominous. Neptune/Pluto, Venus/Saturn, and Mars combine as four T-Squares, major formations of aspects in which two points are in opposition while squaring a third point. Each of these portends sorrows. Neptune/Pluto square Venus/Saturn brings losses of loved ones that she, Rose Kennedy, can only attribute to the will of God.

While *fear* might not normally characterize this brave woman, what dread she does allow herself to entertain will be connected to what she cannot know of the will of her God. After all, she, like Job, has been a faithful and righteous servant all these years, has she not? Can she have good reason to fear God's wrath? An honest self-analysis will no doubt reveal a human being's share of sins spread over a long lifetime, but it cannot reasonably conjure up an explanation of so vast and merciless a punishment. Can her God be at fault somewhere in this? Can He be *unjust?*

From the looks of her chart and because of the deeply entrenched beliefs that have accompanied her all her life, it is unlikely that she would become a complaining agnostic as a result of tragedy, but rather that she would look deeper into herself and seek in her own life the answer to this agonizing puzzle. Ultimately, she must find blame in herself; this is not to say that I feel it belongs there, only that she would sooner cut out her own tongue than deny her God.

Hence, *guilt* enters the picture through the aggravated ninth house of its religious provocations and subconscious nurture, a guilt symbolized clearly in the square to Saturn, a guilt that inevitably attaches itself to what Rose Kennedy loves dearest.

It's hard to say exactly what the earliest causes of that guilt might have been, or when they might have first occurred to her. She was very sharp as a young girl, and it is likely that little of her illustrious father's political reputation escaped her. "Honey Fitz" wasn't exactly your benevolent despot, though despot he was. Boston was then one of the political hotspots of the nation; tycoons and empire builders began their financial careers there, power was centered there before New York usurped geographic control of Eastern financial interests. Wheeling and dealing and every sleight of hand or backhand shuffle was employed by political hopefuls and incumbents alike in the name of a new political force—the boisterous emergence of Irish Power.

Was a devout Catholic girl able to reconcile the cold hard facts of political life, and their responsibility for her social standing, with the words of the humble carpenter, delivered in the brief but eternally effective Sermon on the Mount? How could a ward heeler be compared with the meek who shall someday inherit the same earth politicians roll human dice for every day? Perhaps Rose Kennedy may be characterized as having gone slightly overboard in her faith; she may also be accused of being naive, in dread of the demands of her father's career. Nevertheless, something in her kept an accounting of deeds that demanded redress, while another part of her refused to consciously deal with such matters, preferring in devotional routine to constantly honor and keep in mind a 2000-year-old sacrifice she was convinced was made for the ultimate forgiveness of sins.

Saturn in Virgo is able to confer deep analytical talents; however an equally marked propensity to *not* notice that which is ultimately discordant or threatening. All the mental functions and motives are present for Rose to have suppressed a realization that, for all her prayers, little could be done to reform the irascible father so many hated or feared—or deeply loved, as she did, perhaps blind to any fault he might have had. At the same time, all the religious conditioning in her life convinced her subconsciously that eventually a debt would have to be paid.

The foreboding that accompanied the death of her eldest son probably rekindled these uncertainties connected to her past and ultimate fate. As the pace of tragedy mounted, certainly these feelings crystalized, perhaps into opinions of what was going on that she would not even reveal to her closest confidant.

If, at any point, Rose Kennedy has entertained the concept that the sins of the fathers are visited unto the third generation—given her firmness of faith and dedication to the dogma of the Catholic Church—one might expect that she believed the Kennedy Fathers, as well as her own, to have been judged rather severely. Consciously, of course, she revered all three men for their talents and accomplishments, but a deeper, suppressed, religious consciousness was taught to condemn much of this behavior.

If questioned on this matter, she would defend the men and reject the entire concept I've offered—I don't doubt this for a minute. Neither would she characterize what has been happening to her family as a "curse." Yet it is currently her very strong wish that Teddy, her youngest son, not run for president. (Saturn and Venus are in the eleventh, the house of politics.) As she begins to sense the patterns in her life, she instinctively fears the same arena she once dreamed of as the place of highest accomplishment for her father, husband, and beloved sons. Stoically, she will deny the fear but impress upon those interested in her opposition to Teddy's candidacy that much has already been given to the political life of this country and that now the family's needs are foremost. In one way of looking at things, of course, this is true.

But, again, what of that *fear?* Can it be, *itself,* an element of the so-called "Kennedy curse" I seek to identify? Is it the *effect* of a tragic *cause?* Which *did* come first, or do such distinctions matter in this case?

Many new-wave astrologers will not be held by concepts of cause and effect on the cosmic level. We don't like to say "Mars on your Sun makes you angry," but, instead, "Mars is on your sun—this is a time of anger." Although the distinction seems slight, the word "makes" signifies all the difference in the world. It is a medieval brand of pride to believe that, since the motions of the heavens correlate closely with human affairs, we humans on earth are somehow *objects* of the heavens' concern. In light of a more highly developed understanding of the earth in relation to the rest of the universe and of concepts implied in the term ecology, we accept only that matters in affinity with one another tend to undergo changes at similar intervals, and that all things are *connected*—not that everything causes everything else.

These statements serve as an introduction to an admittedly strange concept that I feel should be applied to Rose Kennedy, without anyone necessarily believing, as a consequence, that she is in any *real* sense a cause of what happens, or in the case of the following conjecture, what *seems* to happen.

Those in endeavors like my own, exploratory expeditions into crusty truths buried in antiquity and abandoned by ignorance, if they are responsible and hard working, will, at some point, stumble over the concept I mentioned earlier—that of the self-fulfilling prophecy. Behavioral disciplines, from the modern

70   THE KENNEDY CURSE

psychological to the ancient occult, will point out that, if you consistently expect something to happen, it likely will. This is particularly true of negative expectations.

Astrological or occult "truths," like most other "truths," are more true for some than for others. This particular truth is relevant, especially to Rose Kennedy. Any guilt-bred fears that grip her are like currents of fate that she helps maintain by her subconscious powers; these have affinity with greater currents which inevitably emanate their influence at her offspring, most dear of life's gifts, associated with her Venus of affections and Saturn of loss.

As the Moon in the twelfth receptor of nightmares as well as of dreams, rises, Rose Kennedy tends to *help manifest* her own fantasies through the vehicle of the strongly negative or indrawing psychic strengths in this chart. Once, this was fairly princesslike, tending to manifest fond dreams. Now—as in the popular science-fiction movie *Forbidden Planet* (based on Shakespeare's *The Tempest*)—these materialized fantasies have become true "monsters of the Id."

She has geometrically tight aspects in her chart connecting consciousness with supernatural realms of existence (the Moon is in the twelfth, conjunct the ascendant and trine Neptune/Pluto in the ninth) that help to *actuate events*—they do not *cause* them. Since each member of a family studied thusly is like an inseparable organ of a greater body, these powers are partially responsible for maintaining conditions hospitable to tragedy.

Rose Kennedy may have been experiencing turbulence in recent years in areas of her faith, but her real soul need is to undergo serious fantasy therapy. She must find ways to mellow or deny negative images planted in her as a child (Neptune/Pluto trine twelfth house Moon trine fifth house Jupiter). She must forgive evil, in general, before she can shed her own sense of guilt.

Joseph Patrick Kennedy
Born: September 6, 1888; 8:00 P.M. EST
Boston, Massachusetts

The Brightest Lights 71

Joseph Patrick Kennedy
September 6, 1888,
8:00 P.M. EST
Boston, Massachusetts

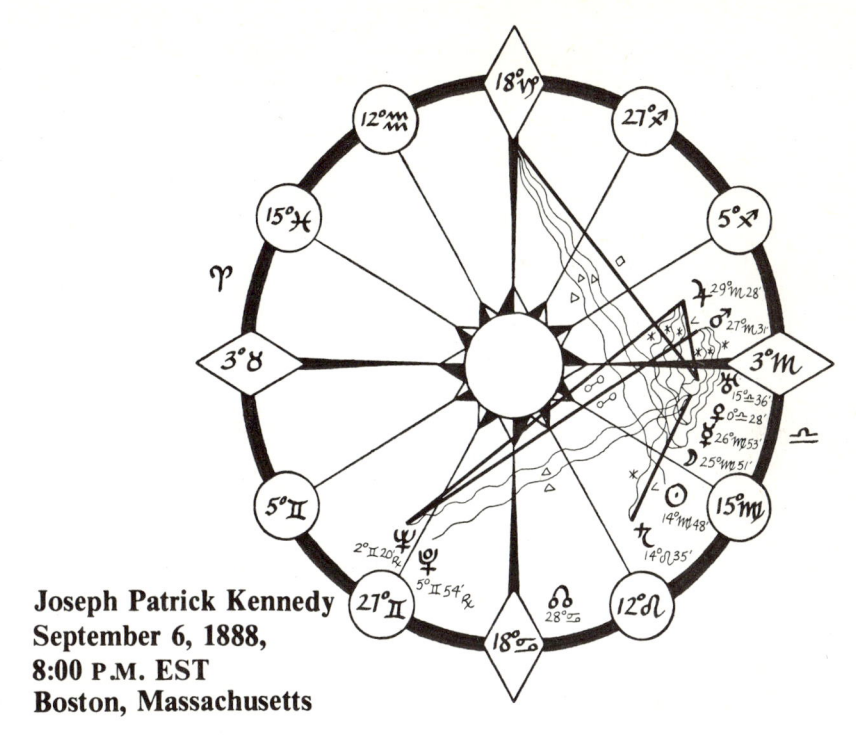

The undisputed patriarch of the Kennedy family was this man, father of two senators and a president. Joe Kennedy was born with the Sun and Moon in Virgo. Taurus rises in this chart as it does in that of his son Robert. The Lord of the Horoscope, Venus, sits at the critical zero degree of the only other sign it rules, Libra, in the midst of a powerful grouping of planets in the sixth house.

The practical element, Earth, prevails in the chart. All three apparent divisions of his unified self are in Earth elements. Earth houses are heavily emphasized: the major conjunction of Neptune/Pluto is on the second house cusp; this is the natural Taurus house cusp; the Sun is on the cusp and the Moon and three planets are within the sixth house, the Virgo house. The only difficult aspect the Lord of the Horoscope receives is a semi-square from Saturn, ruler of Capricorn. This is the remaining Earth sign, and Saturn is a planet of physical caution. All of these qualities combined to make him a likely candidate to continue and further the family's interests, holdings, and political influence.

There is nothing less than a sevenfold symbolic spotlight on the very important sixth house of this chart: 1) there are three planets and the Moon within its cusps; 2) both the Sun and Moon are in Virgo, natural sixth house sign; 3) the sign Virgo is on its natural sixth house cusp; 4) the Lord of the Horoscope, Venus, is in the sixth in its other sign, Libra, in a critical and public degree; 5) Mercury, traditional ruler of Virgo is there; 6) Mercury is also *in* Virgo; and 7) the Sun, conjunct both the Moon and Mercury in the sixth, is exactly on the cusp of that house.

Normally, we see the sixth house involved in a limited number of life's matters. For most, this is the area of routine, a matter few give much thought, by very definition. Such heavy emphasis, however, concentrates the majority of Joe Kennedy's personal power in that realm. Since he was, of course, blessed with a talent for details (Virgo), it may well indicate his varied work and career involvements. He was known to be able to earn money in more unique ways than had occurred to his contemporaries.

Industriousness, therefore, is the least of the natural talents promised. This is the chart of a man of the people. Virgo is the sign of the common laborer. It sweats to earn its good health and is not afraid of dirty work. Still, it may tend one to adopt situational ethics of the narrowest conceivable kind. It is certainly convenient for a politician for that reason.

The support of the people for Joe Kennedy's political career is clear with so much Virgo, because Irish voters were primarily of the working class. The two planets in Libra also promise political success, especially the planet of reformist zeal, Uranus, even though the midheaven afflicts that planet, suggesting, perhaps, a higher power to be dealt with. As powerful as Joe Kennedy became in Boston, it was always the political star of John F. "Honey Fitz" Fitzgerald that lit the New England night.

Joe Kennedy had another, more sinister grip on the Irish community of Boston, yet, for all appearances, it was more accurately a cordial one. Liquor interests slowly accumulated in the family's name. Begun by Joe's grandfather, the Kennedys' service to the alcoholic needs of fellow Bostonians soon accounted for the greatest bulk of the family's wealth.

The Brightest Lights 73

Service and control stem from the sixth house phenomena I have just explained. The result of this empire building, or its consequence, for traumatically displaced Irish immigrants, is generational alcoholism, a disease that filled Kennedy coffers (Neptune/Pluto on the cusp of the second).

This is approximately the same Neptune/Pluto conjunction we examined in Rose Kennedy's chart, due her and her husband being born within about a year of one another and to the fact that the two planets involved are the slowest moving in the solar system. On the cusp of the second, it brings illusion and compulsion to money affairs and unquenchable thirsts for wealth and power. It represents the myth (Neptune) and dark powers (Pluto) that controlled the resources (second house) of a community (Gemini).

This conjunction is opposite the joining of Mars and Jupiter in the seventh house of opponents, indicating that the aforementioned powers were used ruthlessly against opponents, attacking their very sources of wealth and sustenance and, since the sign Scorpio is there, not excluding matters of both life and death. Since Jupiter also rules the eighth house of this chart, there may have been those who died as a direct result of their opposition to Joe Kennedy's power plays or, perhaps, the stakes for *all* of the players were sometimes death.

Much yet remains to be known about the fateful Neptune/Pluto combination, but since the specter of tenacious enemies has arisen again it serves us better to track these figures down. To be sure, some very long-term, though conventional enemies are symbolized in Neptune/Pluto opposite Mars/Jupiter.

Hidden enemies are found in the twelfth house. As in the natural zodiac, Pisces is on the cusp of the twelfth in this chart. Its rulers, Jupiter and Neptune, are opposite one another in the major enemy aspect. Therefore, definitely, there are powerful hidden enemies to contend with at all times.

With Mars on Jupiter, we know them to be capable of violence, and we can safely assume that Joe Kennedy employed violence against them. Their symbol in Scorpio, these men are unforgiving. All signs point to major expenditures of resources in the fighting of inner-circle wars but also guarantee the depletion of enemies' resources in the process. The superficial enemy aspects, in fact, point to a total vanquishing of opposition. The semi-square between suddenly violent Uranus and Scorpio Jupiter once again emphasizes that lives have hung in the balance in these struggles and that several of these lives may have been lost.

To the extent that he succeeded in his political ambitions, one might assume that Joe Kennedy had to totally vanquish a lot of opponents in his lifetime. Total victory isn't always desirable, of course, especially when you have to live within a stone's throw of those you defeat.

Since he was the founding father of his family's political fortunes, his ambitions ultimately rested on his sons. Those who felt a hate-fed need to pay Joe Kennedy back in some way didn't, theoretically, have to look very far to see what cherished prize they might snatch away, using any means available.

But returning to the ominous conjunction of Neptune/Pluto—that shared by both Kennedy parents—we see in its modifying connections with other planets the various ways an owed fate of eye-for-eye, tooth-for-tooth might be expected to materialize. Although they are trine Venus, Lord of the Horoscope, no aspect between, such as Venus and Pluto, should ideally occur at all. Earlier, I called this conjunction a "price" that was demanded; Venus is all a person loves. The unfortunate circumstances of the Venus/Pluto connection become more evident. Saturn in the fifth house, in the natural fifth house sign, Leo, invokes the seriousness with which he regarded his children, as well as his hopes (Saturn co-ruling Aquarius, sign on the eleventh house of hopes) and ambitions (Saturn sole ruler of Capricorn, sign on the tenth house of career and ambition). This sensitive planet is squared by the same Venus of the unfortunate aspect with Neptune/Pluto, a sure promise of tragedy connected with his children.

Saturn is always the past. Ruling, as it does, Joe Kennedy's midheaven, or tenth house of ambition and career, it represents past matters that attach themselves to one's career. This is still another indicator that the enemies of Joe Kennedy may have actually been instrumental in the tragedies that have hounded his family since the crest of their wave of success and popularity.

Patrick Joseph Kennedy
Born: January 8, 1858
Boston, Massachusetts
(Solarscope)

Although his own father first established the family in America, and pioneered the family fortune by becoming owner and operator of a lucrative tavern trade in Boston's Irish neighborhoods, it was "PJ," father of Joseph P. Kennedy, who hewed the real power from the granite shores of Boston harbor. It was this Kennedy who first aspired successfully for public office and firmed a political base of power that would one day lead to the hub of world power at 1600 Pennsylvania Avenue.

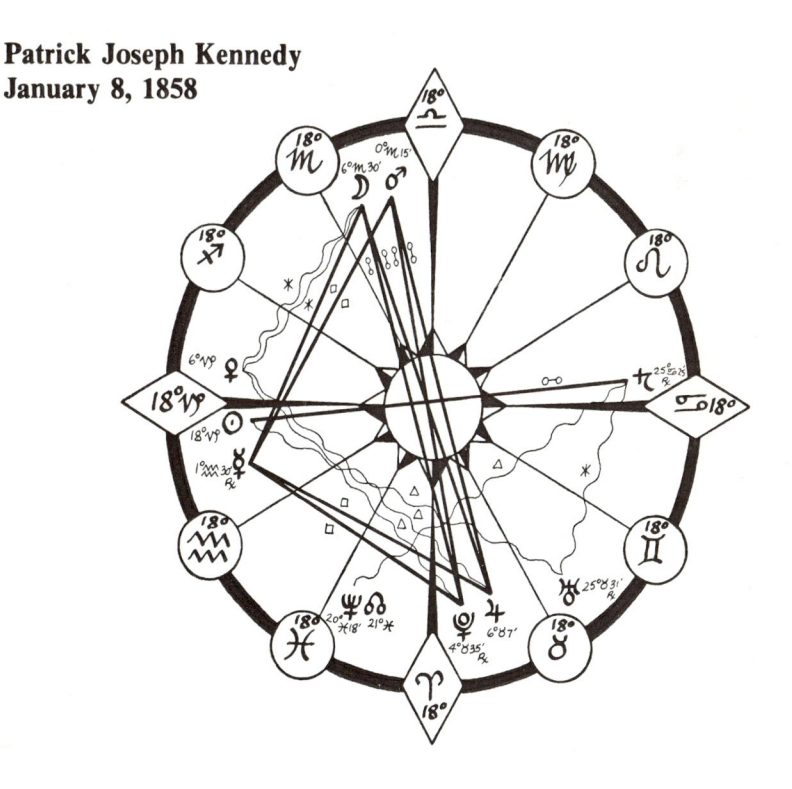

Patrick Joseph Kennedy
January 8, 1858

PJ Kennedy's chart contains some of the most unique geometric formations seen thus far, and, because it is a solarscope, aspects to the ascendant and midheaven are not even included. The only traditionally beneficial combination of aspects is a Grand Sextile, full of opportunities, between Uranus, Saturn, and Neptune. Four major stress formations drive him to take advantage of every opportunity offered by the one good formation. The first generation in this new land has always been the wave of new ideas and methods that sink or swim within clear sight of the shores of a Promised Land.

An Irishman born in Boston in the middle of the last century had the chips stacked against him. He had been sired by refugees from every imaginable deprivation, as well as death by starvation, who, late of a dying land, were washed upon shores promising everything and nothing at the same time. Someone with as many obstacles as an astrologer might read into such a four-to-one ratio of easy-to-difficult aspect formations would be assessed to have very little chance of amounting to anything much.

The four adverse aspect formations are called T-squares, which, as I've pointed out, involve two points in opposition, both squaring a third point. Besides four of these, involving the Moon, Mercury, Mars, Jupiter, and Pluto, there is also a significant opposition of the Sun to Saturn, the most telling of the indicators in the chart. Saturn is the epitome of obstacles in one's life; it also rules PJ's natal Sun, and, in such a relationship with the man's will and driving force, promised a life of struggle for, and the ultimate drawing in of, power.

It's a miracle that he got anywhere, it would seem, with so much against him; yet, a closer investigation reveals that the miracle is a scientifically explainable phenomenon, a geometric one, in fact. Counting the oppositions in the T-square formations, there are five. In each of the five, a third planet benevolently aspects either end of the opposition; one end receives a trine aspect and the other a sextile, the former implying talents and the latter opportunities.

So, while four of the five oppositions received aggravating aspects from a third planet, all five of them received aid from still another planet. I consider an opposition thus aspected a *popular opposition,* one in which the struggle implied sits well with the person's image in the eyes of those he will need to impress or convince.

I refer mainly to the position of PJ's natal Venus, in Capricorn, the sign of his Sun. It is in wide conjunction with his Sun, identifying itself with the man's personal struggles (Sun opposite Saturn) and bringing a good deal of sympathy and popular support. At the same time, this planet becomes responsible for four of the popular oppositions, and, in this capacity, emphatically underlines the degree of popular support the man could muster. In fact, where the opposition of Moon and Jupiter exposed itself through Mercury, the planet that both square, as boastfulness and lies, the often put-upon charisma of Capricorn/Venus convinced constituents and followers alike that these were all too necessary in a political arena; and, where Mars opposite Pluto indicated dirty dealings, Venus could explain them away in the light of an expediency that seemed altogether necessary to down-and-out immigrants for whom the system made rules and constructed barriers meant to keep them in their place.

The fifth of these popular oppositions is benevolently compounded by two planets: Uranus, the popular reformer, and Neptune, the shrewd politician and behind-the-scenes schemer. Uranus sextiles Saturn and trines the Sun, an aspect of political success examined earlier, while Neptune sextiles the Sun and trines Saturn. This particular combination probably was PJ's greatest asset. The Sun opposite Saturn specifically involved two political matters: the struggle against insurmountable obstacles and entrenched power, and the man's public image. The talents and opportunities offered by the two interloping planets not only assured his political ascendancy, but, with the very sudden Uranus in Taurus, the sign of riches, increased his family's wealth in quantum leaps.

These four planets together form an interesting geometric formation perhaps best characterized as a trapezoid—for the benefit of future textbooks, a lucky trapezoid—which does not just double the easing influences working on the opposition but seems to cube their influence. Thus, to an opposition of any two places in the chart, a lucky trapezoid is like four popular oppositions. The key to the base of the formation is the sextile between the two interlopers. Thus tied together, the geometry of this moment of time assures that this is the chart of an able pioneer and a brilliant innovator.

Astrology is sometimes like the most profound of enlightened poetics. Supersaturated as this generation is with knowledge of the Kennedys and of some of the most intimate moments of their lives, it stirs my sense of the awesome to ponder a chart with so much potential eternally suggested. A chart, like any moment, lasts forever; like any moment, it surrenders its meaning to a greater whole and thus becomes meaningless. Here is a beginning whose spiraling ending(s) have leveled a million square miles of pine-forest newspaper pulp in a flash fire of tragic news and sensationalism.

Here are the beginnings of the Kennedy fortunes. Jupiter, symbolic of those matters more than any other of the planets, is closely conjunct the fateful Pluto, planet of inevitable and irresistible forces. Together, they are the basis in this chart of the major afflicting formation that consists of the four T-squares examined earlier. Immediately opposite this combination in the formations are Mars and the Moon, the latter symbolizing PJ's family; square as the two were to Mercury in Aquarius, it promised to manifest in the following manner: Pluto/Jupiter in Taurus (hatred and the accumulation of destructive forces, with motivation in wealth and enmity for all that is cherished) is bound to the same fatal axis as Moon/Mars, in Scorpio; the latter augurs possible disaster, death, and danger to family. Mars, the violent and spiteful ruler of Scorpio, tied karmically to Scorpio's other ruler Pluto, sorely afflicts and excites the domestic scene; the two combinations "work themselves out" through the third party to the T-square, Mercury sitting in Aquarius, specifically, through young men in reform or political arenas.

Generally speaking, however, the immediate fate that confronted the owner of this chart, although beleaguered with active struggle, was on the whole benevolent. This seems to be the first of the vital charts we've looked at that finds Pluto with a benefic planet in conjunction. The frantic activity could be borne, especially with the natal Moon in Scorpio; the man's Capricorn Sun gave him endurance and strength and enough craft to climb, like the proverbial mountain goat of the heavenly ecliptic, to as high a place as could be reached. He succeeded brilliantly. The pendulum of luck that spans generations was on the upswing for PJ.

It has been shown how a lucky trapezoid formation of planets was of vast benefit to the man's political career and helped him undercut every enemy who ever stood in his way. These unfortunate lame ducks could only sit and watch as Kennedy strength grew and theirs declined.

Saturn opposite PJ's Sun is ruler of the Sun, itself in Cancer and, so placed, involves all matters of family and political power. It is very probable that these enmities were not of a life or death sort, yet Saturn in Cancer teaches its children well and, where this planet characterizes Patrick Joseph Kennedy's enemies, the scions of this injured power grew and established their own, relatively quiet power bases. One day, these shadowy enclaves would become points of resistance in a battle for a key senatorial district in a business that refused to heed a presidential guideline, or in matters that involved the nod of a powerful head condoning far darker purposes.

        John F. "Honey Fitz" Fitzgerald
        Born: February 11, 1863
        (Solarscope)

The father of Rose Fitzgerald Kennedy, John Fitzgerald, was an Aquarian Sun with Scorpio Moon. The dynamic tie-ins with these two lights and both Mercury and Mars reflected an impressively convincing temperament; the two T-squares formed by these four activated the Sun/Mercury conjunction in the Aquarian field of politics and stimulated the man with an unswerving drive to consolidate influence and power. With assists from the Jupiter of established power, in Libra, and progressive and politically popular Uranus, he was lucky; with the dynamics of the T-square always at work, he was also one of the most aggressive figures of his age, never satisfied with what he had and always planning his next step, scarcely taking the time to celebrate the victories of the moment. He satisfied this great power hunger in a successful career as a reformer, especially when he was a young hopeful. He lifted entire neighborhoods from despair and built a network of patronage that provided countless job opportunities for young Irish immigrants' sons. This was a positive way the T-squares worked themselves out through the Sun/Mercury combination.

Honey Fitz's notoriety grew, however, from the less humanitarian of the manifestations. Sun/Mercury are squared by

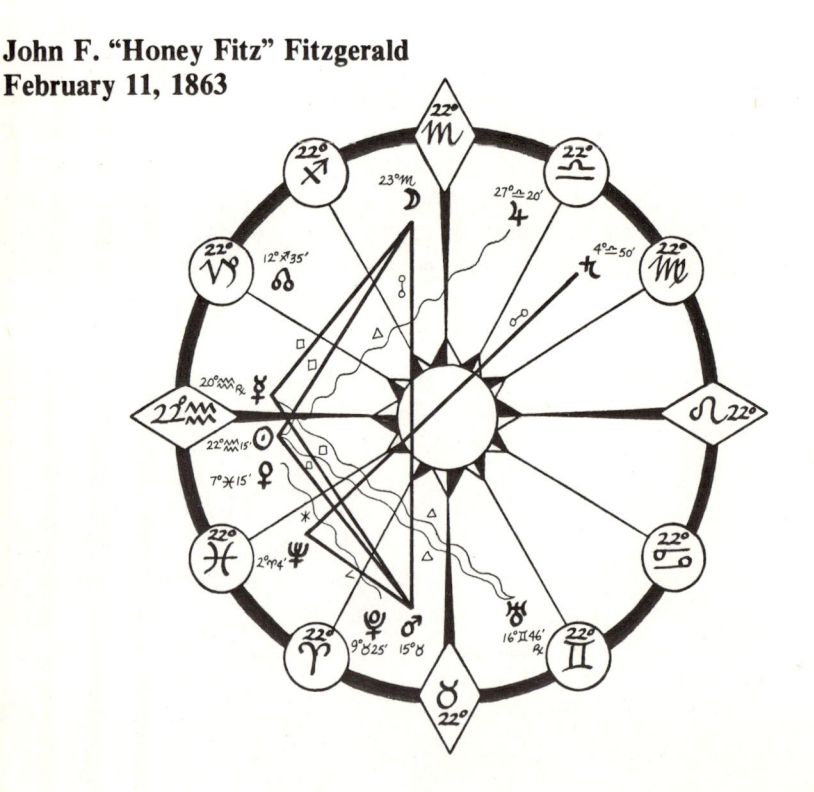

John F. "Honey Fitz" Fitzgerald
February 11, 1863

both the Moon in Scorpio and Scorpio's co-ruler, Pluto. Let it suffice to say that deeds represented here would have embarrassed Richard Nixon. When the T-squares operated on the emotional balance of this man, as they probably did quite often, he could be downright ruthless, if not a very real threat to lives. The trine from the ruler of Aquarius to the birth Sun of that sign does, at the same time, give opportunity to control sudden, destructive impulses.

While these very personal aspects served to enhance or, at least, expand his reputation as boss of bosses, a benevolent trine from Jupiter in Libra expanded his material wealth, as it assured him support from both the law and Boston's established elite, and another trine from the modern Uranus gave him valuable insight into the needs of the Irish community, which were many, and inspired him with the progressive programs that ultimately enabled him to deal successfully with those needs.

Thus far in the many Kennedy charts examined, one of the most fateful of the planets, Pluto, has been involved in a majority of the tragic afflictions. Honey Fitz was a Fitzgerald, not a Kennedy; his Pluto receives only one aspect—a benevolent one from pleasure-giving Venus, in Pisces, the sign of its *exaltation*. (An exaltation is an ultimate expression of planetary characteristics.) Venus in Pisces carries the deepest of joys and, since this planet represents a man's daughters, Rose, exalted in Boston society, was surely one of his greatest joys.

The Pluto connection may be seen as a legacy of wealth, ease, influence, opportunity, and eventual increase of power. There is, therefore, nothing apparently ominous about the impact of this man's life on his daughter, Rose Fitzgerald Kennedy.

Yet if we are to look to the planet co-ruling Venus' sign, Pisces, we find it—Neptune—involved in a morbid opposition to Saturn. (Before Pluto, remember, it had been Neptune's insidious influences that seemed most often connected to planetary pictures symbolic of tragedy.) Saturn, ruling the past and opposite Neptune, represents some promise of repayment, perhaps fatally assured by those whose fortunes were drained by the bulldozer politics of John F. "Honey Fitz" Fitzgerald.

No promise, of course, need come true when only hinted at once. This is the rule of the aspects of a chart. If something is suggested once, it is seriously considered twice, it becomes a matter of probability a third time, and it is even more of a certainty a fourth time, and so on. Nothing in Honey Fitz's chart indicated a tragedy that was unavoidable; let us say, rather, that the karma that attaches to such a career—while possibly not clearly sketched for readers of an astrological chart—certainly has to at least occur to people of conscience.

Public distrust of politicians has left the realm of the cliché and entered that of genuine public concern—with good reason. As a people, we were once content to allow our elected and appointed officials free reign in defining what was best for America and Americans. If we were too vague about those important matters that kept our democracy strong, our lazy deference to politicians worsened the situation. Power has but one purpose in the long run: its own preservation. If this means the violation of the purposes for which it was first granted, so be it. For those still dedicated to preserving what the Constitution guarantees, the road will be a long and arduous one—karmic payment for allowing government to slip from our grasp while we pursued bread and circuses.

> Joseph Patrick Kennedy, Jr.
> Born: July 25, 1915
> (Solarscope)

After all has been considered, Joe, Jr. must come to be seen as the quintessential Kennedy. He was the firstborn of the most powerful branch of the Kennedy family to make its torn and battered way onto the pages of American history books; he had six planets in rulership signs and seven in signs of high authority. His four-planet stellium in Cancer is indicative not just of domestic politics in general, but of American politics in particular (as mentioned before, we are a Cancer-born nation).

The Brightest Lights 83

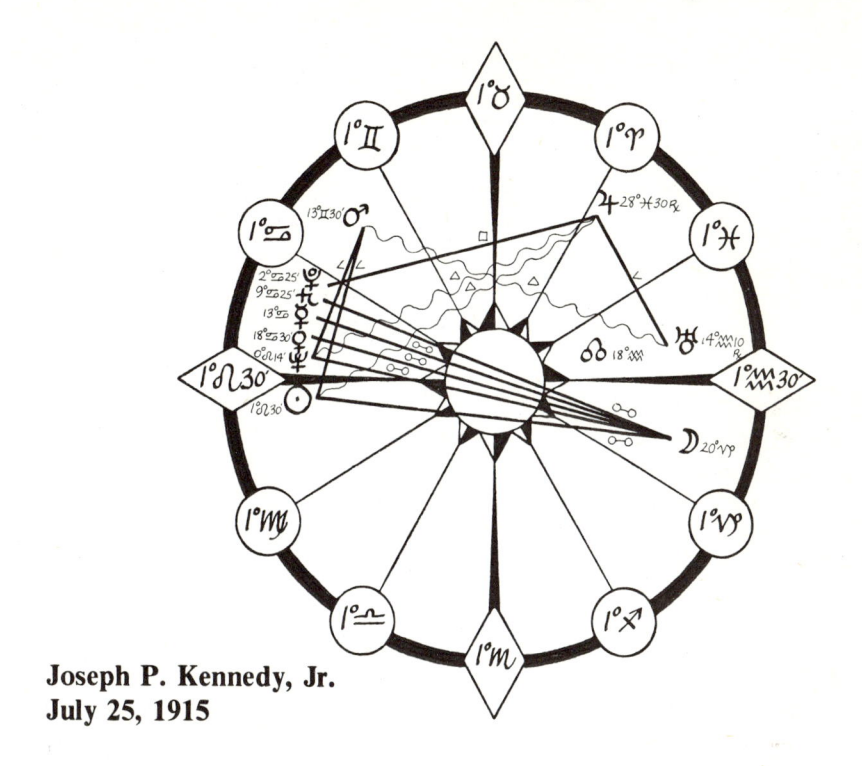

Joseph P. Kennedy, Jr.
July 25, 1915

A man of great ambition, like Joe's father, often subconsciously affirms a moral need to return to the land something of what has been taken out, returning to people some of the excess fruits one has garnered from their labors. This was the guiding early American imperative known as the Protestant Ethic. Wealthy industrialists of the late 1800s would contribute tithes to the nation in the form of endowments, funds, and every other sort of charity. Now taxes help them remember to kick back. But Joe, Sr. was raking in his first millions before incomes taxes, and—while known to be generous at times, he was no philanthropist. He was egotistical above all, with a burning desire to assert his manhood at every turn. Thus, what may have been a Protestant Ethic to American millionaires who preceded him became in Joe Kennedy an Irish Catholic instinct to give the nation a sprawling and public-spirited brood as his legacy.

The firstborn of so determined a man would have to embody all these aspirations, and embody them he did. Joe, Jr. was a natural. Not only did he exhibit all the characteristics of the sign of American political savvy, Cancer, and that of born leaders, as promised by his Sun in Leo, but he also seemed to promise fulfillment of every other dream of Kennedy glory the paterfamilias may ever have dreamt.

Joe, Jr.'s chart has the Sun conjunct Neptune, a planet of great illusions. Thus, he was the most charismatic of the entire brood. But he was also likely to seem to be what he was not to a great many. That, too, is the nature of Neptune. And so it happened that he did not, in fact, fulfill the promises his father saw incarnate in him. So it has gone with the rest—but, perhaps, as we shall see, not for all the same reasons. Each has seemed able, against most odds, to carry something off that may make them great. And then they realize that they are not up to all the odds, and we become aware that they are, in fact, mortal like the rest of us.

Maybe America was conceived by the wizards Jefferson, Franklin, et al, to be *fatal* to kings. For that's what they were, or hadn't you noticed their entourages, their culture, their glamor?

Since the exact time is unrecorded for Joe, Jr.'s birth, I am using the solar chart that you see here. Immediately, we can see a second great affinity between the father and son in the *shaping* of the charts, or where the planets fall. Like his father, Joe, Jr. so often found it his lot to concentrate his life energies in very specific areas so that other matters—what might be called normal areas of interest—were left untended.

Besides the close association of the signs Cancer and Leo with politics, and the association of the Moon's sign, Capricorn, with authoritarian matters, all three signs figure heavily in the lives of people with a lot of parental instincts. In this chart, the parental falls in two house areas mainly: the sixth and twelfth houses of service. The Moon, standing for children, is in the sixth, showing service to whom. Five of the Cancer/Leo planets are in the twelfth house—again, a house of service, but on a less practical and a more spiritual level, or else moved by great charity, and always self-sacrificing.

All of these labels fit Joe Kennedy, Jr. His responsibilities grew with each new baby born to his parents. The absence of planets in so many of the houses of his chart shows that, coupled with his services to his brothers and sisters, working toward his father's goals *and* heeding his mother's religious expectations (the twelfth house is highly religious), he had very little life of his own.

Character builds gradually in an oldest child whose responsibilities grow by percentages every two years or so when a new sibling is added to his care. And when your parents guide you so closely, you are apt to avoid not just the normal temptations, but the normal obstacles as well—for in their guidance was every sort of assistance, whether it helped in the long run or not.

Joe, Jr.'s chart has very little stress upon which to build the character to accomplish election to the presidency. His major dynamics stem from the stellium conjunction of Pluto/Saturn/Mercury/Venus in Cancer, of which Saturn, Mercury, and Venus oppose the Moon in Capricorn, and an out-of-sign square between Jupiter and Pluto. In the latter aspect, Pluto is in the twelfth house, right on the cusp. In the natural zodiac, the sign Pisces rules that cusp. Jupiter is a co-ruler of Pisces, and *in* that sign at Joe's birth. This further identifies him as someone whose life is dedicated to the service of others, but also as one with urges to negate the self—a form of self-sacrifice—especially for the sake of one's nation. The sun conjunct Neptune—Pisces co-ruler—helps triply emphasize this.

Joseph Kennedy, Jr. was not suicidal. His strong moral sense would have been sufficient to quell any such stirrings. Yet he was hard-pressed shortly before his death: His position as sibling chief of the Kennedy clan was being challenged by Jack, the next in line, and he had fallen deeply, tragically, in love. The woman was already married (her husband died, ironically, two days after Joe), and brother Jack had made the British news, as well as having been acclaimed a war hero at home.

Hard-pressed, males with heavy concentrations of planets in Cancer will feel their very manhood challenged. They will react with more compulsive machismo than males of any other sign. Apparently, although he had served out his tour of duty in the navy as a pilot, Joe, Jr. signed up for one last mission, to transport a dangerous load of high explosives. Before leaving, he called a friend in London and said: "I'm about to go into my act. If I don't come back, tell my Dad—despite our differences—that I love him very much."

Leo is the sign of great actors, as well as kings. Throughout history, great kings have been great actors, and vice versa. For a person denied (be it by fate or parents) a chance to grow strong in character against adversity—for whom, perhaps, responsibility and accountability had been the only prerequisites for parental favor—times when they are hard-pressed can suddenly become too much.

The immediacy of the conflict can cause the worst, instead of the best, of them to emerge. Faced with a need to express great romantic disappointment (it is said it was the first time he had fallen in love) and, at the same time, to wax more heroic than another, all the negatives of all the signs he possessed emerged. The machismo of Cancer demands physical extremes. The Capricorn depression of the Moon can sink human beings into the lowest of depths; it probably did. The Pisces of Jupiter demanded a final renunciation, and all the twelfth-house, Piscean phenomena of his chart doubtlessly brought him to the brink of the ultimate renunciation, for the imagined love of the Neptune on his Sun, with the corny gesture of that kind of rampant sentimentalism. But those weren't the only values that guided Joe, Jr.'s last moments. The patriotism, now stoked to its most blinding heat, was there every step of the way.

Questions of responsibility—or karma—are eventually aimed at Papa Joe: How much, in fact, is he to blame for all these Kennedy tragedies? In later sections this idea is examined more closely. Here, however, it might be fair to say that Joe, Jr.'s may be the tragedy most taken to heart by the fate-battered father for such reasons of responsibility—if we can be so precise in our judgment. I prefer karma, because it implies a composite of action, an entire life, whereas "responsibility" usually implies "for actions at a certain time, in a certain place, and with a certain intent in mind."

Most people can be *responsible,* legally, only for things it can be proven were *planned* by them. You don't *plan* the attitudes, prejudices, and conditioning that get absorbed in human families. It just happens. Joe Kennedy, the paterfamilias, was no different in that respect from any of us.

The old man never got over Joe Jr.'s death. As to whether we are to assume that he felt any deep responsibility—even if he had been the most unimpeachable of influences on the young man—he would have probably felt so. Did Joe, Jr. obviously go out in a blaze of glory because he had been taught by his father so thoroughly that "second place is no good"? We'll never know the answer to that one. Did Old Joe think so? We can never be sure. But he assisted the widow of his son's copilot in the raising of her three children, even to the point of sending her sons to college and acting, at times, as their surrogate father and adviser.

Those who knew the old man attest: he carried his grief to his grave.

**The Unwritten History:
Sexual Exploits of the Kennedy Males**

The double standard for men and women never got as much play as it did within the Kennedy Clan. It has been a basic structure within a civilization in which women have been forced to accept the inferior role, and, in a substructure of that civilization so dominated by the male mystique as the Kennedy family one could only expect such a standard to be tantamount to divine directive or dispensation.

That's how the Kennedy men treated the male-female role division. They kept their women pregnant (if not barefoot, as well) and in the kitchen (if only to supervise a complement of cooks, maids, and butlers) and continue to do so. Meanwhile, they saw no reason to respect the marriage vows they wholeheartedly expected the womenfolk to obey. Rules of marriage were for women; and, as long as the men were going about their important political, diplomatic, and business affairs, they felt they had every right to have a few frivolous affairs on the side. Whispers conveyed the bits of news, the general message throughout New Frontier Washington, D.C. Camelot was full of sexual intrigues.

Like most of the other dominant traits of the recent generation of adult male Kennedys, it had all been learned at Old Joe's knee—or, rather, by noting what the gossip columns were saying about *who* was on Old Joe's knee.

Old Joe's promiscuity is legendary. Because of the sexual double standard, the Kennedy males—and most Western males who preceded them over the past few millennia—would consider their pop's exploits sufficient to make him a hero. They certainly all emulated him. On the other hand, should one of the Kennedy *womenfolk* have dared carry on so, she would have been declared a witch and damned—if not actually stoned to death.

Rumors and verified accounts gathered from all the media and more intimate sources surrounding the Kennedys give us a somewhat rounded picture of Kennedy extra- or premarital escapades. Vignettes provide us with new perspectives on this, one of the most powerful families in the nation's history. Does lust for power automatically turn on other lusts, drives that were as basic to the Kennedy males as their quest for higher and higher elected office? Henry Kissinger has said, "Power is the ultimate aphrodisiac." Of course, we know how Henry likes to use superlatives like "ultimate," being one of the world's biggest power-trippers; however, we may assume that his statement is essentially correct when it is applied to the sexually magnetic onslaughts of Kennedy males on American female society.

While most of the sexual inferences made about them seem to be true, these remain baffling to an extent because of their great devotion to their families. Yet there needn't be any mystery here; after all, it's all in keeping with the path they have been on. All of the Kennedy males have married and raised large families. But they've had good reason to: First and foremost, they've all been Irish Catholic politicians and it is *expected* of them; secondly, having a large family prevents ardent admirers from getting *too* ardent, while it forces the wife to stay out of the way of both business and pleasure. The world-famous author Pearl Buck has written about this acquiescence in Kennedy women:

"The Kennedy men were never celebrated for faithfulness to their wives, but their wives found it worthwhile to continue as wives and mothers."

But Old Joe was the prototype. Everything his sons did was only a matter of following in his footsteps. He began as one of the youngest bankers in Boston, making his first million that way. It is said that he got his biggest account as a young man by spending an inordinate amount of time with a wealthy Boston matriarch; in fact, the account took up many of his nights as well.

Joe Kennedy became a movie mogul in the rip-roaring days of Hollywood, so he was naturally seen every night with a new starlet on his arm, while Rose tended to the family at Hyannis or Palm Beach. He was up-front to his sons about the differences between a mistress and a wife, warning them never to confuse the two. He rarely ever broke his own rules. Yet he was constant companion to the great movie goddesses of his era: Greta Garbo, Norma Shearer, Janet Gaynor, and Jean Harlow, to name a few.

The one time it seemed that he had forgotten his own advice, he fell madly in love with Gloria Swanson. The affair was creating quite a stir and, back home, rumors had reached scandalous proportions. Instead of going a bit easier, as friends advised, Joe further defied the tongue-cluckers. He and Miss Swanson, together in a new movie production company, made such films as the one in which she plays a nun who is seduced by a Prussian cavalryman and then inherits a string of bordellos. The affair became so flagrant that Kennedy even invited his lover to come with him and Rose on a European vacation. The austere Rose Kennedy was absolutely true to the code of the Kennedy women whose model she had become; she hardly noticed. In her autobiography she gives the "visit" of Gloria Swanson barely two lines.

Joe generally didn't give a damn what people were saying about him. When in New York, he hung out regularly with playboys Porfirio Rubirosa and the Cassini brothers, Igor and Oleg. His reputation prompted the president, Franklin Roosevelt, to call him in for a private chat before naming him Ambassador to England. "Go easy," said FDR, in so many words. Joe simply shot back that the president should get rid of his own mistress

(Missy Lehand) before peddling such advice to *him*.

His namesake, Joe, Jr., was no slouch. He followed his pop's slippersteps as closely as he could, compulsively jumping from one woman to another. For the father, what might have been part of a great drive to assert himself in every social arena, as well as in every worthy bedroom, became for the sons—and young Joe was the first to go through the paces—an almost painful compulsion to prove that they were as good a man as their father.

While at Harvard, Joe, Jr. became particularly boastful about his "way with women" one evening, sticking his neck out by saying that he could get a date for an upcoming dance with none other than Katharine Hepburn, who was appearing at a Boston theater. To save face, he laid his plea before the actress, who was so amused that she accepted—but on her own conditions. The two were seen the evening of the ball, but they were in the company of Miss Hepburn's mother.

While his conquests were many, Joe, Jr. was usually in control of himself. On leave during the war in St. Moritz, the young flyer nearly lost his legendary cool over a shapely Balkan princess. Unfortunately, after a few days of heavy romancing, she broke her leg coming down a slope (during one of her afternoons alone). Undaunted, he bribed her night nurse and spent the remainder of her nights with her, keeping her company at the hospital and no doubt displaying his athletic prowess. He usually stopped short of falling in love. In the solitary case where he did not remain true to the pattern, he apparently fell too deeply in love. It was something of a tragedy—he certainly took it that way—for, as we have noted, the woman was married; soon after that he signed up for the "suicide" mission in which he was killed.

Jack Kennedy inherited his older brother's place in the expectations of Papa Joe. He certainly showed signs of surpassing Joe in every way. His exploits, in fact, rival those of his father. At least there seems to be more collected about him, perhaps because he has been the only one of the brood, thus far, to have made it to the White House.

In the war, while a naval trainee, JFK was in the habit of dating the wives of navy men who were at sea. Once a husband returned so unexpectedly that the man who would be president one day had to shimmy out the window and run home barefoot, not having the time or the presence of mind to look for his shoes.

He would visit his parents at Palm Beach while on leave. During one particular summer of feeling his oats, his romantic exploits became a matter of local record when a society editor, Charles Ventura, wrote of him:

> "Palm Beach's social colony wants to give the son of Joseph P. Kennedy its annual oscar for achievement in the field of romance.
>
> "The old-timers here say that young Mr. Kennedy managed to rescue its sinking faith in the romantic powers of Florida, the Moon and You.
>
> "Worried dowagers were voicing the belief that the divorce court bench had taken the place of the love seat in Palm Beach when Jack saved the situation by giving Diure Malcom Desloge (and many others) the season's outstanding rush."

While a young legislator, he spent a good deal of time in New York City, where he became a denizen of the nightspots. He had a thing for chorus girls in those days and seemed *driven* from one affair to the next, a compulsive trait that has characterized all the Kennedy men.

Once while his father was in town carrying on his share of New York courtships, Jack was also seriously on the prowl. What happened then was not entirely inconceivable. Old Joe had been violating one of his prime rules again, getting too involved with a certain woman whom he had seen every night for a week. The next night, she called to say she couldn't make it—she said she was visiting a friend. Nevertheless, the old man thought he would try his luck at the Stork Club, his favorite haunt. As he entered, his "unavoidably detained" date came walking out with another man. If it had been anyone else, the old man might have made quite a scene; instead, he let out a slightly injured, yet swollen-with-pride bellow. Only his own son Jack—the young lady's escort—could pull *that* sort of stuff on him!

There was never a more insatiable romantic among the Kennedy men than Jack. What drove him on? While there are few known instances of Jackie, or any other Kennedy wife, for that matter, complaining, it is known that none of the wives, especially Jackie, stayed in the dark for long. Certainly, Jack didn't try that hard to conceal his hobbies. While a fledgling congressman, he would return at all hours of the morning, blaming the dedication of legislators who sit up in committee all night for the good of the country. One morning, rumor has it, after she had returned from a trip, Jackie found a strange bra in her drawer. Handing it to the then president, she said, "You might want to return this to its rightful owner. I'm sorry, but it's too big for me."

It was said that JFK *never* lost himself to love—not even with Jackie.

Once at a party in the Paris home of the former Peggy Bedford Bancroft, the Duchess d'Uzesn, JFK fell to necking with one of the prettier guests, when someone took pictures, for the Duchess' scrapbook. Right after JFK was sworn in, the pictures disappeared—a feat of magic the duchess sagely attributes to the CIA.

What did the opinion of a mere duchess matter, anyway? It is said that he and the future Princess Grace of Monaco were close friends at one time. And there have even been rumors that family ties didn't dissuade the man, that he may have once had an intimate relationship with Jackie's sister, Princess Lee Radziwill.

Of course, he probably did his duty as a husband as well—and as thoroughly. He ordered a DO NOT DISTURB sign hung on the Presidential bedroom doorknob after lunch, earning himself the title, among the regulars at the White House, of "Jack the Zipper."

Recklessness characterized his span of months in the White House. He was rumored to have seduced even the female reporters who came to White House dances, to throw wild, swinging parties on the premises, to transport sex toys through the whited porticos, and to skinny-dip in mixed company in the pool at Camp David.

The night before he was nominated at the Democratic convention in Los Angeles, he gave reporters the slip and roared off to a "Rat Pack" hideaway and to a beautiful young starlet whom his Hollywood friends had invited for the occasion. Before the inauguration, there were several such small-scale scandals. His father gave a party in a posh New York restaurant. According to those who were there, the president-elect made a slight spectacle of himself dancing very close to a buxom woman, constantly kissing her on the neck and shoulder. The next day, Earl Wilson wrote of the incident: "On the night before his inauguration as president, the swingers' swinger arranged for one of his several fixers to assist him in carrying out a rendezvous with a divorceé who had a child." Later, even less-substantiated rumors had him fathering a love child by a woman who fit that description.

On the eve of the inauguration, JFK asked a friend for the loan of his apartment. When the friend registered shock about the timing, Kennedy pooh-poohed him, saying, "If tonight isn't the night to celebrate, there never will be one."

Perhaps the most widespread rumor about JFK's sexual exploits centers on his reputed relationship with Marilyn Monroe. This rumor has had so much play that it emerges and re-emerges in the most bizarre ways. The most notable of late is the fiction piece, "History," that appeared in the June, 1975, issue of *Swank*. It is the story of a present-day, bearded hipster whose boat runs aground on a small and uncharted island off the Carolinas. It happens that two people who amazingly resemble Marilyn Monroe and Jack Kennedy live there with every imaginable creature comfort—even though the island paradise is all but totally isolated from civilization. The hero puts two and two together, discovering that the two are, in fact, *exactly* who they seem to be: The pressures of life in America have grown too great for them, so they have arranged for doubles to die in their places in order to drop out/opt out for paradise. But of course, once revealed, their secret happiness is forever jeopardized, so our fictional JFK stabs the young intruder to death.

What *is* substantiated about this relationship is that Marilyn was a main guest and celebrant at JFK's birthday party, thrown by his show-biz pals, and sang "Happy Birthday" especially for him. While this is the only time they were seen together in public, it is widely believed that she was smuggled into the White House, or that the two lovers met in a Rat Pack pad or in JFK's own apartment in the Hotel Carlisle in New York City.

Marilyn's tragic death preceded JFK's by a year, but it is said that she had gone through a good many changes by that time. Two years had passed since JFK's inauguration, and almost as much time since their romance smoldered at the time of his birthday. In that interval, it is said that her eyes turned to younger brother Bobby. No one thought she took him seriously at first, but they were all soon doing double takes. It is believed, by some in fact, that the tragedy of her last moments was tied to her confused and painful relationship with RFK.

Of all the Kennedy men, RFK's record of infidelities seems to have been the smallest. Few could lay a glove on him. He had the longest list of offspring and the shortest list of known romantic conquests. But that's not to say that he was a slacker. Compared to the average healthy young man, RFK's exploits were legion. It's just that he seemed to pale in the light—or glowing heat—of the records of his older brothers. Marilyn may have been a turning point in his life, in terms of reputation. Only he may not have been prepared at the time to handle the notoriety. He was far more secretive than any of his brothers.

Stories appearing recently connect RFK to Marilyn's death. There seem to be two general theories about his culpability. Both stem from the contention that she had reached a critical period of nervous confusion and was threatening to sink him and his brother—the whole administration—into scandal. Some say that RFK ordered her killed; others say that it was a case of overanxious aides who responded, as did the murderous barons in the service of Charles the Second of England, when he said of Thomas à Becket, "Will no one rid me of this meddlesome priest?"

There are those who say that she was killed by splinter groups of the cloak-and-dagger community, who tried to lay the scandal in the young attorney general's lap, as well as a greater number who contend that it was a simple suicide, or an "accidental suicide." The latter idea might hold the secret to the mystery for the average person, reading the newly revealed details of Marilyn Monroe's death.

Some theorize that Pat and Peter Lawford were in on a plot

along with the blonde bombshell to get Bobby to prove his love for her. She was to fake a suicide attempt by taking a fatal dose of barbiturates. Then she was to call Bobby, who would be having dinner at the Lawfords. Her call and farewell message would then, supposedly, cause Bobby to rush to her side and save her life.

There is evidence that Marilyn was setting the scene shortly before she died: the major medicinal aid for such a fatal dose of the barbiturate would have been oxygen, and she is known, in one of her last statements to her maid, to have inquired whether there was any oxygen in the house. She also asked the maid to make sure that she had the number of a certain doctor handy. If these things are true, it doesn't look as if she wanted to die.

But if this theory is true, then something went wrong. Bobby never got the call. She was dead before help could arrive.

Researchers contend that someone *prevented* the call from coming through; they claim that someone close to Bobby probably intercepted the call. Some say that it was Frank Sinatra, who had soured considerably on Bobby after the young attorney general had set the government's legal hounds on the crooner for his Mafia connections. Sinatra had invested a lot in his relationship with the Kennedys. He had even added a half-million-dollar wing to his home to house the President of the United States whenever he visited. Yet Bobby's released findings on his pal's criminal connections proved too embarrassing for JFK, who had to curtail the relationship publicly. It is said that, with mob help, it was Sinatra who engineered the whole thing. However, some observers believe that if it was an "accidental suicide" it was pulled off by aides, friends, or intelligence operatives close to Bobby. And then, of course, there's the ever-present CIA . . .

As for the youngest of the Kennedy boys, the incident at Chappaquiddick seems to characterize—extreme an example as it may be—the astonishing recklessness displayed by Ted Kennedy in his relationships with other women. *Time* magazine once wrote of him: "The thing that most baffles politicians is Ted's lack of caution. Some who have long watched the Kennedys can say, with certainty, that Sen. Edward Kennedy often flirts with pretty girls in situations indiscreet for someone in his high position."

Some observers believe that this is because Teddy really wants nothing to do with the presidency. He is using, it seems to them, the behavioral extremes of other Kennedy males to ensure that he won't ever be elected.

Someone supposedly has a picture of Teddy streaking naked down a beach with an equally naked blonde. And Arthur Egan, writing for the New Hampshire *Sunday News* (and echoed in the pages of *Newsweek* and the *Washington Post*), stated: "Two high-stepping playboy U.S. Senators, taking advantage of a Congressional recess, spent a pre-Labor Day holiday sailing around Penobscot Bay with two lovely females who were definitely not their wives.

"Senators Edward M. Kennedy and John V. Tunney spent at least four days aboard the *Curragh,* Kennedy's power sloop, with the two women.

"One of the women with the senators has been identified as Mrs. Amanda Burden, the pretty twenty-six-year-old wife of Carter Burden, New York millionaire socialite and Democratic Councilman."

Perhaps in Teddy we will witness a rebirth of purpose, divorced by time and the grave from the traditions that went before. His driving father has been dead for a decade, his brothers Jack and Bobby long gone. There is no longer anyone to emulate, no one's reputation to live up to. Maybe his excesses are preface to a long sabbatical from the Kennedy power hunt. He has shown himself to be the best politician of all the Kennedys; perhaps he will heal himself by deciding he doesn't need to prove himself to women any longer—or to the men who measure personal success by sexual conquest—but to the American public instead.

In our look into the astrological chart factors that are held in common by the Kennedy clan, we will see the repetition of the planet Neptune and emphasis on the eighth house, that of Scorpio, sign of the sex drive. Neptune is a planet of illusion and charisma; so, fed by the illusion of sexual conquest, did the Kennedy men use these powers to achieve purely eighth-house ends. As Scorpio is also the sign of compulsions and psychoanalysis, we may come to understand and forgive them for even their most blatant indiscretions. Among the Irish, as among other highly religious immigrant groups, the need for psychological aid has often been equated with a most unmanly weakness. Perhaps the whole brood needed analysis after leaving the nest. Yet they plowed right on through life as their father had and dealt with each compulsion to succeed—no matter how unhealthy the expression—as it came.

4

What the Charts Tell Us About the Curse

These thirty charts, taken as a whole, reveal a great deal about the Kennedys. When salient positions are extracted from the Family Composite Chart, they disclose shared propensities, weaknesses, directions, and pitfalls. Eventually, from these extractions will emerge the essence of what we have come to call "The Kennedy Curse."

Time Charts: So marked, these eight are the only ones of the group of family charts for whom reasonably accurate birth times were recorded. (The remaining charts are solar charts—symbolic of the birth occurring at sunrise—which I have apologized for previously; they are still valid, however, especially when viewed as a part of a group of charts.) Those included are of Rose, Joe, Sr., John, Robert, Ted, Caroline, her brother, John-John, and their mother, Jackie.

Solar Charts: I looked at all aspects between planets and lights in the larger survey, which also contains the untimed charts that follow. My main interest in looking at time charts was to see what was happening in what houses—specifically, what planets were there? You can be *sure* that a planet was in a house with a time

The Kennedys by house

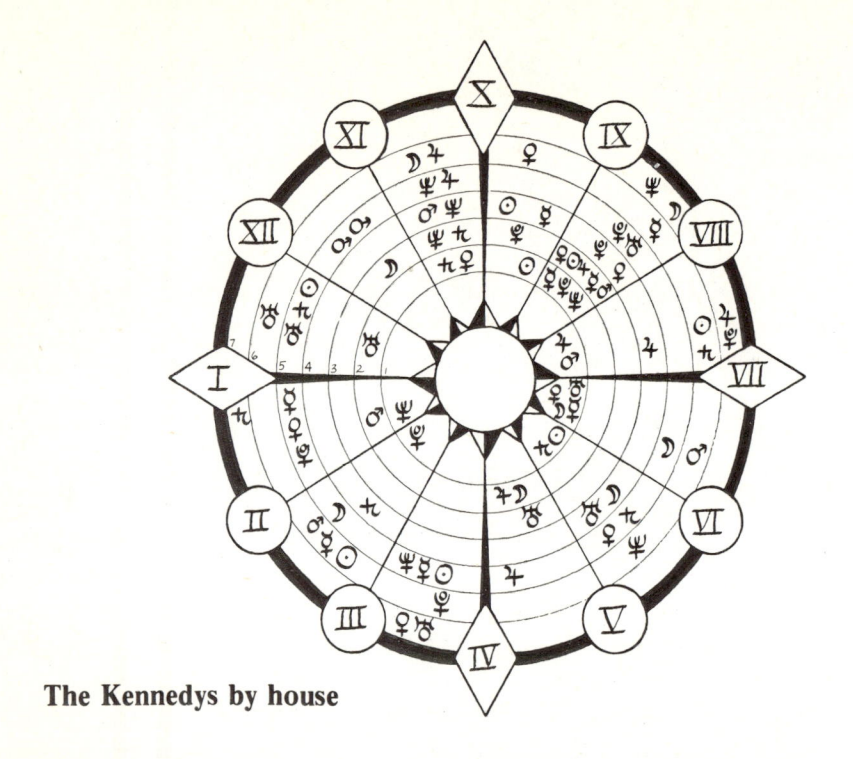

chart, whereas you only symbolically take this to be true in the case of solar charts. House activity shows the emphasis of certain areas of life in the individual's behavior and motivation. In showing general direction for the individual, and, thus, for the group when in a composite form, it speaks very clearly to the notion of a common destiny. This would be difficult to stretch out over the other 22 (solar) charts as well, without being symbolically supported in some way by the findings in those charts.

Ideally, the findings in such a study should be easily interpreted to show what we already know—or practically, anyway. This shorter survey did not disappoint me at all.

First, remember that we are looking for the houses of each of the eight time charts that contain the most planets or lights. Of the latter group there are eight planets and two lights, or ten "planets," as astrologers are wont to call all those *wanderers* that seem to cross our skies each night and day: ten bodies falling anywhere among twelve sectors, or houses. The odds are that .833 planets will be in each house of an individual's chart, or in the case of eight charts, 6.664, or about seven planets per house. Results (see graph on page 112) show that distribution among the twelve houses was quite uneven, so that eight houses had below the average expectancy of planets present. Imbalances are to be expected to some degree; however, these are heavy biases and point to what is well known about the guiding lights of the Kennedy family.

Seven planets each fall in the fifth and seventh houses. This is the average that we would expect. It indicates that of those studied there is always sufficient attention paid to the matters of children (fifth) and mates (seventh).

The second-most occupied house is the tenth, that of government, authority, the public eye, older people, and matters that take a long time in their development. There are ten planets in this house of the composite time chart. In three cases, the planet Neptune is there, clearly showing both the charisma that brought the family to high places (also, alcohol and cinema—the true sources of the family's wealth) and the illusory quality of that power. For Joe Kennedy himself, it represented the slow and tragic fading of the dream.

Again, we know all these things about the Kennedys already. But the house that remains to be studied is the most significant of them all. The eighth house of the composite contains a lopsided fifteen planets. The eighth house is the sex house (Scorpio, in the natural zodiac) and represents the reproductive urge. Being a secretive house and sign, such a concentration of planets there would assure clandestine or illicit sexual relations—not just among the men, but probably, on occasion, among the women as well. But—sex and procreation—they're not *all* of what Scorpio and the eighth house are all about.

Astrologers stress birth *and regeneration* when referring to this zone of the chart; and by regeneration we mean the process beginning with what we have taken to be an absolute ending: death. The eighth is the main house of death in fact; but it is death implying "change of form."

We tend to sensationalize in saying that the Kennedys are all destined to die—who among us isn't? We're on the same cycle they're on. We'll all be around in some form or another when our bodies no longer contain our souls. What is it to be concentrated in the eighth house, but to bear many offspring while constantly remaining aware of one's own mortality? As a matter of fact, people tend to want to reproduce themselves in children en masse, particularly when they feel they are about to die. Witness, if you will, the postwar baby-boom phenomenon—especially children. Those children were conceived between men and women who were uncertain that they would ever see one another again. With that simple tie-in, we can perhaps wrap up what this heavy eighth-house concentration tells us about the Kennedys and let it go at that.

But other details gnaw at one's explorative spirit. What about the "extraneous" assassination facts rejected by the voices of officialdom? There is little doubt that the report by the Warren Commission is being repudiated. If astrology tells us anything, it should at least be able to say whether, in the immediately recognizable common family destiny, there is a propensity for meeting the kind of fate implied by unofficial assassination researchers.

The eighth house answers that question in a bellowing affirmative, with no mouth-filling expletive deleted. Assassins—conspirators of every type and persuasion, murderers of every variety—are found under the rulership of Scorpio and the eighth house. Yet, this only whets our appetite; the next question is, if astrology can affirm running up against this type, can it also help to *identify* them? Again, the answer is yes—only, a bit more tentatively: Many occupations and types are ruled by the eighth house and its natural sign, among them counselors, surgeons, teachers, and, in general, many others not in any way involved in conspiracies.

In fact, no occupation falling under the rulership of the eighth is intended slander by any association I draw here. All I am saying is that certain *types,* and members of certain professions, have been, if only peripherally, implicated in conspiracy theories surrounding the death of President John F. Kennedy. A complete list of such types and occupations ruled by Scorpio and the eighth house can be found in the glossary at the end of the book. For

What the Charts Tell Us about the Curse 103

now, a few should be pointed out: secret agencies, espionage groups, detectives, writers of mystery novels, tramps, those who have (or betray) a great trust, and coroners. Each of these types figures somewhere in current, private investigations of the assassinations. If astrology hasn't provided absolute identification of the guilty parties, it begins, in this analysis of the minor grouping of time charts, to narrow the field. What remains is to discover to what extent the findings in the entire composite, that of the time and solar charts, will bear out any of the findings.

The Total Family Composite: Planets in Signs

Again, I'm including the Sun and Moon when I say planets here. Of the thirty charts studied, the average for the appearance of planets in signs remains the same for each individual chart as for the twelve houses: Planets appear in each sign at the rate of .833

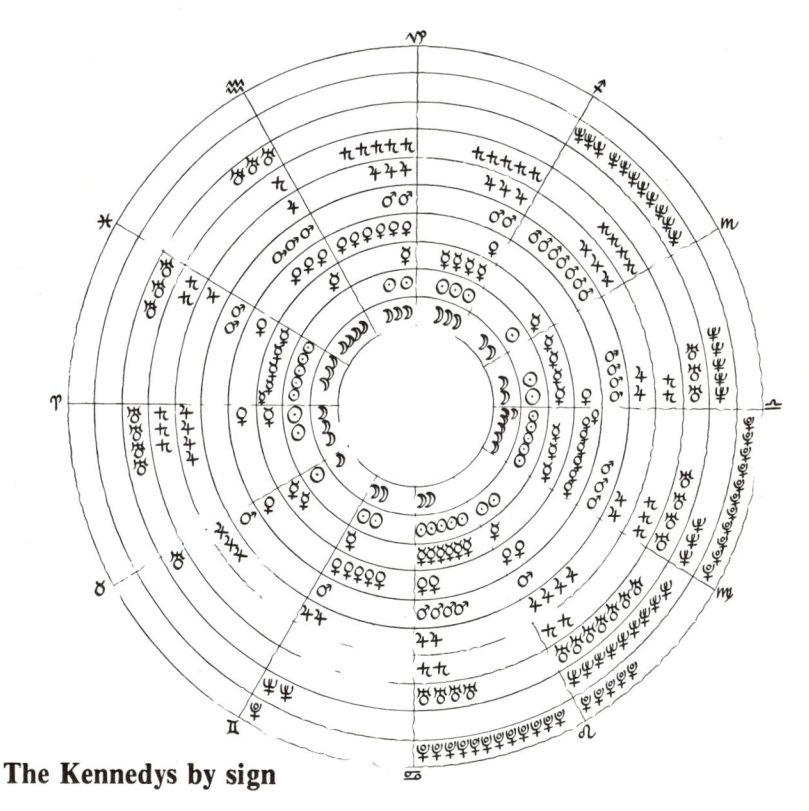

The Kennedys by sign

per chart. In thirty charts, then, there should be an average of 30 x .833, or 24.99. Thus, in any sign you ought to be able to find an average of twenty-five planets.

Seven signs have a below-average number of planets present. One is about average—the sign Libra, containing 24 planets. Once again, *sufficient* attention seems to be paid marital duties, and a sense of decorum in these matters seems to have been observed in spite of extramarital carryings on. And the family continues, in this greater analysis, to have its "fair share" of *open* enemies— again, Libra (the twelfth and eighth houses indicate one's hidden enemies).

Of the signs that are inhabited more than an average number of times, Scorpio is the one that so concerned us in the previous, shorter study. The appearance of thirty planets in Scorpio begins to provide the study with symbolic backing for the earlier findings of concentration in the eighth-house/Scorpio area.

Of the thirty planets present, only seven could be construed to be benevolent or otherwise harmless. The other 23 promise tragedy. What is most significant here is that eleven of those twenty-three danger planets are placements across the thirty charts of the natural twelfth-house ruler, Neptune. It appears eleven times in Scorpio. Although this may in fact be a *generational* phenomenon, Neptune serves to combine the symbols of hidden enemies, death, and endings in one sign, Scorpio, or that of the lethal eighth house. Also, if you'll recall, Neptune was the main tenth-house planet of the time charts, the tie-in here representing one of the roads to tragedy (from high authority to assassination—tenth to eighth houses) and all the mystery (Neptune) surrounding those tragedies.

The sign Cancer has thirty-eight planets in it, and the sign Leo has thirty-four, far above the average, and here, for the first time, indicating the very heavy emphasis in the Kennedy family on the family itself, or on having large families, and, in a greater sense, on the family in the United States. Cancer is both our nation's Sun sign and the sign of politicians, so these house placements present a picture not only of a large family, but also of the virtual first family of American politics.

Before looking at the most populated of the signs in the composite chart of the Kennedys, I must digress to explain something about the order of the houses and the signs that rule them. Looking at a natural zodiac chart with Aries rising, you will note that the signs Aries through Virgo are beneath, while Libra through Pisces are above. We speak of this as above and below the horizon. All the houses and signs below the horizon are associated with matters that are for the most part concerned with inner motivations and developments, while those above the horizon are concerned with outer attractions and the needs of others.

The greatest number of planets in the composite chart—forty-seven to be exact, including five birth Suns and six Moons—fall in the sixth house sign, Virgo. The main principle is inescapable: Virgo is the sign of service; thus, an essential part of inner development entails answering various calls to service. In terms of this larger study, a secondary grouping of motivations stems from the great grouping of planets in the Cancerian field of American politicians (thirty-eight) and the Leonine sign of leadership and great popular love (thirty-four). Once again, this is a below-the-horizon influence and as much a part of their family nature as summers at Hyannis; a growing family and a prospering America go hand in hand. Motivation from *above* the horizon may be seen as a set of inevitables. The heavy concentration among the eight timed charts of the most prominent family members shows that most of these eight dream(t) of inevitably being in high authority. Service, especially in elected office, often leads to this kind of power for the Kennedys. But then, so too does it inevitably call upon the forces of death—embodied, perhaps, in powerful enemies—to be always hot at their heels.

Bobby Kennedy, who was the only Scorpio among the family lights, was once a rackets investigator, making him an eighth house type. Death always is a hazard of that tenuous trade. It may have become an inevitability, somewhere along the line, that he be "paid" for all the mafiosi he sent to prison. However, had he stayed a lawyer instead of running for high office, he might be still alive. If Jack had stuck to his eighth-house dream, instead of bolstering his father's tenth-house dream of the American presidency, he might still be teaching writing at some ivy league college and living quite nicely, independently, at least, on royalties from his books.

But becoming president was an inevitability for JFK; running for the highest office was inevitable for RFK. The needs of others that brought Jack Kennedy to Dallas on November 22, 1963, were of a long set of responsibilities and inevitabilities that came with his job and that led, fatally, from the earliest days of his father's urgings to a motorcade past Dealey Plaza.

Further Breakdowns of Thirty Planet-in-Sign Charts

Thirty charts with 10 planets in each gives us 300 planets to distribute. The sign breakdown, as I have shown, is quite uneven. Where the unevenness is even more revealing, however, is in the breakdown among the elements in astrology and the so-called qualities. The elements are Fire, Earth, Air, and Water; the

Sign/Planet	Sun	Moon	Mercury	Venus	Mars	Jupiter	Saturn	Uranus	Neptune	Pluto	Total
♈	2	3	1	1	0	4	3	4	0	0	18
♉	1	1	2	1	1	2	0	1	0	0	9
♊	2	2	2	5	1	3	0	0	2	2	19
♋	5	2	5	2	4	2	2	4	0	12	38
♌	2	0	1	3	1	4	2	7	9	5	34
♍	5	6	3	6	3	2	4	4	3	11	47
♎	2	1	4	1	4	2	2	3	5	0	24
♏	1	2	1	0	8	3	4	0	11	0	30
♐	3	3	4	1	1	3	5	0	0	0	20
♑	2	3	1	6	2	3	5	0	0	0	22
♒	0	4	1	3	3	1	1	3	0	0	16
♓	5	3	5	1	2	1	2	4	0	0	23

qualities are Cardinal, Fixed, and Mutable. These are explained more fully at the end of the book; brief explanations will suffice here.

There are seventy-two planets in the element Fire, seventy-eight in Earth, sixty-nine in Air, and ninety-one in Water. The average expected is seventy-five. In the Kennedy charts, Fire and Air—the creative, communicative faculties—are generally weak. This—except for JFK, who excelled in communication and took deep interest in the arts—may account for the predominance first of Earth (though associated with simple wealth, enough *money* to buy all the culture and breeding that was necessary, or *possessions* to compensate for the lack of refinement) and Water—the family and public element—which sublimated the urge to create into the building of a large family or the manipulation of the public mood.

All in all, however, this breakdown tells us little. The most telling of these larger-category breakdowns is that among the qualities of the signs. There are three: Cardinal, which includes the signs Aries, Cancer, Libra, and Capricorn; Fixed, which includes Taurus, Leo, Scorpio, and Aquarius; and Mutable, or Common, which includes Gemini, Virgo, Sagittarius, and Pisces. You will note that each quality contains four signs, one from each of the elements. In the thirty charts studied, and with an expectancy of 100 in each of the three qualities, I found that there was an average number of placements in Cardinal signs—102. A below-average 89 planets were present in Fixed signs, however—which shifted the balance to the Mutable signs, for there were 119 planets present in this group.

Now, there is a Jungian way of looking at the qualities: We may see the Cardinal influence as being quite similar to extroversion, the Fixed group to exhibit characteristics akin to introversion, and the Mutable group to be like what Jung's student Neumann called the centroverts.

The first group, the extroverts, live very much in an external reality, constantly interacting with people; the second group, the introverts, live according to a very subjective reality—they interpret what sense data they receive and fit it into some overview, and thus take a very long time to act or reach critical decisions. The chief distinction between these two groups is that the latter includes thinkers and the former, doers. The world needs both.

However, members of the third group fall somewhere in between. Poised between thought and action, the centroverts are constantly tilting in either direction; sometimes they go heavily one way or the other, but not for long. While extroverted-Cardinal-sign types charge ahead insensitively, centroverted Mutables pause to see the consequences of their actions. When introverted Fixed sign types enter their 87th hour of meditation on a beautiful phenomenon of nature, centroverted Mutables have already photographed the whole event, written it up, and sold it to a local newspaper; bored easily, they go on to the next attraction. Cardinals are tuned to accomplishment, Fixed to reflection and private thought, and Mutables to the communication that must intercede before the efforts of either of the other two can be applied to the good of the whole.

This can go a long way to characterize the Kennedys. The sign of service, as I mentioned before, is paramount. Virgo, with forty-seven planets, is the chief direction taken by all this Mutability. Mutables are helpful in many ways—more so than most of the Cardinal and Fixed signs—and, with Virgo doubly emphasizing this tendency, we once again see the fatal calling to serve exerting its influence.

Repeated Aspects Between Planets and Lights

The aspects in the Kennedy charts that repeat most often are also indicators of the course of family destiny. In the following listing, only those aspects that repeat in more than 20 percent of the cases have been considered as relevant. Unlisted are the so-called generational influences that stay in aspect over a long period. Included in this unlisted group are the long-term effects of Uranus conjunct Pluto (occurring mostly during the sixties, when the majority of the latest brood of Kennedy children were born). This conjunction, promising vastly disrupting and fateful influences, occurs in 20 percent of the charts we are studying. Also left out of this study is the sextile between Neptune and Pluto—or the fated, forced study of mysteries, the effects over a long period of confusion and deep psychological uncertainty, the place of Providence in the fate of the family, as well as the part played by secret groups—which occurs in 48 percent of the charts.

The first planet, or light, we should look at is the Moon. It forms several aspects to the Sun and other planets, but none occurs in more than 20 percent of the charts, save the adverse square between Moon and Sun. *Moon square Sun occurs in 22 percent of the cases.* Several family traits can be attributed to this combination. Generally, this is symbolic of very basic male-female polarities, or, more correctly, difficulties in blending the masculine element with female attributes. Many astrologers believe that when such adversity occurs at birth there were, at the same time, difficulties between one's parents. Moreover, there is no ease in relating the roles of male and female either in the family and in the greater arena of life. This pertains, too, to the womanizing habits so highly developed in Kennedy males. From a purely personal point of view, whenever this aspect occurs in an individual's chart we can expect that one's public image (Moon) is at variance with one's basic drives (Sun).

The next set of aspects pertains to the planet of intellect, *Mercury, which is conjunct the Sun in over 50 percent of the cases.* Normally, because of this small planet's close proximity to the Sun (from our Earth-bound point of view) the conjunction would occur in about 37 percent of the cases in any sampling. The greater-than-average frequency in which the conjunction occurs indicates a strong intellectual bent among members of the Kennedy family. Also, it indicates a quest for self-understanding and objectivity. Being the planet of business, it further indicates a certain ingrained wheeler-dealer propensity.

Mercury is also conjunct Venus in 26 percent of the cases. This combines the intellectual, communicative faculties with the appreciation of the finer things in life. Again, because of the close apparent proximity of these two planets, conjunctions occur rather frequently. While this fact makes the frequency of conjunctions here a bit less than an important phenomenon, it points out the direction of both communicative and business faculties. Business, being carried out since the early days of the family's history on these shores, has been with a mind toward improving status and life-style. Education has been toward the same ends. In national politics, the family drive has been toward developing broader-than-sectional appeal and a gracefulness of communication.

Venus semisquare the Sun occurs in 20 percent of the charts. This, too, is a more or less frequent aspect, given the apparent closeness of the two bodies in the astrologer's heaven. However, it tends to negate some of the more positive aspects of Mercury conjunct the Sun, as it causes a strain running through the family psyche to *push* for refinement, a concept somewhat contradictory within itself: If you strain to refine sentiments and modes of communication, you tend to show the strain and reveal more the *need* for refinement than its achievement.

Venus is one of the chief feminine planets, in fact, it is symbolic of most women between the ages of seventeen and forty-five. The strained aspect to the Sun—like the squares from the Moon—again points out the problems, or strained life-styles, of Kennedy men (Sun) in their relations with women.

Mars trines the Moon in 20 percent of the charts, indicating an energetic, *physical* appeal—a trait that is obviously connected to the Kennedy charisma. It normally gives a great deal of energy in responding to public needs; however, *Mars is also square the Moon in 20 percent of the cases,* indicating a harmful precipitous, or gut-oriented, responsiveness that may be, at the least, counterproductive. It also promises widespread attacks in the public arena—both attacks of an overt, honest, and above-board nature and those that actually put the body (Moon) in danger. *Mars is also square Saturn in 20 percent of the Kennedy charts,* promising great obstacles as well as conflicts and dangers. These two, aside from being the most immediate of the *malefic* planets, are also great frustrators when combined in this manner. Mars is energy and Saturn, restriction. Together, they symbolically become the "irresistible force" that meets with the "immovable object." Mars is personal, active zeal, and Saturn is the intransigence of systems and authorities. At times, in the family's history, the fervor of the reformer has met with fierce resistance from the powers that be; in some instances, zeal has forced reforms, while at other times a great wall has been erected against those efforts. Current theories have it that the forces of Saturn, biding their time, as they characteristically do, waited only as long as it took for the Kennedys to reveal a single chink in their armor. Dallas and Los Angeles, it is postulated with probable accuracy, were the Saturn forces' *right moments*.

Next, *Jupiter is trined by the Sun in 20 percent of the charts*—as good a symbol as we need to represent great wealth and perhaps even its sources (indulgences in alcohol, *big* business, and political appeal, Jupiter governing each of these), as well as the generally good opportunities that have presented themselves to members of the family and, of course, the rather hearty state of their health. On the other hand, *Jupiter squares Uranus in 20 percent of the cases*. The active side of this aspect allowed them to "push their luck" successfully at several times in their composite history, as well as to use willful methods (Uranus) in dealing with benevolent authorities. It also represents, to some extent, the liberalizing attitudes they developed toward the distribution of wealth. On the negative or passive side, it represents fanatical responses to their liberalism. Mostly, it represents the sudden loss of the more positive qualities of Jupiter—including wealth, health, and public position.

The Great Inhibitor, *Saturn, is conjoined by the Sun in 20 percent of the charts.* Again, the whole matter of serious restrictions is highlighted. Saturn, representing the skeletal system, was JFK's back troubles. Saturn is also one of the great father figures of astrology, and in a very real way—while his urgings forced them to succeed (success is a Saturn factor) in entering the rarified atmosphere of great leaders—Papa Joe Kennedy's great ambitions also led his sons to disaster. The Ringed Giant represents the entrenched systems faced by all the political Kennedys. It is a great weight, a great sense of responsibility. It is also the past that demands accounting for, as well as more conservative elements of society that oppose them.

Uranus trined by the Sun in 22 percent of the charts represents the modern, and its role in their lives. It is innovation; it represents the reformer. People-oriented, it describes their urge to strengthen democracy and their reliance on the will of the people in achieving elected office.

112   THE KENNEDY CURSE

The placement of *Neptune* in the houses and signs has already been examined. In aspects, it *is trined by the Sun in 26 percent of the charts,* or in one out of every four charts. It represents such matters as public image and charisma, and further points to an urge toward human refinement, but here it also shows a desire to spread such opportunities among the populace. *Neptune is also squared by the Sun in 20 percent of the charts.* As mentioned in the previous sections, this stands for the weaknesses that were and are inherent in their political reign. It is dissipation of strength and hidden illnesses, such as JFK's relatively unknown adrenal problems. It stands, as well, for the hidden enemies that accounted for the lives of at least two of the family stars.

Finally, *Pluto is squared by the Sun in 20 percent of the cases.* This is perhaps the most fateful of the aspects thus far. Pluto is inevitability. Its cycle is the longest in our solar system and thus becomes the longest of term influences. It represents unavoidable and often hidden controls, and, what is perhaps the most important consideration when examining the assassinations, it also represents investigators, detectives and *secret groups,*

Planet / Aspect	Conjunction ☌	Semi-square ∠	Sextile ✶	Square □	Trine △	Opposition ☍
☽	24	6	12	40 (☉ 22%, ♂ 20%)	32 (♂ 20%)	23
☉	25 (☿ 50%, ♄ 20%)	7 (♀ 20%)	8	19 (♆ 20%, ♀ 20%)	27 (♆ 20%, ♅ 22%, ♆ 26%)	4
☿	16 (♀ 26%)	2	13	8	9	2
♀	10	2	10	8	9	8
♂	3	4	7	15 (♄ 20%)	4	7
♃	6	0	8	10 (♅ 20%)	12	5
♄	3	0	2	5	9	3
♅	3	0	0	5	4	0
♆	2	0	10	0	0	0
♇	0	0	0	0	0	0

conspiracies, and *espionage groups.* Because of Neptune's frequent association in the Kennedy composite with the sign Scorpio or its eighth house, Pluto—ruler of Scorpio—is also closely tied in with the Kennedys' hidden enemies.

The fourteen significant aspects listed above repeat themselves with enough frequency in the composite to warrant study here. Of the fourteen, only six are benevolent aspects; however, of those, two, the trines from Uranus and Pluto, may be also seen in a somewhat malefic light. Of the malefic planets from Saturn outward in the solar system, it is said that *no contact at all* is the best of the possible relationships with such planets. In other words, while the Neptune trine brings vast appeal and the Uranus trine brings innovation and reform-consciousness, it is thought easiest if they did not occur at all. Since these planets are chiefly malefic—because the human race hasn't yet developed to the point where it can best appreciate and utilize their qualities—even a trine to or from one of them will have its serious drawbacks.

The populist characteristics of the two aforementioned aspects made the Kennedys as many enemies as followers. The human race—as represented by a good number of our fellow citizens here in the United States—is still very much unready to deal with the greater good that may be waiting for us in each of these planetary principles.

Neptune is tied closely to the principle of brotherly love, while Uranus is associated with democracy. The Kennedy's interests in expanding democratic principles in the South, as well as their growing resistance to foreign wars and murder plots, made them many enemies among those for whom brotherly love and the human implications of democracy were too much to swallow.

The repetition of fated aspects, such as those to or from Saturn and the squares of the Sun to Pluto, coupled with the frequency of adverse aspects, were such that something had to come to a head. The timing of this karmic pay-off is investigated elsewhere. We may note here, however, that the term of the conjunction of Uranus and Pluto (mentioned in the beginning of this section) represents a period during which the heaviest of the fated forces came into their own. This period occurred during the sixties and is now ended. We may come to discover that the most dangerous period for the Kennedys is over. That could, of course, simply mean that no Kennedy will ever again run for high public office, although Ted Kennedy, these days, at least, seems very much a possible national candidate. Then again, it may mean that the issues that have occupied the attention of the political members of the family over the past decade and a half are *dead*. If the "Cowboys and Yankees" theory of the CIA battle for power is true, and if, as some leftist observers have maintained, there has already been a secretive military-industrial takeover here, maybe there will no longer be the *democratic opportunity* to address one's self to the kinds of issues on which the Kennedys have built their political reputations.

5

The Assassins: Everyone's Questions

Strollers on the streets of New York City would have been considerably taken aback in March of 1975 if they had not been aware of the much-publicized story then running in the current issue of *Penthouse* magazine. There, in the traffic, were dark green city buses bearing signboards lettered in bright green: LEE HARVEY OSWALD WAS INNOCENT. It was a gaudy symbol of the times: the assassinations were alive once more.

Consider the charged atmosphere: The nation had just dumped Nixon, seven short years after forcing LBJ from office, and was in the midst of sensational exposés of political and super-spy agencies. Still an unknown entity, President Gerald Ford, having chosen Nelson Rockefeller as his vice-president, had appointed him to investigate the CIA. To private researchers in the assassination field, it seemed as if the man with the biggest secrets in America had taken on the men with the second biggest secrets.

Conspiracy? What about the conspiracy against the most hated man in America, the skeptics asked. They were convinced that new evidence showed Lee Harvey Oswald to be innocent.

If they are right, the question arises: If not Oswald, who? Below are a few charts of people who might have stood to gain by such an act.

In their study of the Kennedys, *Astrology in Action,* Marcia Moore and Mark Douglas have compared the charts of Oswald and Kennedy at the time of the assassination, looking into progressions (a rather esoteric mathematical advancement of natal planetary degrees in each year of one's life and a study of both their shifting relationship to the fixed degrees of natal planets and lights and their response to transits) and transits (the relationship between the actual movement of the bodies of the solar system and the fixed positions in the chart of birth).

The authors took note of the victim-suspect chart comparison—a weak one—and of the aspects that Oswald's chart was receiving at the moment the fatal shots were fired, concluding that if one looked one could find the seeds of violence in Oswald's chart. Yet, "Otherwise there is a mystifying lack of aspects to account for the infamous act. One can only speculate that Oswald may have been the tool of other conspirators, and perhaps not the sole culprit."

The case against Lee Harvey Oswald, after all, is based on one primary piece of historical data: He was arrested and charged with the assassination of President John Fitzgerald Kennedy. And, for all its efforts, the Warren Commission's report is not wholly satisfying. Its critics' perseverence spans a dozen years. The holes they poke in the evidence and the testimony—and in the conclusion that Lee Harvey Oswald was the lone assassin—are still there, and angry winds blow stronger through them.

The newly processed Zapruder film clearly shows that the president was hit from the front by an assassin's bullet; not all of the bullets came from behind—as would have been the case if Oswald, in his schoolbook-depository sniper's nest, had done all the shooting.

In the same week this new piece of evidence caused further outcry for reopening the case, *Time* magazine reported that the CIA had employed Mafia "hit men" to assassinate foreign heads of state who were considered dangerous to our interests. In the March 3, 1975, issue, *Time* claimed reliable information that "contracts" had been successfully taken out on Ngo Dinh Diem, first of the South Vietnamese strongmen to enjoy the political buoyancy that came with the ready flow of the American foreign/military aid dollar in the early sixties, and Rafael Trujillo, then the dictator of the Dominican Republic. Unsuccessful attempts were engineered against "Papa Doc" Duvalier, ruler of Haiti, Trujillo's island neighbor, and against Fidel Castro, for whom the Mafia had little love because he had cut off Havana as a gambling, dope, and prostitution capital of the western world. That the Mafia should have been involved with the CIA seemed to shock almost nobody. Americans by this time had come to accept the fact that the CIA does indulge in external conspiracy and counterrevolution —as clearly indicated in the case of Chile— and that, like the Ku Klux Klan, it is beyond the reach of the law.

But recent findings seem to make it no longer a question of "Did Oswald act alone?" but of "who, in fact, *did* kill JFK?" The article in *Penthouse* magazine touched off the controversy: George O'Toole, the author, is an expert in a new polygraph, or lie-detector, method. What we've been used to in lie detectors has been a complicated technique of measuring four fluctuating bodily reactions to stress: perspiration, breathing, blood pressure, and pulse. The continued use of the standard polygraph has not so much attested to its widespread success as to the fact that it has proven satisfactory in a sufficient number of cases. O'Toole, however, has been experimenting with a far more radical approach to the measurement of stress in determining whether someone suspected of a crime is telling the truth.

It's all in the *telling:* The human voice is all the new technique measures. The instrument, called the Psychological Stress Evaluator (PSE) resulted from a discovery by Bell and McQuiston, a polygraph research team, regarding frequencies in vocal tones. It was found, in the course of their research, that human voice frequencies modulate from eight to fourteen times a second; however, when the speaker is under stress, this regular variance in frequency is frozen so that only the most basic frequencies are emitted. An indication that there is stress at any given moment of a speaker's statement is, according to this growing school of many polygraph technicians and scientific researchers, a sign that the speaker is lying. Police scientists and criminologists at leading university research departments have endorsed both the method and the PSE, the device used to measure the stress.

The bombshell in the article concerns the author's experiments with the only existing tape of Oswald denying, after his arrest, that he shot President Kennedy. In one statement after another—every one of the vital points wherein stress would be present if the man were lying—O'Toole fails to discover stress when playing the tapes into the PSE. He and the other experts in this new field admit that the presence of stress in a speaker's voice doesn't necessarily mean that the speaker is lying; however, all contend that the absence of stress almost certainly means that the speaker is telling the truth. No stress, no lie. If Oswald didn't lie when he claimed at an impromptu press conference that he had killed no one, then who killed Kennedy? Who killed Officer Tippit?

The paranoia is likely to grow until someone finds out for sure. The one point in the Oswald tape at which O'Toole did in fact find stress—and thus an indication that Oswald *may* have been lying—was when the accused assassin said something to the effect that he knew nothing of what was going on in Dallas.

The mystery deepens. At the press conference announcing the publication of his article, O'Toole disclosed that the voice of one of the law officers protecting Oswald had stated on tape that they had in custody the man *they believed had shot the president;* according to the PSE reading, the man showed great stress when he made that statement. While the presence of stress isn't a sure indicator of anything, and while one would naturally expect stress under such circumstances, the absence of stress in some parts of the officer's statement and its presence in the crucial part of the statement, seemingly one in which only a person who was attempting to hide something would be under stress, could be a telling clue.

Yet, if doubts of Oswald's guilt prove true, we would—as a nation—find ourselves in hotter water than we might now realize. An unparalleled crisis of belief might be the result. After all, a president of the United States appointed the group that studied Kennedy's assassination, and the group itself consisted of some of our most reliable officials. The Warren Commission, as its name implies, was headed by none other than the chief justice of the Supreme Court, the final arbiter of the law of the land. How can the decision of so auspicious a group now be held up to question?

The Warren Commission

In 1964, to stifle the charge of conspiracy in JFK's assassination, President Lyndon Johnson appointed an investigatory body, headed by the chief justice who had sworn in John Kennedy at his presidential inauguration. Ostensibly, the commission's purpose was to gather evidence and to determine whether there was any indication of a conspiracy or if Lee Harvey Oswald was, in fact, the lone assassin. Oswald himself, of course, was unable to testify, having been murdered in what was described by his killer, Jack Ruby, as something akin to an act of charity toward the bereaved family of the slain president. (Ruby is covered in a separate section, as a potential conspirator.)

Thus, despite being deprived of a chief witness and main suspect, it was expected that the commission's work would be, at the very least, exhaustive. The *quantity* of work they completed easily satisfied that requirement—there were twenty-six volumes of information and accumulated testimony. However, from the very beginning, the *quality* of the investigative work of the commission has been in question—members of the commission itself have urged that private researchers carry the case still further.

New techniques in investigative research and criminology have been coming up with surprising results. Besides the PSE tale of the Oswald tape, it has been rumored that conspirators (dressed as Dallas cops) pretended, after the president's execution, to round up co-conspirators (dressed as tramps—see section on tramp photos).

What suggests that someone may have posed as a Dallas cop? Well, to begin with, the Dallas Police Department has been unable to identify two policemen photographed by a wire-service photographer as they were rounding up three "tramps"; moreover, there is no arrest record on any of the nine "tramps" rounded up immediately after the shooting on the grassy knoll or around Dealey Plaza that day. Still further, one cop who was photographed has what appears to be an unusual listening device in his ear: But such equipment is neither required of members of the Dallas police force nor used by the department.

The final conclusion of the Warren Commission is that Lee Harvey Oswald, the assassin, fired three bullets, two of which struck the president, one of these passing through the president and wounding Governor Connally. All twenty-six volumes of evidence are meant to support this conclusion. Many motives were attributed to the alleged assassin, and, at the insistence of one member, the then Congressman Jerry Ford, the "motive" that Oswald "was a Communist" was added to the official findings.

What follows are several Warren Commission vignettes, meant to demonstrate some of the gaps in its investigation. These have been drawn from the critiques that are being published almost daily, critiques that appear to ask a fundamental question: Who runs this country?

The Zapruder Film

The second most important witness, next to Oswald himself, probably was the film taken by Abraham Zapruder using his hand-held 8-mm home-movie camera. The Warren Commission never viewed that film. Its members looked only at slides of separate frames, having been told by Earl Warren that the film was "too gory" for them to see.

Time, Inc. purchased the film from Zapruder for a reported $100,000 and offered it for viewing to the commission, but aside from that has kept it bottled up in its own vaults. Later, however, so many pirated copies of the film began emerging from the investigatory underground that the whole matter became an embarrassment to Time, which sold it back to Zapruder's son—for a dollar.

Most readers probably have seen at least part of the Zapruder film. Those who saw it years ago saw a very poor copy. It—and the slides—barely showed the cloud of blood and brain matter that is clearly revealed in the more professionally processed and reprocessed version. This, say commission critics, is the most telling clue of all, for it means that the president was shot from the front, as well as from the rear. The new film clearly shows half his head blowing away behind him, on his left side. Oswald (if, indeed it was he) fired from behind him and from his right, so that blood would have sprayed *forward*.

The Zapruder film, had it been viewed *as* a movie, would have made it difficult for commission members to conclude Oswald's guilt. And, say critics, it must have been inordinately difficult to ignore as official evidence the fact that police officers behind the president's car were splattered with blood and brain matter.

Josiah Thompson, *Time*'s own researcher, went to work on the Zapruder film late in the sixties, ostensibly to put to rest theories that other gunmen beside Oswald were involved. His findings: that the first shot, from the Texas Schoolbook Depository, hit the president in the back; that the second, from the nearby County Records Building, struck Connally. And finally, that two shots hit the president practically at the same moment, one in the back of the head, the other in the front, taking off most of the left side of his head. Observers who have viewed the film say that it is not difficult to determine from which direction the shots were coming.

Kennedy's Brain

Recently, assassination researchers reported that when they attempted to see the brain of the murdered president, supposedly preserved in formalin at the National Archives, they were told that it "couldn't be found." The president's brain *missing?* Anyway, the Warren Commission claims that his brain was blown to smithereens by an approximately thirty-caliber bullet. According to the incorruptible Kodak film of Abraham Zapruder, it is said, the impact looked more like that from the slug of a high-bore elephant gun.

The Magic Bullet

The Warren Commission specifically concluded that three bullets were fired by Oswald, the final and fatal shot hitting Kennedy in the back of the head. The second shot, they claimed, struck a bystander after missing the president and ricocheting off the pavement. Now, and this becomes nearly impossible to follow, the *first* bullet, concluded the commission, struck JFK in the back just below the neck, passed through his body and into the back of Governor Connally, went on to smash through the governor's rib and came out his chest below his right nipple, then continued on striking his wrist, passing through, and finally lodging in his thigh. This was reportedly accomplished by a relatively low caliber Mannlicher-Carcano—seven holes from one bullet.

Although these are official findings, the evidence gathered in pursuit of these findings calls them in to question, say the critics. An early FBI report claimed that Kennedy and Connally were wounded by separate bullets, but this report was later repudiated by the FBI.

When viewing the shots in the Zapruder film one cannot miss the fact that a full one-and-a-half-second elapses between the time Kennedy is hit and Connally hunches over. The speed with which such a bullet would have to travel to pass through so much bone and flesh would allow for no more than *tenths of a second* in reaction time. Warren Commission supporters insist that Connally was suffering from "delayed reaction," whatever that means. In any event, the "magic bullet" miraculously appeared on the stretcher alongside the governor as he was being wheeled into Parkland Hospital. It was turned over to the FBI for lab tests, after which J. Edgar Hoover himself submitted a memo on the bureau's findings.

Hoover claimed that the "magic bullet," and the bullet fragments found in the bodies of the two victims, were subjected to spectrograph analysis. These tests were inconclusive. A Neutron Activation Analysis was performed; this measures the differences in material that has been bombarded with extremely low-level radiation. But, Hoover claimed, little was to be discovered from the results, since there were only "minor variations" found between the bullet fragments taken from Kennedy's body and those taken from Connally's. What the commission apparently was not well enough informed to notice in this report, critics say, is that *any difference at all* would have been enough to conclude that two separate bullets were involved. Now, in the case of the lead mixture used to make bullets, as in most other things in this world, the whole is equal only to the sum of its parts—and each part shares intimately all the characteristics and the elemental makeup of the whole. The fragment of a bullet must contain the same measure of ingredients as the rest of that bullet. There can be no variation.

Private investigators claim that they have weighed the fragments and the bullet and have discovered that if you returned the fragments to the bullet they supposedly came from you would have a bullet that was far bigger than when it was fired. A bullet doing that much damage will naturally leave a lot of fragmentary matter behind and will invariably become twisted and misshapen. The "magic bullet," on the other hand, retained almost all of its original contours and is reputed to have lost very little of its original content.

The Mannlicher-Carcano Rifle

Many critics of the Warren Commission claim that the report had to assert that only three shots were fired because tests on the rifle showed that it could not be primed and fired more than three times in the six seconds witnesses claimed it took for the shooting to end.

Even then, they say, tests further proved that Oswald couldn't have done the shooting: His marksmanship record in the Marines was poor. Yet, when the commission employed the services of NRA-registered marksmen, shooting on *level ground* at a *stationary* and *larger* target, using the Mannlicher-Carcano, these riflery experts were unable to reproduce Oswald's feat. In fact, before they used the rifle they had to shim (boost with thin supports) the sight to make it accurate. Also, the rifle was fitted with a left-handed scope, while Oswald was right-handed.

A famous photo shows Oswald posing in his backyard with

socialist literature and what is purported to be the Mannlicher-Carcano. Besides the question as to whether Oswald's head was cropped onto another man's photo, there are also those researchers who have measured the rifle in the photo every which way and have come to the conclusion that the rifle in the hands of the man reported to be Lee Harvey Oswald is *not* a Mannlicher-Carcano.

The Autopsy

The President's brain seems to be missing: perhaps there's good reason. Based on their independent study of the autopsy findings, the American Academy of Forensic Pathologists recently declared that the official autopsy conducted by the Dallas County Coroner's Office at Parkland Memorial Hospital in Dallas was so sloppy and incomplete as to be no autopsy at all.

The Witnesses

The greatest of the mysteries subsequent to the major mystery has to do with the witnesses themselves. Many of them are dead—unexplainably, to observers who hesitate to assume the worst. To other researchers, however, there is no mystery surrounding the death of so many witnesses, save perhaps how some of them may have managed to survive as long as they did.

Such researchers theorize that the conspirators were and probably continue to be very powerful people. If they could engineer the blatant execution of a president of the United States, they could certainly manage to squeeze out a few more executions of lowlier citizens whose versions of what happened that day could not be allowed to become history. In its April 18, 1975, issue, *New Times* magazine reported ("The Greatest Coverup of Them All") that the facts of the deaths of eighteen witnesses to the assassination were submitted to an insurance actuary, who estimated that the chances of those deaths occurring in that space of time were approximately 100 trillion to one!

Patrolman Joe Smith was summoned to the grassy knoll by a woman who shouted to him that "they are shooting the president from the bushes." In his report to the FBI he claimed, "I pulled my gun from my holster and I thought, 'This is silly. I don't know who I'm looking for,' and I put it back. Just as I did, he (the suspect he had covered) showed me he was a Secret Service agent." However, Secret Service records do not list anyone assigned to the grassy knoll.

Fifty-two witnesses testified that shots came from the grassy knoll—almost twice as many as those who said they came from the Texas Schoolbook Depository. Many of these fifty-two are dead, and, for the critics, mystery will always shroud those who came to an untimely end. (How, in fact, did columnist Dorothy Kilgallen die?) Abraham Zapruder himself seems to have died a natural death; critics like to suggest that he was an exception because his name had become world famous. Zapruder was one of those who claimed that bullets came from sectors other than the Texas Schoolbook Depository. He said that he heard bullets whistling past his right ear, which argues in favor of those who claim that a gunman was stationed on the roof of the County Records Building nearby.

Further supporting those who claimed that gunmen fired on the president from the grassy knoll are images that appear on films of the assassination. In the Zapruder film, on frame 413, researchers claim to be able to distinguish the figure of a man in the bushes, his shoulders, arms and head extending from the underbrush, pointing a rifle. Because of the relatively poor quality of the reproduction, however, it is hard to be certain.

Orville Nix, another home-movie buff, took his own films that day. Standing across the street from Zapruder, he also caught in his lens what researchers claim appears much more clearly to be a man pointing what is apparently a long-barreled, telescopic-sighted pistol, while supporting himself against a cream-colored station wagon parked behind the grassy knoll.

The picture of this man was shown to a witness who volunteered his testimony, a railroad worker by the name of Lee Bowers. While working his post at the top of the nearby switching tower, Bowers had a view of the whole scene. He told the Warren Commission that he had noticed an "unusual commotion" in the vicinity of the stockade fence as the assassins' shots rang out. Researchers showed him blowups of the Nix film. "That's exactly what I saw," Bowers was reputed to have said, in the *New Times* article. He was also reported to have claimed that he'd seen a man talking into a microphone in one of the cars behind the grassy knoll. He died soon after, when his car, traveling at moderate speed in full daylight and under the best of driving conditions, struck an abutment.

John Connally

If you are going to kill a president, Warren Report critics suggest, you need a lot of local support. You must be sure of allies on all fronts. It is logical then to assume, they say, that if local Texas politicians were involved there had to be some dealing with the highest authority in the legal life of the state, the governor. In 1963, that man was John Connally. The question is, how did the conspirators deal with this matter? Did they in fact simply aim to cut Connally down along with Kennedy, or was his getting shot a mistake? You will note in the section dealing with motive that John Connally's antipathy toward JFK was strong. Even though it is astrologically true that personal dislike between the two victims does register strongly on the objective charts of the heavens, I am somewhat reluctant to suspect a man who almost lost his life in the crime of being involved in its perpetration, and I do not suggest that either he or his wounds lie. Several grains of lead were taken out of the many passageways the single bullet that struck John Connally was supposed to have made, along with at least four points of entry or emergence. The "magic bullet" itself was found to contain only a few grains less than it weighed before being fired, while the addition of the grains of lead removed from the governor's body would have made it several grains too heavy. This does not faze the supporters of the Warren Commission, as it did not faze its members. The commission's findings depend entirely on the three-bullet theory—all of them fired by Oswald. We are told that all the holes in John Connally's body were caused by one bullet that defied the laws of physics and *increased its mass* before it entered the governor's body so that it could leave behind more leaden particles than it had to give.

He could have died, sure enough. Maybe, the commission's critics say, the conspirators meant him to die. The critics recall that, as the hail of lead that snuffed our highest elected official skewered his own body, John Connally was heard to cry out: "My God, they're going to kill us all!"

Fidel Castro

The connection between Oswald and supposedly pro-Castro groups is enough, for many people, to lay the assassination guilt at Fidel's door. But if Oswald was a double agent working with both pro- and anti-Castro groups in the pay of the CIA, as some observers claim, the fact that his pro-Castro connections were publicized and his anti-Castro ones concealed, at the time of his arrest, tells us that if you're going to try to pin a presidential assassination on an agent, you'd better make it impossible for him to defend his good name. Someone did just that, say the critics—at least, they made sure that JFK's accused killer would never get a chance to say *anything* in his own defense by shutting him up once and for all.

Observers also theorize that quite likely he told all to the lawmen who held him. He was too intelligent to think that he'd live very long with a frame-up like that being laid on him; he *had* to declare himself in their presence. The officials know who and what Lee Harvey Oswald was, but perhaps they have good reason to say nothing. Oswald had used the intelligence agencies to get himself out of minor fixes in the past, the critics recall; he didn't have to send for an agent in Dallas. But it's unlikely that these officials gave him any recognition beyond convincing him to say nothing to the press.

Despite so much evidence of Oswald's connection with the CIA, the Castro-phobes will continue to claim—as did LBJ until his death—that "it was Castro." Johnson's role itself is most questionable, say the critics; however, his thesis has some strange support—notably from Jack Anderson, the investigative columnist.

But private researchers doubt the logic of this argument. JFK, they say, had only recently *thwarted* an invasion of Cuba by withholding air support, and Castro knew long before the American public that Kennedy's intentions were to end the CIA's

Caribbean adventures. Furthermore, there was a discernible liking for the American President on the part of the Cuban leader. Little that is substantial links Castro personally or by policy to the conspiracy that is now being reinvestigated.

Jack Ruby

If there was in fact a massive conspiracy against JFK, then undoubtedly, say the critics, Jack Ruby was involved. He murdered Lee Harvey Oswald and, in doing so, kept the matter a mystery.

Ruby's only defense for his crime was that he had acted under extreme duress brought on by sympathy for the Kennedy family. However, months after he began to serve his life sentence, it was publicly announced that Jack Ruby was dying of an advanced cancer. If his shooting of Oswald was in fact the act of a vengeful and grief-stricken semipsychopath, critics say, then it was just one more incredible bit of unexplainable sloppiness on the part of law enforcement authorities that the man should have been allowed anywhere near Oswald, and especially without first being checked for weapons. However, they suggest, had he known in advance that he had only a short while to live because of his cancer, he might have been tempted to commit such a crime for a price: the security of those whom his dying would leave helpless, perhaps. Many conspiracy investigators believe that he was not only the triggerman in the Oswald hit, but one of the conspirators in the JFK assassination itself, and that it was prearranged that he should be the one who slipped into the midst of sheriffs and deputies in the labyrinth beneath the Dallas County Jail.

Jim Garrison, then the New Orleans district attorney, was the first to ride the conspiracy roller coaster to the heights, as well as the first to encounter the sudden stone wall of silence (and the countersuits, and the unofficial or official harassment, stemming from his trying Clay Shaw, David Ferrie, and others as having been associates of Oswald and connected to the conspiracy to kill Kennedy) that greets most conspiracy researchers. Garrison pinpointed Jack Ruby's involvement in the part of his book that deals with the testimony of one Julia Mercer, which had been given to the FBI and passed on to the Warren Commission. According to Garrison, Mercer was driving by the grassy knoll shortly before the motorcade arrived. She noticed a man in his early twenties, or thereabouts, dismount from a plain green pickup truck and remove an object wrapped in brown paper; Julia Mercer claimed that its outline, even from a distance, clearly revealed that it was a rifle. She got a good, long look at the man who was driving the pickup; when studying pictures that the FBI showed her, she said, she fingered the photograph of Jack Ruby.

However, according to the testimony Garrison claims to have evoked from the witness, her statement was later altered for its presentation to the Warren Commission to read that she *could not* identify the man who drove the truck from among the photographs shown her. Her statement was further revised to read that the witness claimed that the plain green truck had black lettering on the side that read AIR CONDITIONING.

Some writers will insist that Ruby's involvement with the CIA and anti-Castro groups was extensive and easy enough to trace. It has been claimed that he even used to run guns for the anti-Castro Cubans. One final note on this man: After Oswald had been arrested and taken into custody, the Dallas district attorney gave an apparently impromptu press conference, revealing, as though by some vehicle of computerized magic, the wealth of information his men had gotten on the accused assassin in less than the two hours since his arrest. The district attorney kept saying that Lee Harvey Oswald was a member of the "Free Cuba Committee." This is a group actually quite hostile to Castro and among the most violently inclined of the Cuban refugee groups in the Gulf area, having been originated by the CIA and personally supervised in its inception by the ever-present E. Howard Hunt. The district attorney, however, was corrected by Jack Ruby, who stood at the back of the room. Smiling, Ruby reminded him that Oswald was a member of the Fair Play for Cuba Committee, *not* the anti-Castro Free Cuba Committee.

If we have been dupes of the cover-up to end all cover-ups, then even the astrologers were taken in. Back in 1963, astrologers didn't have the extensive availability and resources of computer programs, accredited university research facilities, or occasional state, local, or federal assistance, directly or indirectly. In short, the application of their all-but-forbidden art was not in behalf of existing sciences and technologies: These were the segments of society that wished to keep astrology an outcast. Astro-criminology is still a developing field, even though prominent astrologers have lent their expertise to the solution of every type of mystery throughout history. Actually, little of scientific worth has been passed down to aid the future astro-criminologist.

For the most part, astrologers all over the country, although there were many who intuited the smell of conspiracy that seeped through the TV tube that black November weekend, accepted the theory that Lee Harvey Oswald was at least one of the assassins of John F. Kennedy. They then proceeded to demonstrate the efficacy of their art by comparing the charts of Oswald and JFK to show the fatal connections and to demonstrate how each man was severely aspected by the planets of the moment.

Of course each man was heavily aspected by the patterns in the skies—one was assassinated, and one was charged with the assassination and within forty-eight hours was himself assassinated. Astrology works, as anyone who has looked very far into it can tell you; but even if it had only half the validity it is credited with, a basic premise of strong celestial activity affecting the birth chart at significant moments would have *had* to have been satisfied at so heavily significant a moment in each man's life. If two men have fatal accidents at opposite ends of the globe at the very same moment, it is likely that they share common birth configurations somewhere in their charts, yet this can be no reason to assume that the accidents or people are *causally* related. All that the aspects from the planets and lights prove, when demonstrating what many astrologers have tried to pass off as Oswald's fatal connection to JFK, is that the two men were in for hard times at the same time.

6

The Assassinations: Some Astrological Answers

Synastry is the art of chart comparison in astrology, the biggest of the field's draws, for it is usually used to judge the compatibility of a couple and the chances for enduring love. In judging love and attraction, synastry also reveals areas where dangerous conflicts might lie.

So it is that astrology can be used by criminologists to determine the extent of motive in crimes of violence. Chart comparison is merely the noting of areas of interplay between charts. *There must be some violent interplay to provoke one of the two to violence toward the other.*

In a birth chart, the planets and lights aspect one another; they are in geometric relationship to one another. If a planet is 90 degrees away from another, we say they are in "square" aspect, indicating challenge and adversity. When an astrologer compares charts, he puts the planets and the degrees of the rising sign and midheaven, or zenith, of one in the chart of the other. In the case of a violence reading, he would put the planets of the aggressor in the chart of the victim, since it is a case of the one acting on the other. The astrologer then compares the geometric angles between the planets, lights, and angles of one with the other. A preponderance of trines (120 degrees) and sextiles (60 degrees) would indicate a relationship of ease and would cause most of the violent motivations attributed to a suspect to evaporate. Such a chart relationship would not be conducive to sudden flare-ups of violence, much less a carefully planned and executed, cold-blooded murder. Should a criminologist, using all the tools available, discover that the chart of a suspect in a murder contains such unexplainable benevolence toward the chart of the victim, usually it would hasten his investigation if he dropped that suspect. This would *astrologically* hold true, of course, only if the murderer was of a normal frame of mind at the time of the murder.

My own approach to the list of suspects, semisuspects, and ringers (the latter being the control group) begins with a synastry analysis of each of their charts placed within the circle of the birth chart of John Fitzgerald Kennedy. I searched diligently for all

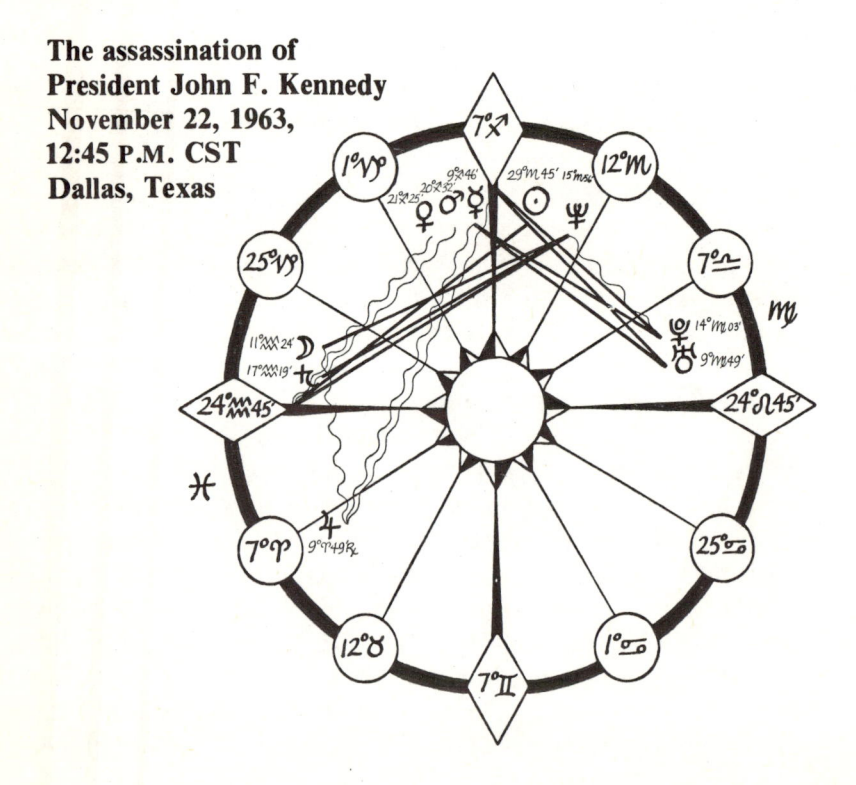

The assassination of President John F. Kennedy November 22, 1963, 12:45 P.M. CST Dallas, Texas

The Assassinations: Some Astrological Answers   133

pertinent aspects between the inhabited degrees of each chart, listing them and giving each easy or difficult aspect a numerical value. In this and the final chapter of the book, I have given both the birth information on all the suspects, as well as my methodology, which is somewhat technical yet by no means esoteric. Any amateur astrologer, if he or she wishes to spend two months double-checking me, could repeat my clearly explained steps.

Below is a list of those whose charts I analyzed. Percentages give a degree of basic antagonism toward President John F. Kennedy that is relative to the strength of adversity I found in the charts as a group. That is to say, I chose to assign the value of 100 percent adversity to a negative numerical value of −400. (Since the highest of the negative scores of suspects studied was −378, I called 400 maximum adversity for this *group*.) It is quite probable that there were in the world many who hated Kennedy more than any of those in this study. It is also likely that my choice of twenty-five does not encompass anything near the scope of the conspiracy that killed our thirty-fifth president; very few of those I list below were possibly or probably involved.

Part I: Motive Potential

Not everyone with adverse imbalances toward JFK wanted him killed. Many of the suspects were, and continue to be, up-front fighters for the most part and, although they disliked the man, would not have thought to counter what they probably considered a great evil with a still greater evil. Those who might employ undercover means to accomplish their ends, on the other hand, are easily identifiable in this list.

Suspect	Motive Potential
John Connally	94%
Mao Tse-tung	86%
Frank Sturgis	66%
J. Edgar Hoover	62%
Virgilio Gonzales	61%

134   THE KENNEDY CURSE

Nikita Khrushchev	52%
Howard Hughes	52%
Central Intelligence Agency	47%
G. Gordon Liddy	44%
Billy Graham	41%
Richard Nixon	41%
Lee Harvey Oswald	*32%*
Gen. Charles Cabell	27%

The Range of Normalcy

Adlai Stevenson	19%
Dwight D. Eisenhower	17%
E. Howard Hunt	14%
George Wallace	12%
Ronald Reagan	11%
Eugenio Martinez	11%
Lyndon Baines Johnson	10%
Jack Ruby	10%
Nelson Rockefeller	5%
Aristotle Onassis	4%
Fidel Castro	4%
Thomas Dewey	0%
Barry Goldwater	0%

Part II: Critical-Moment Analysis

Like any event or birth, the execution of JFK has its own chart. It, too, bears comparison to the charts of those involved at the moment or suspected to be. Although we don't use the term synastry to describe this kind of analysis, it is similar enough to be thought of in almost the same way. Astrologers call this a *horary* analysis—from hora, or hour—a study of a time and the relations of all its principals.

The Assassinations: Some Astrological Answers 135

The next step the astro-criminologist must undertake is to place the planets, lights, and angles of all the suspects into a chart drawn up for the exact moment of the crime. If there is no adversity, it is unlikely that the suspect had much to do with the crime.

In my analysis of the twenty-five suspects, semi-suspects, and 'ringers' stress relationship to the moment of JFK's execution, I gave special consideration to the planets and angles that most adversely aspected the chart of the president himself. In a slight digression into the technical, I must point out that I began my study of each suspect's chart by noting which areas were the most explosive or otherwise malevolent. I assigned to these the status of *high-frequency malefic* (HFM) so that their aspects to JFK's chart, and aspects from the moment of the execution to those critical points, would receive more attention and be scored higher in violence or ruthlessness potential. (*See* chapter 10.)

It should be noted that there is a world of difference between the average violent criminal and conspirators involved in killing Kennedy. For the most part, they were not all driven by violent impulses. If violence is heat, then the greater number of those involved were cold as ice. To be a triggerman implies that you *are* the violence, and those few of the many received a majority of violent aspects from the heavens. The rest received violent aspects as well, no doubt, but the ruthless and inhumanly detached vibrations were the strongest in the air for those with fingers on the trigger. The polar fury ruled when that day in November was suddenly, unnaturally sapped of its heat for all of America.

In the list below I have assigned percentages based on the intensity of stressful relations between the suspect's chart and the chart of the moment of JFK's execution:

The Moment of JFK's Execution:
Stressful Aspect Analysis

Suspect	**Stress**
Virgilio Gonzales	77%
Nikita Khrushchev	56%

Central Intelligence Agency	55%
Howard Hughes	48%
Adlai Stevenson	46%
John Connally	43%
Frank Sturgis	40%
Gen. Charles Cabell	37%
E. Howard Hunt	36%
Fidel Castro	33%
Billy Graham	33%
Richard Nixon	31%
Mao Tse-tung	28%
George Wallace	27%
G. Gordon Liddy	21%

Range Of Average Stress Conditions

J. Edgar Hoover	20%
Ronald Reagan	20%
Lee Harvey Oswald	*18%*
Lyndon Baines Johnson	16%
Eugenio Martinez	15%
Jack Ruby	12%
Aristotle Onassis	12%
Dwight D. Eisenhower	9%
Thomas Dewey	5%
Nelson Rockefeller	0%
Barry Goldwater	0%

After having judged the purely astrological connections between JFK and our group of real and hypothetical suspects, it becomes necessary to show, by weight of evidence, those who are "ringers" and those who are authentic suspects. But what is weight of evidence? If we go to official sources, for example the Warren Commission, we come away unsatisfied with the conclusions. The alternative is to judge evidence on our own.

Researchers such as Mark Lane have been chopping away at the official version of the JFK assassination for a dozen years.

Lately, a veritable army of independent researchers have been joining the ranks, producing volumes of new evidence, new questions, and new refutations of the official line.

I have considered all this new data in an admittedly arbitrary way. All such independent conclusions must remain arbitrary for the present. Someday we may all agree on a single, unified conclusion; but until then, bear with mine regarding what the new evidence seems to tell us.

I have interpolated subjective conclusions regarding existing evidence with the astrologically objective findings related to, first, motive and, secondly, stress at the time of the assassination. This triple-pronged assault on the enigma has helped me understand who among the group studied *might* have had as much, if not *more*, culpability in the president's murder.

Three-Part Analysis

(For those preferring to weigh evidence on their own, to reject anything of what I have claimed to be evidence, or to add any of their own information. I have included a second analysis of the tests that excludes subjective evidential analysis and takes into consideration only the astrological testing.)

Part I: No Evidence Against Any of the Subjects
Thomas Dewey
Dwight D. Eisenhower
Barry Goldwater
Virgilio Gonzales
Billy Graham
Mao Tse-tung
Aristotle Onassis
Ronald Reagan
Nelson Rockefeller
Adlai Stevenson
George Wallace

Part II. Circumstantial Evidence—or Less

Lyndon Baines Johnson: LBJ stood to gain most—or so it seemed. It was generally well known that he had grown restless in his role as vice-president. And, of course, the assassination occurred in his home state. To many observers, the Dallas police were "in his pocket." Add to this the fact that many of the other possible conspirators named would have been men Johnson might very well have had dealings with, and give LBJ: 10 percent.

Eugenio Rolando Martinez: Although no evidence exists to place him in or near Dallas on November 22, 1963, he has been closely associated with Frank Sturgis in the past and has been deeply involved with anti-Castro agencies—notably, some of those Oswald himself seems to have been connected with (see section on Lee Harvey Oswald) that were disguised as *pro*-Castro fronts—and with counter-insurgency plots against the Cuban regime. Many of these schemes included plotting to assassinate Castro, as well as anyone else both vulnerable and vital to the cause of the Cuban Revolution. His arrest at Watergate demonstrates that his undercover work for the CIA, as well as his freelance involvement in dirty tricks, did not end with the Bay of Pigs fiasco. I give him: 10 percent.

John Connally: His relations with JFK were characterized in many quarters of government as poor, to say the least. Although there is no evidence connecting him with the crime, the astrological findings make it possible to infer that the man who was shot along with Kennedy in Dealey Plaza that day might have been informed of the plot but expected not to be in the line of fire. When he was hit, he was heard to cry out, "*They're* going to kill *all* of us!" (emphasis my own). For this, I have given him: 10 percent.

Gen. Charles Cabell: Most influential in Texas right-wing politics, an ex-deputy director of the CIA, he was reputed to have been the man responsible for changing JFK's motorcade route at the last minute. I give him: 10 percent.

G. Gordon Liddy: Though there is nothing in the way of hard evidence to place him in Dallas that day, Liddy's extensive con-

The Assassinations: Some Astrological Answers   139

nections with cloak-and-dagger operations, his pre-Watergate connections with both the CIA and FBI, and the rumor that he had volunteered to assassinate columnist Jack Anderson to prevent further leaks from hurting Nixon, all contribute toward making this "swashbuckler" a natural suspect in the JFK murder case. I've given him: 10 percent.

Richard Milhous Nixon: Nixon has been blamed for much, why not blame him for Dallas as well? Well, there are all sorts of rumors floating about that he was in Dallas that day, but I haven't seen an iota of proof. What connects him most is merely an assumption that he had more against Kennedy than did even the militant anti-Castro Cubans. It was felt by many that the 1960 election had been stolen from the Republicans. There was reason enough in that charge to demand some kind of retribution. However, this is all less than heresay. The strongest piece of *evidence* connecting him to Dallas is that tying him to the mysterious background of conspirator E. Howard Hunt.

While president, Richard M. Nixon presented to the Congress and people of the United States, in late 1973, a transcription of tapes, made in the Oval Office, of conversations between himself and several of his aides earlier in the year. According to Nixon, transcriptions were accurate enough to serve as stand-ins for the actual tapes, which he then refused to turn over. At last the courts and Congress forced the turning over of the tapes, and they were checked against the transcription. The House Committee hearing the tapes indicated several places in which the Nixon transcription did not match, as well as several places where there were actual omissions. In one such place, Nixon and John Dean (later joined by H. R. Haldeman) conversed on March 21, 1973 about E. Howard Hunt's blackmailing of the administration for defense money in his Watergate trial. The president and Dean agreed that it would be best if Hunt did not tell what he knew. However, in the president's version (according to the House Committee), the following statement of Nixon's has been deleted: "The main person to keep quiet is Hunt, because he knows about a lot of other things." Later, he says of Hunt that his case is "a scab that shouldn't be picked." Just what did Nixon mean? There are those who believe he was referring to Dallas. If Hunt was involved in Kennedy's assassination, so too, was Nixon. Anyone who merely *knows* the secrets behind Dallas is guilty as a conspirator after the fact. On this basis, I feel it necessary to give Nixon at least: 10 percent.

Howard Hughes: Lately, the disclosure that the Hughes Corporation-owned Glomar Explorer was used by the CIA and the navy to help salvage parts of a sunken Russian submarine has further linked the empire of the CIA to private industry. Hughes himself has always projected an image of rich soldier of fortune, and he has been a gambler by life-style for as long as he's been famous. His only hedge is his anonymity, a quirk making the appeal of CIA cloak-and-dagger activities something he wouldn't likely resist for very long. Maybe it's simply an example of one hand washing the other; after all, while Hughes's facilities may be made available to the CIA, the agency, in return, throws Hughes all the backing the corporation needs to land expensive defense contracts in the next fiscal year. Because of his connections and former headquarters in Nevada, especially Las Vegas, many have conjectured, with probable justification, that Hughes would then most naturally have had many dealings with the local Mafia, which practically controls every aspect of tourism in the state, including legalized gambling and prostitution.

At the time of the Kennedy assassination, the big man in Las Vegas was John (Don Giovanni) Roselli. He referred to himself then as a Hollywood movie producer and, according to some researchers, was introduced to CIA agents in 1960 by a Howard Hughes executive who had formerly worked for the FBI. Whether or not Roselli corresponded with the CIA via these means does not matter; what does matter is that the purpose of these meetings between the mob and the CIA was the setting up of an assassination attempt against Fidel Castro. Roselli appeared late in June, 1975 before Sen. Frank Church's committee studying CIA activities, where he did not admit to such a deal. Frank Sturgis, however, admitted to six million readers, via the *New York Daily News,* that Roselli had been a part of the plot and gave lengthy details of other such plots. Since it was possible that Hughes or Hughes's people were connected, directly or indirectly, with other assassination plots around the time of Kennedy's assassination, and since Hughes represented some of the most highly organized and powerful business and industrial interests in the area, he may have needed to be consulted—he may have volunteered. Also, he, like others, may have feared the Kennedy administration's cutting back on the defense spending that had made Hughes one of the richest men on earth. He should be considered at least a suspicious party in the matter and given: 10 percent.

Part III. Evidence and Major Clues
Lee Harvey Oswald: The man accused and officially assumed to be the only culpable party to the Kennedy assassination is given considerably less than the potential 100 percent many might think he should get. There are several reasons for this, the first and foremost obviously being the gathering evidence that there were others involved. Opening comments in Chapter 5 point out that recently developed and scientifically irrefutable technologies available to criminologists have tended to prove Oswald innocent. The PSE (Psychological Stress Evaluation) studies done by George O'Toole and others speak in Oswald's behalf. Nevertheless, I have given him the greatest percentage of the group studied because he seems to have been severely implicated, if only set up to seem the solitary perpetrator.

Even though the above considerations would seem enough to warrant lowering the probability on Oswald from 100 to 70, other questions are thrown into the picture regarding not just the accused assassin's activities on November 22, 1963, but also his activities long before that date as well. There's even some question whether he was the person we thought him to be.

This latter bugaboo has been named the "Other Oswald Theory" and stems from some of the following facts: Late in September, 1963, Oswald went by bus from New Orleans to Mexico City hoping to obtain a travel visa to visit Cuba. On October 10, the CIA sent a cable to the Office of Naval Intelligence (O.N.I.) and the State Department saying that a "sensitive and reliable source" had reported that a Leon "Henry" Oswald was seen entering the Soviet Embassy in Mexico City. The CIA communicated that it had reason to believe that this was the same L.H. Oswald who lived in Texas and had once defected to the Soviet Union, and went on to request that State and O.N.I. furnish photos of Oswald so that the identity could be confirmed. In its cable, the CIA described Oswald as "approximately thirty-five years of age, six feet tall, athletically built, with a receding hairline." Later the CIA released pictures of the Mexico City "Oswald"—and the only resemblance between this man and the Lee Harvey Oswald arrested in Dallas on November 22, 1963 was the receding hairline. The CIA will only refer to the matter as a "mix-up," nothing more.

According to the Warren Commission's findings, however, Oswald was riding the bus to Mexico City on September 25, 1963; yet, on that same day, a man calling himself Lee Harvey Oswald walked into the Selective Service Office in Austin, Texas, and announced that he wanted to speak to someone about his dishonorable discharge from the Marine Corps, presumably switched from a medical discharge after his defection.

What was Oswald doing in Mexico City? It's hard to know the full truth, but if we keep in mind that he was leaving the United States via New Orleans, one of the biggest CIA—and, at that time, Cuban exile—bases in the states, we might then pay some heed to the claims of assassination researcher Mae Brussell, who claims that Mexico City is the location of a secret FBI base where twenty-five to thirty professional assassins are briefed and trained.

Following up on this apparent familiarity of Oswald's with both the CIA and FBI, researchers have uncovered what has come to be known as "the Hoover Memo." On June 3, 1960, the late director of the FBI sent a confidential memo to the State Department raising the possibility that an *imposter* might be using the credentials of Oswald, who then lived in the USSR. Neither this memo, however, nor any of those in response from State were ever forwarded to the Warren Commission. They were buried in the National Archives and only recently uncovered.

Another strange hitch in the government's case against

Oswald comes from Warren Reynolds, a witness to the murder of Officer Tippit. Reynolds chased Tippit's murderer and, oddly, was not interviewed by the FBI until January, 1964. At that time, he told the FBI that he could not identify Oswald as the man he was chasing. Two days later Reynolds was shot in the head by an unknown assailant. Miraculously, he survived and later reflected that "it must have been Oswald after all."

During the preliminary investigation of the accused assassin, while in Dallas police custody, it was discovered that there were nitrates (from gunpowder) on Oswald's hand, yet not on his cheek, where they would be had he been sighting in on the president with his rifle. There was a palm print on the rifle that was *not* identified as Oswald's. Whose palm print was it? When checking on the purchase of the rifle, the Warren Commission discovered that it had been sold to an A. Hidell. When he was arrested, Oswald supposedly had such an I.D. on his person, yet the picture looked nothing like him. How does a man purchase a rifle with an I.D. bearing a picture that doesn't even resemble him? Or—was the I.D. planted on him, or simply reported to have been in his possession?

In 1969, Jesse Curry, who had been chief of Dallas police at the time of the assassination, was quoted as saying: "We don't have any proof that Oswald fired the rifle. No one has been able to put him in that building with that gun in his hand." So, was Lee Harvey Oswald the "lone assassin"? It seems quite unlikely. Was he involved in any way? Maybe. Oswald gets: 70 percent.

The Central Intelligence Agency: The name keeps coming up wherever private researchers snoop. At one time people tilted their heads at you if you implied that the CIA—defenders of our liberty, are they not?—would participate in so heinous an act. But this is 1976; we've come a long way. We now *know* that the CIA has been involved in foreign "dirty tricks" so intensely that murder is not ruled out. Why then should we assume that people who violate natural law would respect civil law? It seems more likely that they would ignore the respect the populace accords to the office of chief executive if that particular executive threatened their existence. Machiavelli, and not Jefferson, wrote the rulebook that secret police groups—CIA included—follow.

Ex-CIA assistant director Victor Marchetti, who bolted the agency to write the blockbuster *The CIA and the Cult of Intelligence,* which has been all but totally suppressed by court injunctions brought down on the publishers by the CIA, says: "The more I have learned, the more concerned I become that the government was involved in the assassination of President John F. Kennedy. Maybe it was just in the covering up . . . but sometimes I wonder if it doesn't go deeper than that."

In 1963, the Cold War was then worth $79 billion in annual appropriations and no one, least of all the CIA, wanted to see that joyride ended. The Kennedy Administration intended to cut these figures drastically and, soon after the Bay of Pigs, threatened "to break the CIA into a million pieces and scatter them over the ends of the earth." When you play around with ultimate forms of power (as the CIA does daily) your chief care is to preserve that power—at any expense. Obviously, the CIA had many reasons for wanting JFK out of the way, and, as the evidence continues to pop up, so does its name, especially in direct or indirect relation to that of Lee Harvey Oswald in his adventures both here and abroad.

Some say that two of the CIA's most illustrious agents, E. Howard Hunt and Frank Fiorini (alias Frank Sturgis), were caught with their secretive pants down at Dallas on that crucial day. "Tramp photos" taken in the vicinity of the grassy knoll at Dealey Plaza of persons rounded up as possible suspects reveal several showing three men, two of whom look remarkably like Hunt and Sturgis. Both, of course, deny that they were anywhere near Dallas at the time, Hunt going so far as to swear he'll sue anyone who says he was—but more on these two later. However, it should be pointed out here that both men figure heavily in my assigning the CIA so high a score on evidential materials. They were both then in the agency's employ. Add to this our knowledge of the lawless methods the CIA uses (and forget, if you wish, the motivation, which is admittedly circumstantial), that it has murdered and attempted the murder of foreign heads of state and has not held back in such tactics against heads of state elected in popular elections, and the CIA must be awarded: 60 percent.

E. Howard Hunt: We all remember Everette. He's the hack writer turned chief-Nixon-dirty-trickster who's had a bad run of luck lately. Actually, if he'd had any luck at all at any time in the past dozen years, he wouldn't be ending up here and at the end of a thousand researcher's microscopes. But, as I mentioned, some say that Hunt was *photographed* in Dallas along with Frank Sturgis, and that thus it's a sure thing that he had something to do with the goings on.

Let's consider those photos taken by a wire-service photographer who happened to be in the area: They show men arrested behind the grassy knoll. While they are shabbily dressed, they have neatly trimmed hair. They are flanked by police, one of whom is carrying what appears to be a shotgun. He also seems to have a listening device in his ear. No one can identify this policeman, though—and it was determined that no one knew of any Dallas policemen wearing hearing aids (which would disqualify them from service), nor have any similar sorts of hearing devices been issued as equipment. The Dallas police have never released the names of the arrested men, nor have they ever revealed what happened to them.

First the rumor: It is said that the tramp who does not look amazingly like Hunt and Sturgis was identified as having been at the same CIA training camp on Lake Pontchartrain where David Ferrie was supposed to have been seen with Oswald. Ferrie, of course, was a key figure in the Kennedy assassination investigation carried out rather heavy-handedly by District Attorney Jim Garrison in New Orleans in 1969.

Now the apparency: Apparently, some feel, the two other men *are* Hunt and Sturgis. Aside from Hunt's own vehement denial (he says he was eating Chinese food with his family at the time), there have been some who have disputed the claims of those going about the country—notably Dick Gregory—and their objections seem at first well taken. In the article "The Mystery Tramps in Disguise" that appeared in the April 24, 1975, edition of *Rolling Stone,* the reviewer points out the following in Hunt's defense: 1) Hunt was forty-five then, but the picture seems to be of a man of about fifty-five; 2) according to Charles V. Morton, criminologist at the Oakland Forensic Science Institute, the helix of the ear in Hunt's photo is concave, while that of the mystery tramp is convex.

The second of these objections, while seeming to be the most telling, is actually the easiest dealt with if one simply notes that the hat on the tramp in question is pushed back, and obviously pressing on the back of his ears, which would easily cause the concave shape to buckle out slightly and appear convex.

While the first objection is somewhat subjective—who's to say from a photo how old someone really is?—it can be dealt with both logically and astrologically. Logically, we might assume that Hunt, if he was involved that day, might have reached a state of extreme physical fatigue as a result of all that he was taking on. After all, it must be exhausting to plan and carry out the execution of the president of the United States. If this conjecture is not enough, I refer you to the man's chart. Between ages forty-two and forty-four—at about the time many men face the danger of heart attack—Hunt was entering what is known as the Uranus Half-Cycle. Astrologers have attributed this period to the corresponding physical dangers to the heart. Could Hunt have been undergoing severe cardial stress at the time? His chart shows that he was born with the propensity for facing just such a danger: Uranus and Saturn were opposite at birth, Uranus in Aquarius and Saturn in Leo, the sign that governs the heart muscle. The half cycle meant that Uranus was coming to its own opposition, on the same degree of the Saturn that debilitates matters of the sign that it is in, in this case the heart.

Uranus brings the danger from great tensions afflicting cardial matters. All of us know of people who, while going through severe heart troubles, may look scores of years beyond their actual age, but who regain their youthful looks once the greater danger is past. Also, in astrology, if something seems imminent, the only way to escape is often to sublimate the meaning of the aspects that afflict so that they manifest in some other form. This is another form of transcendence that I will discuss later.

Perhaps fearful that he would soon die anyway, Hunt may have inadvertently stumbled upon the one and only greater manifestation of that powerful aspect of Uranus conjunct Saturn/opposite natal Uranus: it is the symbol of a great rebellion. Perhaps, in dealing with the tensions of assassinating JFK, in committing one of the bloodiest acts of rebellion in history, Hunt put all his troubles on another level altogether.

E. Howard Hunt, author of forty novels, began as an operative in Mexico for the CIA in the early 1950s. Soon after, he helped overthrow the freely elected government of President Jacobo Arbenz of Guatemala. One of his prime involvements, it has become well known, was work that lasted for some two years in preparing Cuban exiles for the Bay of Pigs invasion. In his novel about the famous fiasco, *Give Us This Day,* he wrote of being *betrayed* by President Kennedy, whom he believed only sought "to whitewash the New Frontier by heaping guilt on the CIA."

He had earlier failed to sell the Eisenhower administration on Castro-assassination plots; he tried in 1965 (according to journalist Tad Szulc) and was finally successful with LBJ. The plot progressed. A Cuban physician, Rolando Cubela, was the chosen triggerman. The plot was scrapped, however, at the very last minute because of Johnson's invasion of the Dominican Republic. Hunt later used his knowledge of and participation in "illegal conspiracies" to extort money from the White House for his Watergate burglary defense. Shortly after this extortion, Hunt's wife, carrying a mysteriously large amount of money ($10,000) died in a plane crash. No official connection has been made, and, of course, people wonder why.

Hunt had organized the Cuban Revolutionary Committee, the anti-Castro group in whose name Oswald had been handing out supposedly pro-Castro literature. (While the name at the bottom of the leaflet read Fair Play for Cuba Committee, the address was that of the Cuban Revolutionary Committee.)

Hunt's involvement in dirty tricks, as we know, continued into the early seventies. How much, we ask, is there yet to know about this devious and probably dangerous man? More implications than I've listed here continue to occupy researchers.

In the *New York Review of Books* in April, 1975, novelist

Gore Vidal tries his hand at explaining this man's activities. Hunt's prose, claims Vidal, sounds remarkably like that of would-be Wallace assassin Arthur Bremmer. Hunt, as we have been made aware in the case of the spurious cables linking the Kennedys to the murder of South Vietnamese President Ngo Dinh Diem, has a certain expertise at forging assassination-related documents. At the suggestion of Chuck Colson, the latter dirty trick sprang from the Nixon enclave. Colson tried to peddle the lie to the press but failed. Vidal feels that it is strange and probably not coincidental at all that recent assassins—Sirhan, Bremmer, and Oswald—all showed a penchant for leaving written evidence linking them to their alleged crimes. Vidal wonders if all such documents might have sprung from the same pen. All things considered, Hunt deserves at least: 50 percent.

Frank Sturgis: Hunt and Sturgis were together on the Watergate burglary. They seem to have been photographed together in Dallas. There were, however, objections posed by the *Rolling Stone* reviewer about the probability of the taller tramp being Sturgis. First, he claims, Sturgis obviously looks very Latin, while the tramp looks Scandinavian. The first of the claims is, again, subjective. The reader should study the face of Frank Fiorini Sturgis and decide whether his features are or are not "obviously" Latin. I personally disagree that anything of this sort is obvious. If the reviewer means hair color, however, we all know how many ways that "clue" can change.

The second objection that relates not just to Sturgis, but to both men is this: Sturgis is only a *few* inches taller than Hunt, yet the taller tramp in the photos seems to be about *eight inches taller*. In answer, first the reviewer must be questioned in terms of the *perspective* from which his apparently approximate measurements are taken: Has he taken into account the fact that the taller tramp is in the foreground, while the smaller tramp is behind? How far behind is the smaller figure? What kind of lens was used, and is it free from distortions that would make it difficult to determine the true distance? Also, what was the terrain like? Could the smaller tramp have been climbing *stairs?* Was the area *hilly?*

The Assassinations: Some Astrological Answers   149

Take into account, as well, the health and astrological stress probabilities working on the smaller tramp, if it was in fact E. Howard Hunt, and recognize that, aside from the energy expenditures such an operation would have entailed, the old ticker may have been kicking up as well. The man could be bent over for all we know. There are numerous things that could have shortened the likeness of E. Howard Hunt that day, but few things to allow or force us to totally dismiss as coincidence the fact that two key assassination-minded U.S. Intelligence agents should look so much like two mystery tramps picked up at the scene of the century's most resounding assassination, by mystery cops who gave them a mystery police record.

The third mystery tramp in the photos, by the way, has been identified by some researchers as a minuteman from Washington, D.C., who also amazingly resembles the first police sketch that went out on a man wanted for the assassination of Martin Luther King, Jr.

No one really knew about Frank Sturgis until Watergate. In *All the President's Men* he's described in the following glowing terms: "... an American soldier of fortune ... had been recruiting militant Cubans to demonstrate at the Democratic National Convention ... One leader told Bernstein [coauthor] that Sturgis and others whom he described as 'former CIA types' intended to use paid provocateurs to fight antiwar demonstrators in the streets during the national political conventions." Sturgis wasn't always so easygoing. He once operated as a go-between in a deal between the Mafia and the CIA to assassinate Castro. And an attorney in Washington said he could positively identify Sturgis as one of the several men who had attacked "Pentagon Papers" defendant Daniel Ellsberg outside a memorial service for the late director of the FBI, J. Edgar Hoover.

Sturgis has apparent knowledge as well of the activities of Lee Harvey Oswald, which he claims were as a pro-Castro infiltrator in anti-Castro groups. Other than that, he was deeply involved in every sort of espionage in the Caribbean in the late fifties and into the sixties and was angered when Kennedy's refusal to aid the invaders destroyed all he had helped plan for for so long. In his memoirs, published in the late spring of 1975 in a five-part series in the *New*

York Daily News, Sturgis mentions his deep personal regret, and his hatred for Castro, after the Cuban leader executed a close friend. Thereafter, his involvement in his work seems to have evolved into a warped sort of dedication. Was he among a vast and powerful police underground in this country who resented and feared Kennedy power and what it might do to their war games?

For all of this, but especially for *seeming* to be so absolutely photogenic, I have given Sturgis the rating I gave Hunt: 50 percent.

Nikita Khrushchev: Lee Harvey Oswald spent two years in the land controlled, at that time, by this powerful Communist leader. He did so with the status of a defector from American democracy and, according to some researchers, may have been a subject of certain diabolical soviet "experiments." His employment at the Soviet Electrotechnical Institute, in the experimental section, has been offered by Alex Bottos as a clue to Oswald's activities behind the Iron Curtain. If this is so, it is possible that he was one of the earliest and most successful subjects of behavior modification. Bottos's theory implicitly presupposes that the Russians saw value in Oswald and primed him to be one of their chief American operatives.

Could he then have been sent back to the United States programmed, like the character portrayed by Laurence Harvey in *The Manchurian Candidate,* to go off at the right time like a thermonuclear time-bomb? Given that all of his mysterious contacts back in the states were with U.S. intelligence and anti-Communist types, it seems hardly likely, although not totally out of the question. Another very serious accusation has been made in some quarters, some might call them the fringes of the assassination research movement, that the Kennedy assassination was the result of a combined effort of U.S. and Soviet intelligence, forces long since out of the hands of a Congress, or a ruling Politburo. Motives given are several, although the chief contentions lie in areas of 1) making sure that no do-gooders mess up the joint U.S.-Soviet handling of the world's heroin traffic, and 2) asserting that both had "reasons" (of self-preservation?) for getting JFK out of the way. Yet, while the Russians may have still been smarting from the Cuban-missile backdown and loss of face in the world press, and the CIA seething at Kennedy's aborting of their pet Bay of Pigs project, there would be no common meeting ground on these matters, as each group would more likely have *backed* Kennedy in his aggravating actions against the other side.

Whatever the truth may be behind the myriad theories, we *do* know that Oswald defected and spent two years in Russia doing God-knows-what. For some reason, his re-entry into the United States and resumption of normal citizenship status came easily. His activities *seemed* to continue along pro-Communist lines here at home; however, there have been serious doubts raised as to the veracity of those pro-Castro charges hurled at him.

If Oswald was primed to act as the government claims he did—alone and with high treason and murder in his mind, not necessarily in his heart (or in any way connected with his emotions)—then it is also very probable that his conditioning made him invulnerable to such methods as the polygraph and, subsequently, to any improvement, such as the PSE, on that technique that measures, essentially, the emotional context of a suspect's replies to incriminating questions. However, this is all a very big if. There is little else in the way of evidence to connect the Russian premier with JFK's death, aside from Lee Harvey Oswald—which may be connection enough. I have given Khrushchev: 40 percent.

J. Edgar Hoover: It is probable, from all accounts, that Hoover may have had a lot to do with a cover-up following the assassination, but there is little, again, except for the accused assassin, to connect Hoover to the actual murder. While I examined the CIA's possible role in the affair by looking at the birth chart of the agency itself, from all we know of the FBI, it *was* J. Edgar Hoover (and vice versa). So I am skipping the middleman, as it were, by looking at Hoover's and not the FBI's chart.

The foremost reason for suspecting the FBI of participating in the cover-up is that all the evidence that was presented to the Warren Commission was first gathered by the FBI. That is to say, the Warren Commission investigators could look anywhere they wished for conspiracy—save at the FBI; and if we abhor the sloppy job done twelve years ago by that commission, we must lay the blame for that travesty of investigative work at the desk of the late J. Edgar Hoover. This, in itself, warrants putting Hoover on our suspects list; but there is more.

One of the six Warren Commission members was Allen Dulles, a former director of the CIA. He was asked if an intelligence officer responsible for the recruiting of an intelligence operative would be aware of what he was up to. This was his answer:

DULLES: "Yes, but he wouldn't tell."
EARL WARREN: "Wouldn't tell it under oath?"
DULLES: "I wouldn't think he would tell it under oath, no."

Even if the Warren Commission had intended to investigate the FBI's role, or the extent to which their gathered testimony was complete, probably they would have gotten little help from the Bureau itself.

When the contents of the notebook found on Oswald were first released by the FBI for the Warren Commission's perusal on December 23, 1963, there was a name missing. It was that of special agent James Hosty. Oswald had his name, phone number, and license-plate number. Knowledge of this omission filtered into the commission hearings long before a second report was issued on January 11, 1964, which included Hosty's name. In his testimony before the Warren Commission, Hoover explained that the first list reflected the FBI's own course of investigating the assassination: It had checked on Oswald's connection with all those listed in the book, but had left out Hosty's name because it already knew his relationship to Oswald. According to Hoover, Hosty's interest in Oswald had been routine; the Special Agent simply had been keeping tabs on a repatriated defector.

A source identified as a Dallas assistant district attorney, William Alexander, has since claimed that Oswald was a paid informer for the FBI—that he received a monthly paycheck of $200 and that his payroll number was S-179. Many of the strange connections the accused assassin supposedly had with the FBI would be made clear if this fact is borne out: After his arrest for creating a disturbance in New Orleans, Oswald demanded to see an FBI agent. The day after this interview, Oswald was released with a slap on the wrist in the form of a ten-dollar fine. In a supposedly routine follow-up survey of Oswald's activities in Dallas, agent John Fain interviewed the ex-defector on August 15, 1962, outside Oswald's home.

What was strange about this encounter was that the agents chose to speak with Oswald in their car rather than inside Oswald's apartment. Questions have been raised as to whether the agents may have wanted to avoid being overheard. Finally, when Oswald was arrested at the Texas Theater and charged, first, with the murder of Officer Tippit, the police were presumably responding to a call that a suspect had taken refuge there. However, FBI agent Robert Barrett was in on the arrest. Why, researchers want to know, was the FBI involved in a local police matter?

Supposedly, before Oswald's transfer to a different jail cell in the basement of police headquarters, the FBI called the Dallas police to inform them of a call that had warned of an attempt on Oswald's life. Oswald was obviously *the* key to the whole case—why, one might well ask, weren't the Dallas police ready when Jack Ruby was? Had "uninformed" elements of the Dallas police participated in Oswald's capture so that it was not possible to kill him and close the case forever there in the Texas Theater? If Oswald was to be the century's biggest fall guy, it was necessary to get him out of the way.

Add to these disturbing questions the disclosure of "the other Oswald" memo sent by Hoover to the State Department—disclosed after his death—and it is necessary to give Hoover a rating of: 30 percent.

The composite analysis follows, showing the most likely possibilities of those having been stressfully involved with the events in Dallas on November 22, 1963, shortly after noon. It is a composite of three procedures: the first, a synastry between the suspect's chart and that of John Kennedy; the second, a horary chart of the moment of the incident compared and analyzed for stress with the chart of each suspect, and, finally, an arbitrary analysis of the weight of evidence implicating the suspects. Motive, critical-moment stress, and evidence each have been given percentile ratings, the higher percentile suspects being, of course, all the more suspect.

In no way do I advocate that the methods I have employed to arrive at my conclusions be used by thoughtful people or even the wildest of assassinationologists in place of existing criminology techniques. This study is a cosmic adjunct to the investigations currently being carried out by citizens across the land. The cycles we call coincidence would allow that a certain percentage of the population would have, at the same moment—in Dallas or elsewhere—experienced equally stressful conditions that were in no way connected directly to the assassination. There are other such variables that have not been considered.

For those who don't wish to go along with my percentile analysis of the weight of existing evidence, I have provided a second list. The percentages represent only the astrologically objective parts one and two of my study; you may assign your own percentages to the evidence, or what you will.

Three-Part Analysis: Conclusion

Name	Probability of Involvement
The CIA	54%
Frank Sturgis	52%
Virgilio Gonzales	46%
John Connally	45⅔%
Nikita Khrushchev	42⅔%
Lee Harvey Oswald	*40%*
Howard Hughes	40%
Mao Tse-tung	38%
J. Edgar Hoover	37⅓%
E. Howard Hunt	33⅓%
Fidel Castro	25⅔%
Gen. Charles Cabell	24⅔%
Richard Nixon	24⅔%
Billy Graham	24⅔%
G. Gordon Liddy	21⅔%
Adlai Stevenson	21⅔%
Lyndon Baines Johnson	15⅔%
Jack Ruby	14%

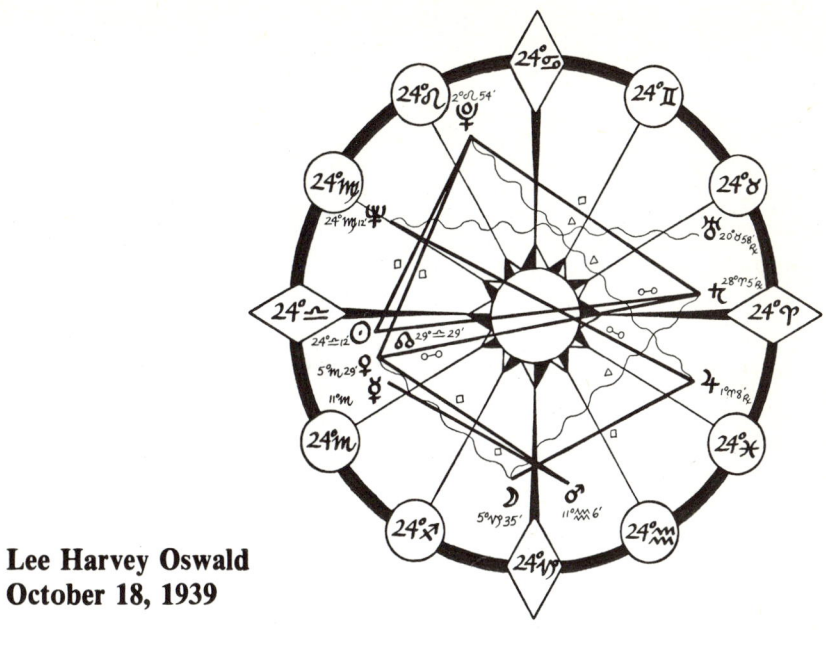

The Assassinations: Some Astrological Answers 155

Lee Harvey Oswald
October 18, 1939

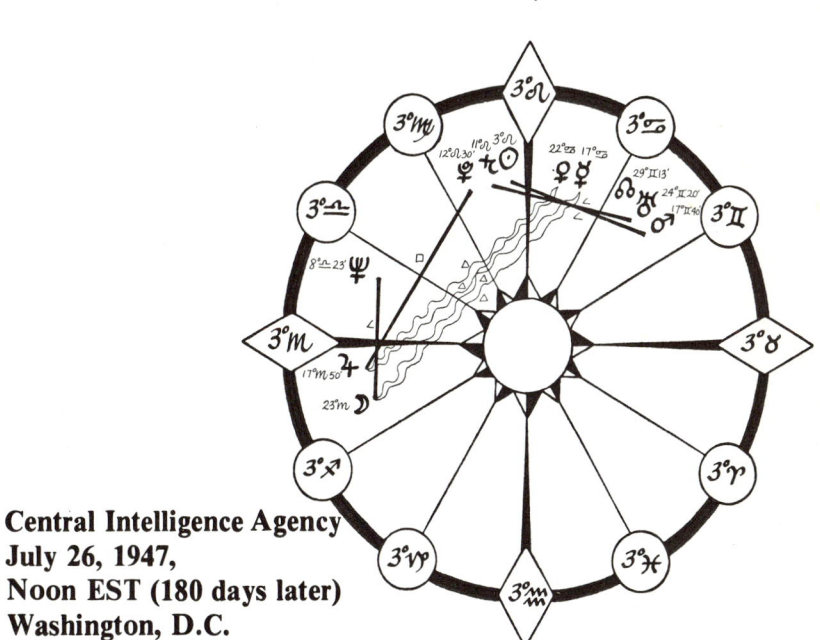

Central Intelligence Agency
July 26, 1947,
Noon EST (180 days later)
Washington, D.C.

156   THE KENNEDY CURSE

George Wallace	13%
Eugenio Martinez	12%
Ronald Reagan	10⅓%
Eisenhower	8⅔%
Aristotle Onassis	5⅓%
Nelson Rockefeller	1⅔%
Thomas Dewey	1⅔%
Barry Goldwater	0%

Two-Part Analysis: Conclusion

Virgilio Gonzales	69%
John Connally (43% stress/*94%* motive)	68%
Mao Tse-tung	57%
Nikita Khrushchev	54%
Frank Sturgis	53%
The CIA	51%
Howard Hughes	50%
J. Edgar Hoover	41%
Billy Graham	37%
Richard Nixon	37%
Adlai Stevenson	32½%
G. Gordon Liddy	32½%
Gen. Charles Cabell	32%
E. Howard Hunt	25%
Lee Harvey Oswald	*25%*
George Wallace	19½%
Ronald Reagan	15½%
Lyndon Baines Johnson	13%
Eugenio Martinez	13%
Eisenhower	13%
Jack Ruby	11%
Aristotle Onassis	8%
Thomas Dewey	2½%
Nelson Rockefeller	2½%
Barry Goldwater	0%

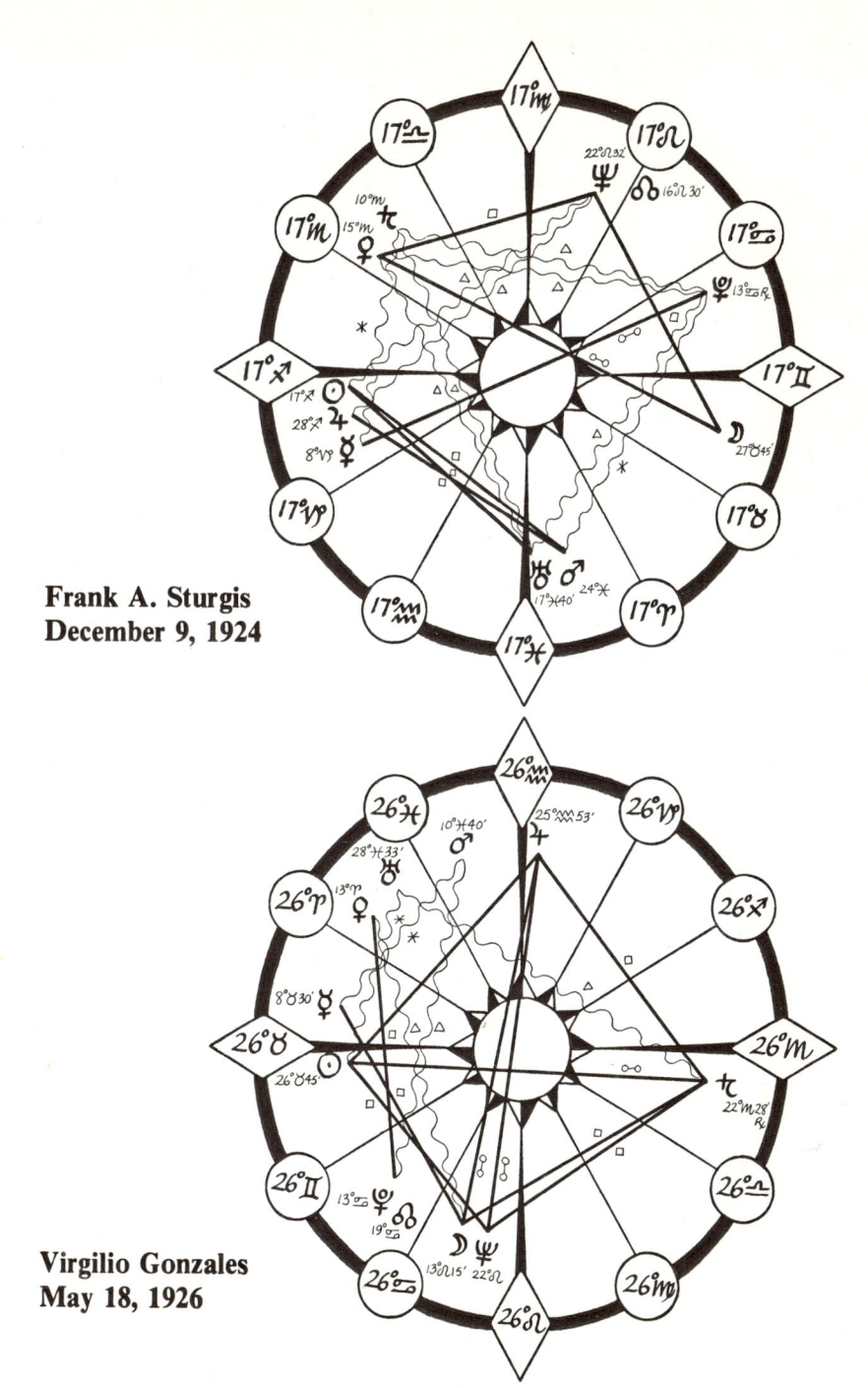

The Assassinations: Some Astrological Answers 157

Frank A. Sturgis
December 9, 1924

Virgilio Gonzales
May 18, 1926

We now sift through the final list and remove the seventeen charts of suspects, semisuspects, and ringers whom no one has connected with Dallas that day in any reliable way. Although there's been a rumor afoot for years now that Richard Nixon was in Dallas that day, I am not including him in the list. I do, however, include the chart of J. Edgar Hoover, although I know he wasn't there in person. Since Hoover *was* the FBI, and as there were many FBI men present in Dallas that day, so, too, was J. Edgar Hoover.

The following represents the involvement potential, based on the three- and two-part analysis, for suspects present in Dallas, or probably present in Dallas, on November 22, 1963:

Three-Part Test

The CIA	54%
Frank Sturgis	52%
John Connally	45⅔%
Lee Harvey Oswald	40%
J. Edgar Hoover	37⅓%
E. Howard Hunt	33⅓%
Gen. Charles Cabell	24⅔%
Lyndon Baines Johnson	15⅔%
Jack Ruby	14%

Two-Part Test

John Connally	68%
Frank Sturgis	53%
The CIA	51%
J. Edgar Hoover	41%
Gen. Charles Cabell	32%
E. Howard Hunt	25%
Lee Harvey Oswald	25%
Lyndon Baines Johnson	13%
Jack Ruby	11%

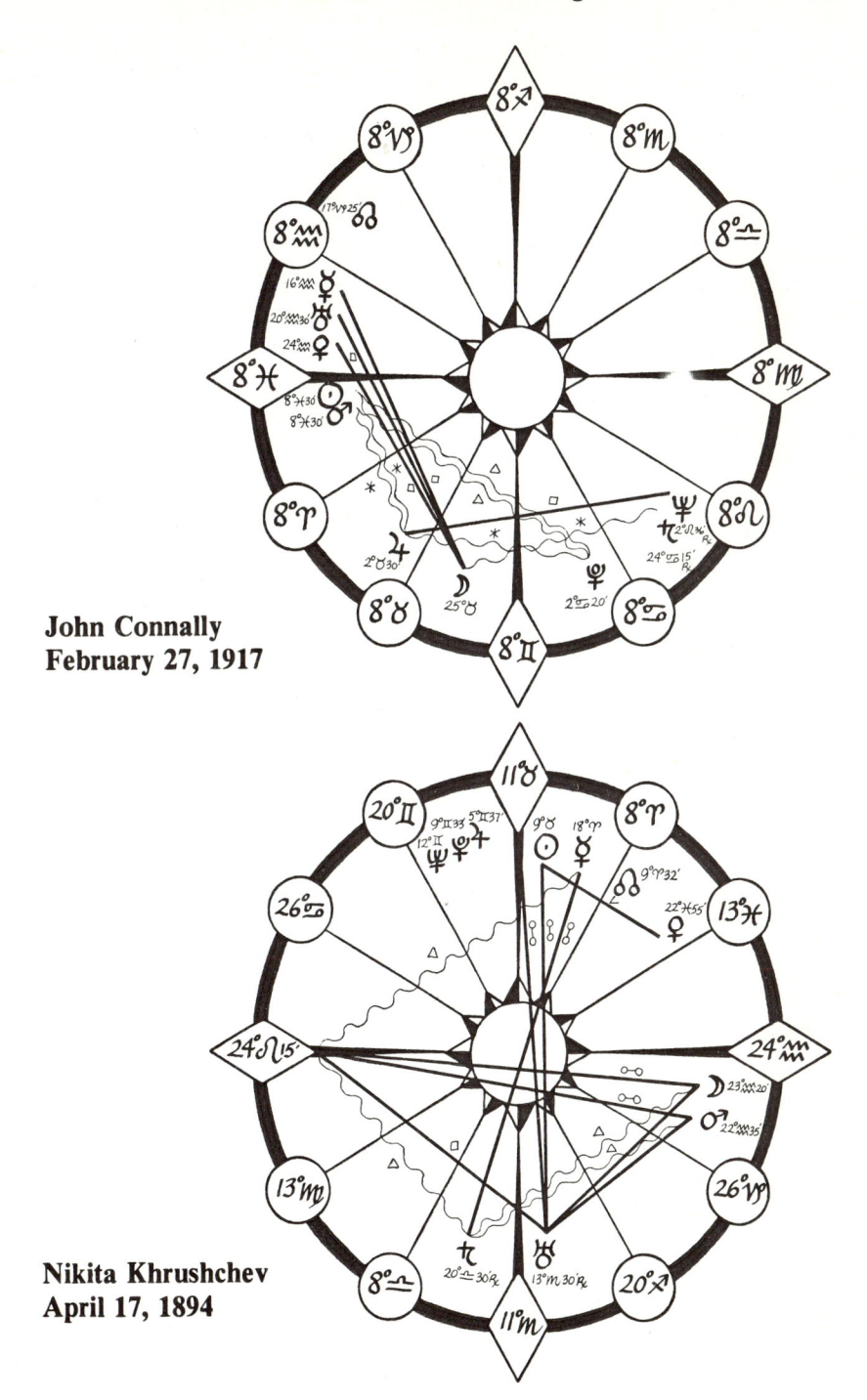

The Assassinations: Some Astrological Answers 159

John Connally
February 27, 1917

Nikita Khrushchev
April 17, 1894

Mao Tse-Tung
December 26, 1893

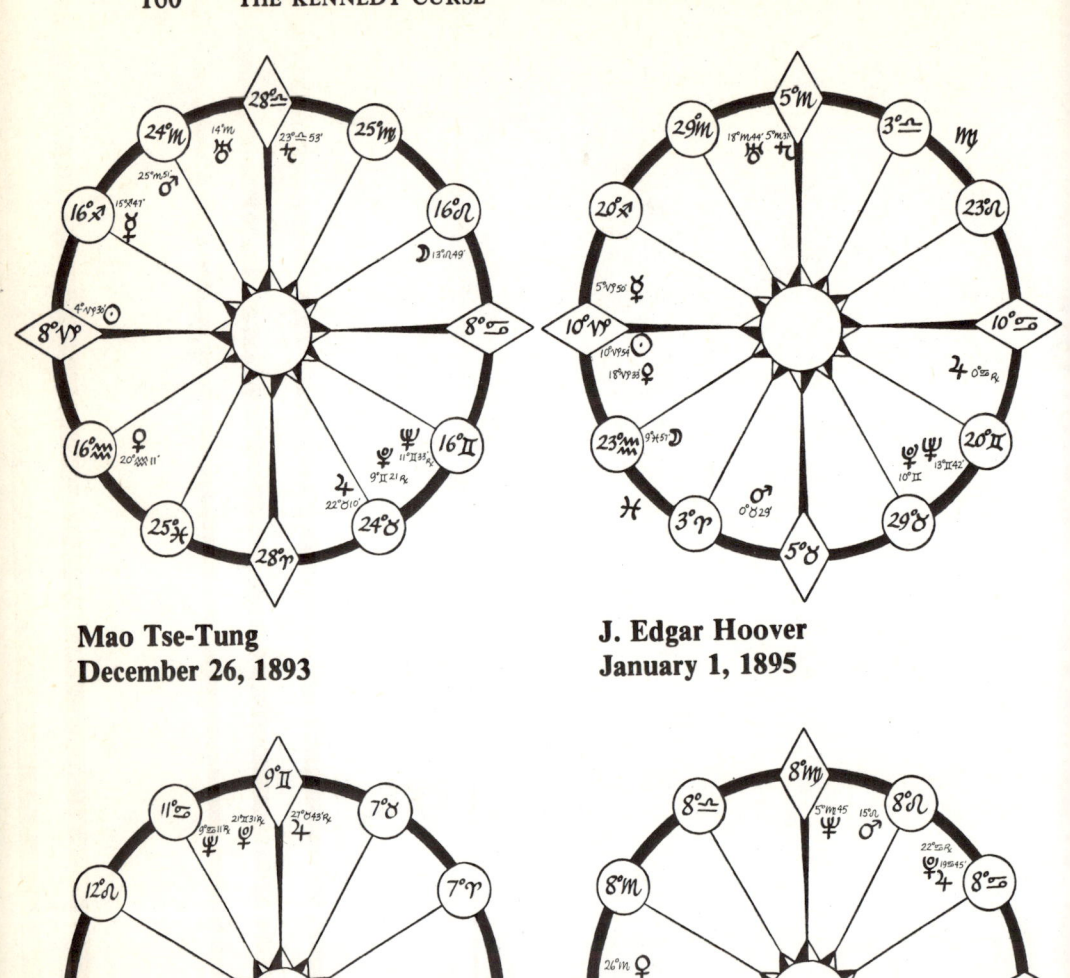

J. Edgar Hoover
January 1, 1895

Howard Hughes
December 24, 1905

G. Gordon Liddy
November 30, 1930

The Assassinations: Some Astrological Answers   161

Billy Graham
November 17, 1918

Richard Nixon
January 9, 1913

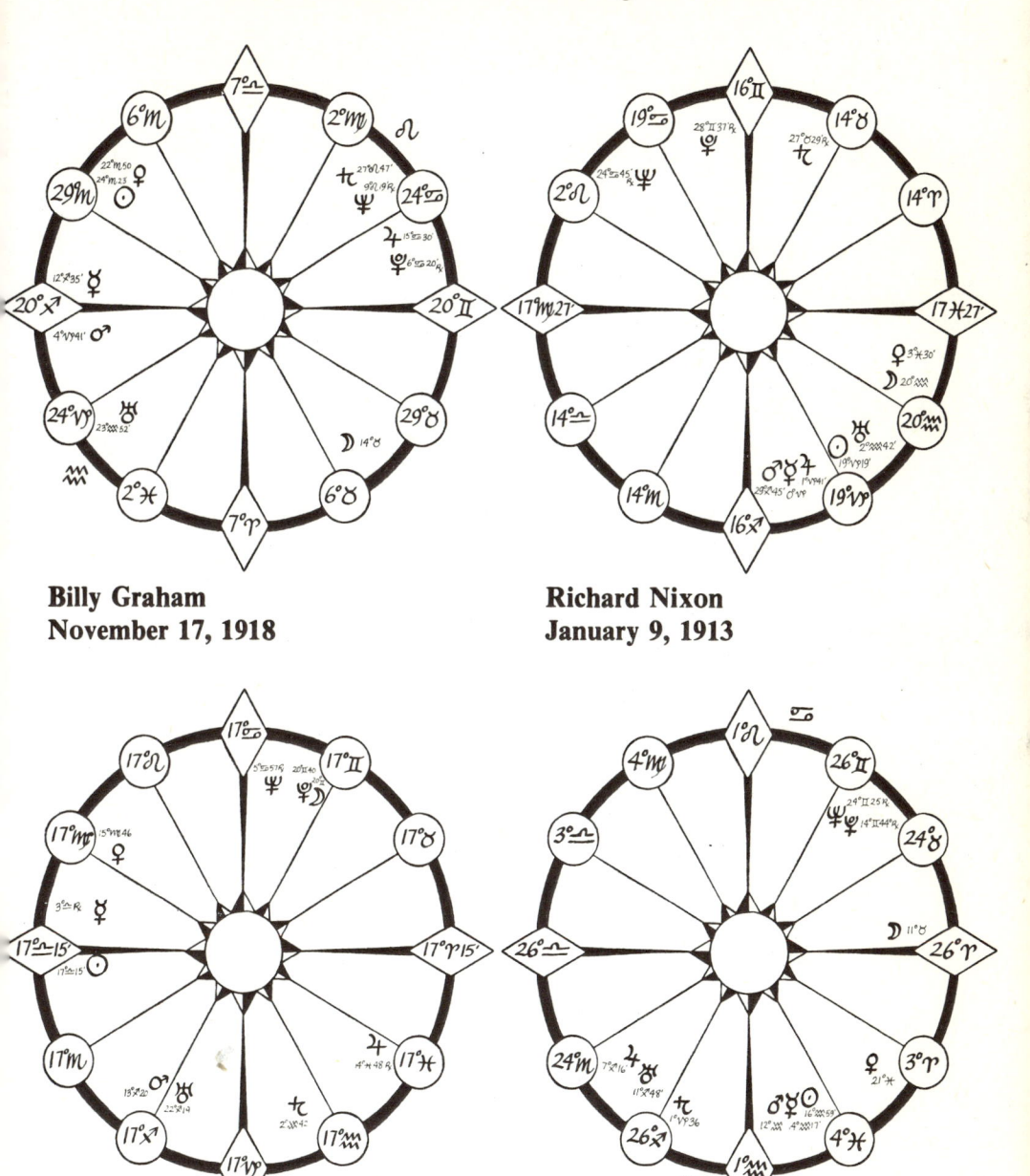

General Charles Cabell
October 11, 1903

Adlai E. Stevenson
February 5, 1900

Dwight D. Eisenhower
October 14, 1890

E. Howard Hunt
October 9, 1918

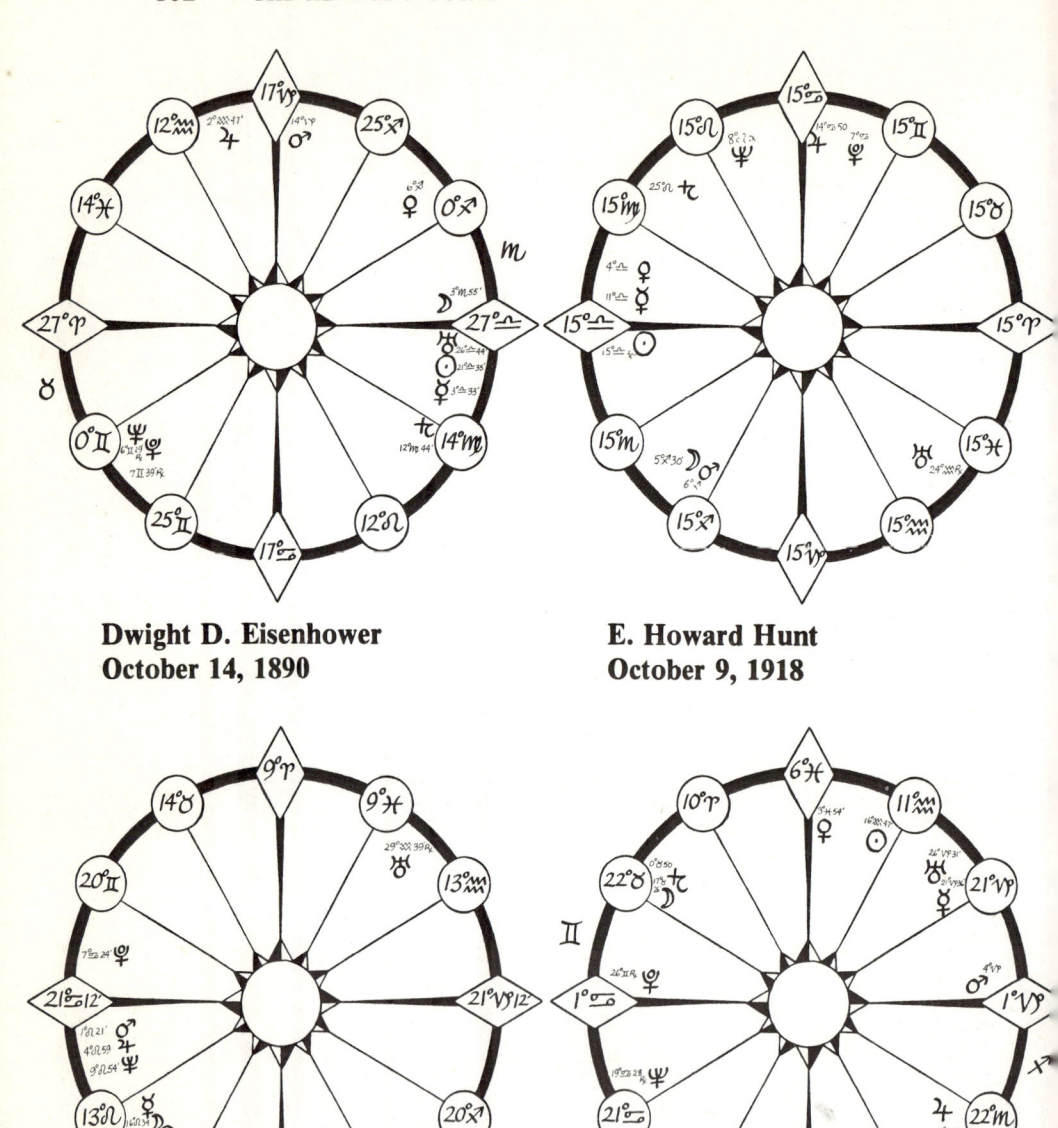

George Wallace
August 25, 1919

Ronald Reagan
February 6, 1911

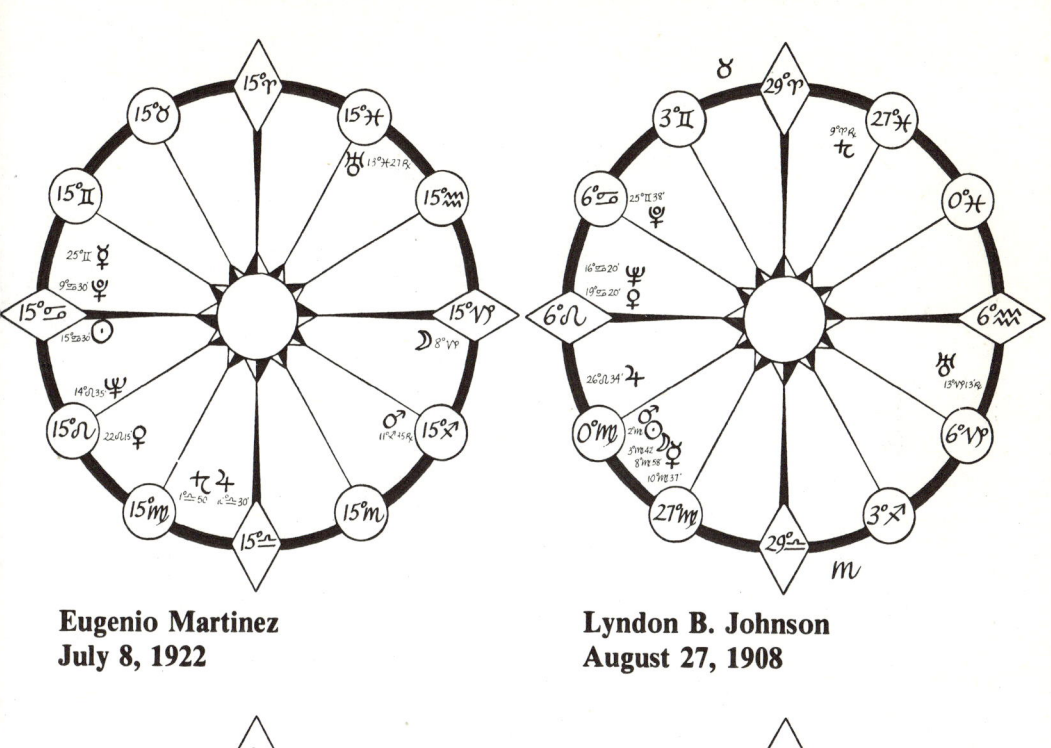

The Assassinations: Some Astrological Answers 163

Eugenio Martinez
July 8, 1922

Lyndon B. Johnson
August 27, 1908

Jack Ruby
March 25, 1911

Nelson Rockefeller
July 8, 1908

164 THE KENNEDY CURSE

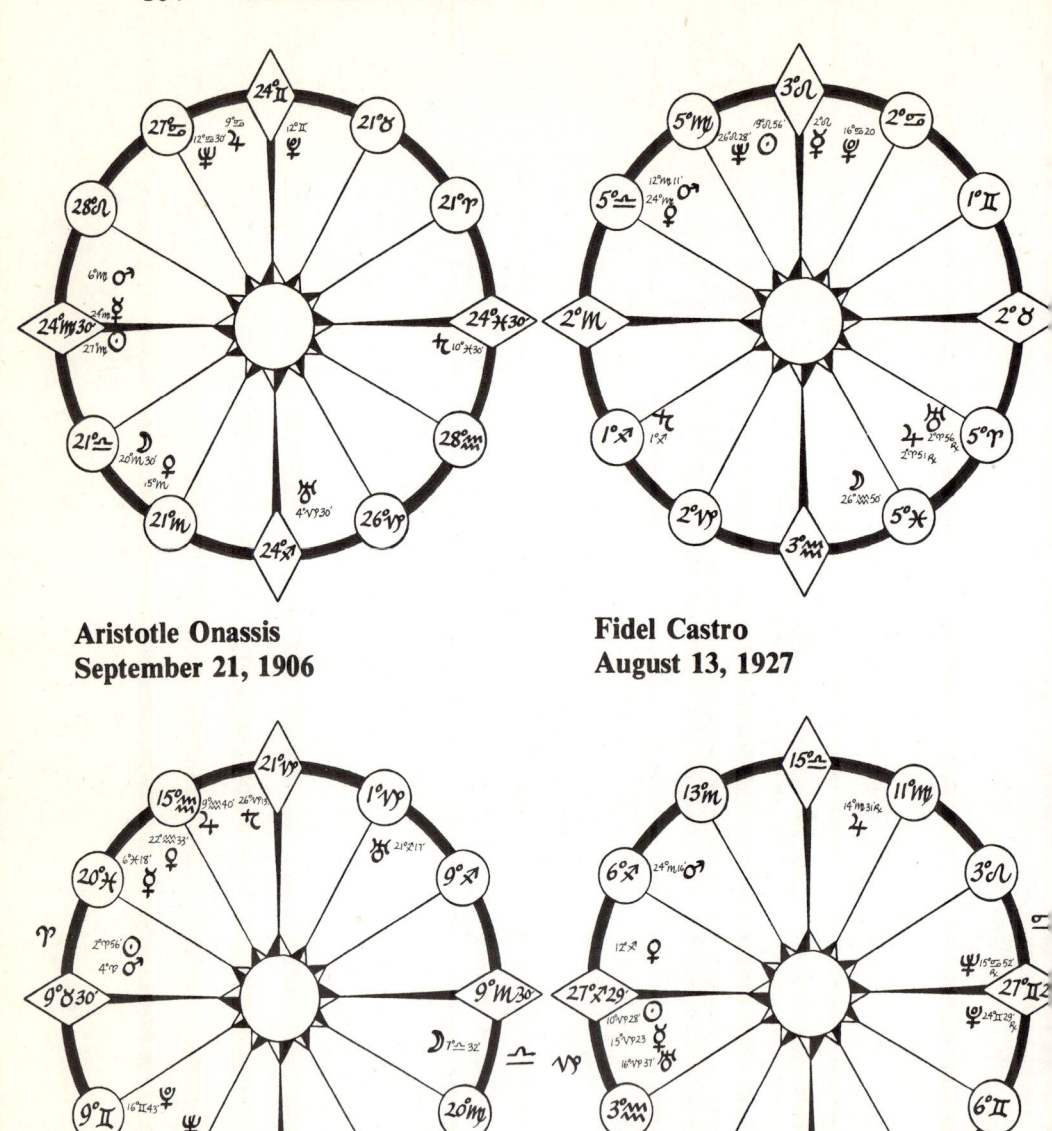

Aristotle Onassis
September 21, 1906

Fidel Castro
August 13, 1927

Thomas E. Dewey
March 24, 1902

Barry Goldwater
January 1, 1909

7

The Kennedy Curse Unmasked

In the widest overview I can take on the entire subject of doom facing the Kennedys, a view that depends on an esoteric understanding of such ideas as curses, it must be pointed out that we all, in some small way, contribute directly to the action of the curse concept. Certainly, all citizens must accept indirect blame for the shape of a government that would allow its most secret, inner operatives to go berserk. Most Americans, we can undoubtedly agree, are lazy about the participatory necessities inherent in democracy. Eventually our elected representatives begin to listen, perhaps, to people who whisper in their ears things like "What's good for General Motors is good for the country."

The E. Howard Hunts and Gordon Liddys of the world become powerful because you and I are not interested in the workings of government. That power groups lie dormant, waiting to rise against any overhaul of government (even against elected representatives as high in rank as president) is the fault of imperfections both within the populace and the system. We must also keep in mind the immortality of thought, as in the case of all the ancient accounts of curses that, while they may have faded in the consciousness of the accursed lineage, remained alive within the legend of the people, so much so that their influence has permeated the spiritual, or second state, of the common mind we all share, helping to manifest the event. What then of an entire population convinced of the fatal connection between a Kennedy in high office and death? "Oh, no!" people will proclaim. "Teddy can't be so crazy as to run for the presidency." What if he should *win*—which he probably would—well, then *he'll die like his brothers before him.*

Forged into the consciousness of half a nation is this vague concept that always lurks in the common mind, in the great subconscious plane on which there are no physical or language barriers: that great tragedy will most naturally plague the Kennedys. To the extent that the Kennedys are tuned in to the common *will*—or needs that are expressed through conscious means—they are also, more than most politicians, subconsciously attuned to the common *mind.*

Afflicted Neptune functions in this way. This astrological co-conspirator against the family links the outgoing charisma of its members to an in-drawing of the less pleasant intuitions—one, at least, being the strong possibility that they are a doomed bunch.

As in the case of more classical curses, even the unconscious awareness of the curse helps its manifestation. While no actual curse may have been ever pronounced (nor would it, in the case of the Kennedys, seem to matter much) the belief that there is one would help it come true. Being hung up on such outdated and childishly harmful psychic concepts may be our current racial karma, such as it were, but that we cannot escape that profound interest in the Kennedys' seemingly inescapable doom makes the inescapable aspect of that doom even stronger.

At this point, the working prognosis must be that there is nothing terribly fateful and like a *curse* in operation here. The eighth house involvements, while among the most fated in the zodiac, cannot be seen to be the only criteria necessary. If you play with fire, you get burned; he who lives by the sword . . . all go to show that we attract what interests us most. The two assassinated Kennedy brothers took on the crooked and the corrupt from the word go; Bobby's reputation was built on these pursuits, making it not at all unlikely or really nepotistic for his brother Jack to appoint him U.S. Attorney General as soon as he was inaugurated. Together, they invited the wrath of murderous elements. Toward the end of their influence over American politics, the Kennedy brothers shifted from one eighth-house area of interest, crime and criminals, to another, the deadly activities of spy and secret groups within our borders and in foreign lands.

Here, they were pitting their American-political-family savvy against the fierce patriotism of such as secret paramilitary, John Bircher or Minutemen types, and against factions of agencies like the CIA, whose autonomy was greater than that of the puny Minutemen, even while under supposed government control, for they had at their disposal your and my tax dollar. You might have sneered at the misguided fanatic who growled that the Communists were all over the place and that we all had to arm to the teeth, but would you please give him a contribution for "the Cause"? Then, as you might have turned indignantly on your heel, some jerkwater government clerk was signing a requisition for a million dollars worth of surplus government landing craft that would be thrown away in the Bay of Pigs boondoggle (it may have been an invasion, as far as the expatriates themselves were concerned, but for the CIA it was just another big tab to justify the funds for a bigger one the following year).

Ted is also involved in eighth-house matters these days. The poor fall under the eighth-house influence, as do the affairs of taxation, and these are some of the main areas the senator is building his reputation on. But he's no longer the chief liberal threat. The country has changed a lot since the sixties. Many people who may have once wanted to hand over full responsibility for governing to their representatives in Washington, and especially to the president, have learned that they must always retain a portion of the control. Now many have called back their proxies and are actively working to shape the decisions and opinions of their local representatives, and even to publicly challenge the President himself with the most irrefutable of scientific data.

Now everybody is the potential enemy of the military-industrial complex; Ted Kennedy is just an old wound to them. In his urgings to spend more on the needy and less on defense, he is just one of many. As for the investigations into the assassination, he is in a very fortunate position as this is being written, he can let private citizens and other lawmakers do all the shouting. The matter, after all, is far too personal. However, if he should be the Democratic presidential candidate in 1976, he would *have* to make strong statements, and the public would expect him to be far more candid than he's been, not just about his brothers' assassination and his suspicions thereon, but about Chappaquiddick as well.

What mystery, one wonders, does Ted Kennedy ponder in the death of Mary Jo Kopechne? Mystery—returning once again to the significant factors repeated so often among the charts—is ruled by Neptune. So, too, are watery depths and bad weather. Chappaquiddick was most typical of the combination of Neptunian things with eighth-house things. But the two also represent the alliances between one's hidden enemies (Neptune rules Pisces, the twelfth-house, or hidden enemies sign, and is associated with secret groups, especially death-dealing ones) and can indicate that trickery played a part in the tragedy.

What, for instance, was E. Howard Hunt doing studying Ted Kennedy and the Chappaquiddick affair while in service to the Nixon White House, and was Hunt studying both Ted and the location of the tragic accident only *after* the event? We now know that it was under direct orders from President Nixon that the CIA entered into what was the bloodiest phase of their operations during the early seventies, the overthrow of the democratically elected government of Chile and assassination of its leader, Salvador Allende. We all know that Ted Kennedy was Nixon's chief fear in his bid for reelection. If Allende, why not Mary Jo Kopechne?

The rest of the tragedies seem to be connected to eighth-house things, as well as to tenth- and fifth-house influences. The latter two houses, remember, are those of "being 'tops' in the field" and "taking risks," respectively; the eighth makes death part of the stakes in the game. Joe, Jr. may have been typical—making a suicide mission to outshine his brother Jack, made hero by that unpredictable, general accident of war—and dying in the attempt. What do you expect from a suicide mission, though? The other deaths seemed to happen to those in small private planes, flying in bad weather, and so on. More of the same: You take your risks, you pay your price.

In a family so large, one retarded child, a few miscarriages, even Ted Jr.'s bone cancer, can be expected. Thus far, there is, as I've said, nothing terribly doomlike in their family astrology.

The distinction between doom and karma is one of transcendance; you can't avoid doom, but you can pay your debts and transcend your karma, even leave it entirely behind. Obviously, no one put an inescapable doom on the Kennedys. You may hear a story or two floating around that this or that old hag put a curse on Joe Kennedy's great-great grandmother, but no force can be that strong when wielded by a mortal. However, it's apparent that a very high price is being paid for *something*. The concept of karma is a good one to view the Kennedy saga through. Just deserts is another way of thinking of karma, although in our Western Christian tradition, we have been led to believe that we pay *after* this life. The concept of karma in one respect is like that of the idea of a living principle of original sin couched in human genetics: The sins of the fathers shall be visited upon future generations. It is revealed clearly in the Bible, but somehow, we've chosen to think that responsibility won't be visited upon us until we're dead. Karma says, don't count on an easy life of sinning in return for eternal damnation (if that's what you really want) because you start paying *here and now,* as well as there and then.

Apparently, Joe Kennedy found this out the hard way. Here is where we first must begin to look for blame.

The eighth house that we have been inspecting so closely here is co-ruled by Pluto, planet of compulsion, of the most insidious kinds of slavery. Aside from all the secretive and death-related matters of the planet, house, and sign, this new association, coupled with afflicted Neptune, brings the topic of *alcoholism* immediately to mind. Neptune rules spirits, Scorpio enslavement. The Kennedys first established themselves on Boston shores as saloon keepers. On the whole, such trades are benevolent and humane. One of the friendliest people on any block is the corner bartender. And there's nothing wrong with alcohol, when (as in the case of any drug) it is used in moderation.

Perhaps this was lost on the early Kennedys, though, because, as they gained local influence, they converted it into political control, which became their new base for power. Now, political power can also be benevolent, if wielded with the best public intentions in mind.

The only *intention* of the Kennedys was to break their way to the top of Boston society, with all the Irish they could muster, buying out anyone who stood in their way, and worse. Otherwise, it was a gut-level hunger that drove them on relentlessly, with no clear intention, perhaps, until Joe Kennedy, Sr. hit the scene.

Thus it was that the family roots were tainted by the alcoholism promoted on a large-scale, dehumanized basis. It was an enslavement that struck the immigrant, poor-as-churchmouse Irish population—their own countrymen—in Back Bay Boston particularly hard. It was no longer an elbow-tilting neighborliness, but a simple promotion of what was becoming a plague-like addiction. The likes of the Kennedys brought on Prohibition. They had bought votes with tabs, lied, cheated to garner political spheres of influence, in short, behaved exactly like the crooks Americans were being warned that all politicians were. But they went one more step to use their influence to further their booze trade—like Richard Nixon using Muzak to deaden the senses of the corporate heart of America, then asking them to back *him,* and getting their help. One hand dirties the other. The associations keep rolling in:

Neptune	**Eighth House/Scorpio**
alcohol	alcoholism
secret deals	taxes
deception	the poor
leadership charisma	secret deals
water	death
mysteries	secret groups, conspiracies
bad weather	fatal accidents
and we might add . . .	
movies	low-budget
romance	lust
fast-talking	covetousness

No one is free of a list of faults that hounds his or her heels. But, in Joseph P. Kennedy, Sr., we may have a key to the strength of the recent karma that hounds the heels of his sons and daughters and their families. If anything can be called a "curse," it may have been the composite of the accomplishments of this one, misguided man *in the name of his children.* JFK's bad back, where the first bullet struck—bushwhackers go for the back first— was his father: Leo, the sign ruling the back, is that of fatherhood, while Capricorn, ruling the skeleton, is fatherly authority.

When Prohibition had wiped out the vestiges of the saloon trade, Papa Joe wangled an ambassadorial post to Great Britain from his old friend, FDR, on the promise that he would lay the groundwork there for Roosevelt's policy of entering the war and helping our English cousins. He used this influence, coupled with the confidential word from the president that Prohibition would soon end, to corner the franchises on major scotch whiskeys. Thus, when the other liquor interests in America had to sell their own grandmothers to get back in business, Joe Kennedy had fleets of cargo ships poised off our shores to sweep in as soon as the band started to play "Happy Days Are Here Again" and distribute the single-most missed drink in America: good, stiff scotch whiskey.

Instead of making better movies (afflicted Neptune, the planet ruling cinema, would make bad movies at first) Joe Kennedy, in this supposed coup, actually only reestablished his family's responsibility for the spread of alcohol. Now, this may seem to be a bit puritanical an interpretation, so I should point out that I still do not condemn good old booze, being one of its many users myself. It's profiting from something that you do not exercise responsibility for and control over that can become dangerous, especially if that something has in its nature elements of danger and harm to other human beings. You may *inadvertently* cause such things to happen, maybe by giving a bum a quarter, or by buying someone his or her first drink, it happens all the time. But when you do it intentionally, time and again, to further other interests of your own (money, power, control), then you are likely to be called to account for your actions.

Joe Kennedy also Neptuned (deceived) the president of the United States, in that he did the exact opposite of what he agreed with FDR he'd do: He spoke pessimistically about Britain's chances of bringing the United States into the war. Thirty pieces of silver, or years later, another president was deceived, this time in Dallas.

The karma this man brought to his family is endless. The romantic escapades he set before them as an example of a man's prerogative was minor, compared to the other impressions he made upon their minds or their destinies; albeit he never gave them a chance to realize themselves as total human beings. Did you ever try to raise *that* kind of consciousness? Male chauvinism that begins on the assumption that you *must* succeed in all areas of life, and then defines women as *prizes,* is among the thickest skull rot to break through. The corollary of that attitude, of course, is keep 'em pregnant and in the kitchen, half of which, at least, has been male Kennedy *policy* for generations.

Much has been said about the patriarchal tyranny of Papa Joe Kennedy elsewhere, and one grows weary of fault-finding. Political corruption, alcoholic addiction and profiteering, unfaithfulness, secret goings on, are all part of the only curse on the Kennedys—the curse of an inhumanly large debt to pay.

The chief astrological characteristic of Joe Kennedy's chart is his Sun/Moon four-planet stellium in Virgo, a Mutable sign. This conforms with the general pattern within the family as a whole and, perhaps for the first time, identifies the negative-most development of the Mutable type, towards becoming a notorious wheeler-dealer.

The Curse Embodied in One Man

This Mutable stellium, it turns out, becomes the salient *grouping characteristic* in the birth charts of all his descendants. When three or more planets group together in one sign, far more are Mutable than Fixed or Cardinal groupings, or stelliums—more than would be indicated by looking at the totals of planets in sign qualities at birth (Fixed: 89; Cardinal: 102; and Mutable: 119). There are six stelliums in Cardinal signs, seven in Fixed signs, and *fourteen* in Mutable signs. Another thunderbolt!

The Kennedy Curse Unmasked

But the electric lightning is in this: Here is the key to the future that may allow the Kennedys to evade the dangers planned, or just waiting for them, because this is the chief aspect that congregated in the heavens at the moments of the past tragedies.

Joe Kennedy, Sr. died the way old empire-builders are supposed to, or so it seems. Born with four planets, including both lights in Virgo, Pluto and Neptune in Gemini, and Jupiter at the very end of Scorpio about to enter the Mutable Fire sign, Sagittarius—six or seven planets in Mutable signs—he died most naturally of a final stroke on November 19, 1969. On that day there was a stellium of four planets, including the Sun, in Scorpio, and two planets in Mutable signs—the Moon in Pisces and Pluto in Virgo. There was nothing spectacularly Mutable about the time, a time, more symbolically, of passing on.

Since there are three qualities in astrology and 10 planets, 3.3 planets in any random chart sampling should ideally be in each of the three qualities. Of course, the times themselves are a cycle, such that if it is Pluto's time in its 240-year cycle to be in such-and-such a place, then it will bias many such samplings over that period toward that place. But then, one's times are just as much a part of objective destiny as they are of the internal pressures and fatal attractions that compel us from without. The two planets in Mutable signs at Papa Joe's death are below average, but then, Joe Kennedy's "curse" wasn't to die, himself, all at once, but a thousand times, as each of his dreams, embodied in his children, died. Death itself, in the Scorpio stellium, is the signature at his passing, and it is a reminder of the great debts that had to be paid. Joe Kennedy died after the three sons he had primed for this nation's highest office. He never lived to see one of them last one term as president. Perhaps now the old debt has been paid.

But what of the Mutable stelliums as a signature of future warning? If the currently overtragic curse has been settled and has run its course, there may be no need to stay alert. But then, neither can we let down our guard in this era of just beginning to discover how far the secret police will go.

This is the key—John F. Kennedy was born with an average weight of three planets (Sun and Venus in Gemini and Moon in

Virgo) in Mutables. Yet, he was killed during a stellium of three planets in the Mutable Fire sign, Sagittarius, and two planets, Uranus and Pluto, in Virgo. This means five in all—a weighty Mutable imbalance and telltale Mutable stellium. His brother Robert was gunned down five years later. Senator Kennedy had only two planets in the Mutables at birth; however, he died during two Mutable stelliums. One was in Virgo, and included Uranus, Pluto, and the Moon, and the other was in Gemini, containing the Sun, Venus, and Mars—in all, six planets—twice as many as the expected amount! Their older brother, Joe, Jr., was born with only two planets in Mutables. They may have been minor, compared to a four-planet stellium in Cancer that occurred at his birth and the conjunction of the Sun and Neptune in Leo, but they were revealing of his end: Jupiter in Pisces symbolized his bold self-sacrifice for motives he probably wasn't even sure of; Mars in Gemini indicated the danger in air travel. When his plane exploded, however, there were six planets in Mutable signs— including a four-planet stellium in Virgo, and the Moon and Uranus together in the Mutable Air sign, Gemini—the planet Uranus ruling sudden events, such as explosions.

What these facts tell us is that the Kennedys must be more than careful when there are stelliums in Mutable signs gathering in the heavens.

Mary Jo Kopechne died at Chappaquiddick with four planets, including the Moon, in Mutables. Teddy is still with us. Surely, if Chappaquiddick was planned by someone, it may represent one of the last efforts for some time on the part of that secretive group to render him politically ineffective. In fact, even the structure of secret groups changes. It would seem that the senator has already had his closest brush with death, if these Mutable stelliums tell us anything. Look what went on in the skies on June 19, 1964—the date of Ted Kennedy's near-tragic plane crash: the Sun, Mercury, Venus, and Mars were in Gemini; Uranus and Pluto were in Virgo; Saturn was in Pisces; and the planet Neptune, ending its stay in chaotic Scorpio, was about to enter the sign Sagittarius. Counting the latter, eight planets in Mutable signs! And, yet, something saved him. Maybe he was meant to do important things. It's hard to know if they'll be the good things so many expect of him, or if he was spared because, like Nixon, he'll set the example that will force us to learn painful lessons.

For instance, maybe charisma isn't the way to appeal to a voter. Maybe we'll have to find out the hard way that good breeding, looks, poise, eloquence, and outstanding speech writers do not a good president make. But if hidden enemies would attempt to murder a family, perhaps we're than led to assume that Teddy is the good guy, and that his works will heal a sick nation (Pisces is the healer).

Therefore—if stelliums in the Mutables are a tip-off to the days or periods during which the Kennedys must be particularly careful—it would serve to list some of those periods here:

---

*August 22–26, 1976: Sun, Venus, Mercury, Mars, Moon in Virgo
September 21–22, 1976: Sun, Moon, Mercury in Sagittarius
**November 22–December 22, 1976: Sun, Mercury, Mars, Neptune in Sagittarius
March 18–19, 1977: Sun, Mercury, Moon in Pisces
June 11–21, 1977: Sun, Mercury, Jupiter, Moon (6/15–17), in Gemini
*July 18–August 2, 1977: Venus, Mars, Jupiter in Gemini
September 12–14, 1977: Sun, Moon, Mercury in Virgo
September 23, 1977: Sun, Venus, Mercury in Virgo
*November 23–December 1, 1977: Sun, Mercury, Neptune in Sagittarius
*December 5–21, 1977: Sun, Venus, Neptune in Sagittarius
February 22–March 9, 1978: Sun, Mercury, Venus, Moon (3/8–9), in Pisces
June 5–7, 1978: Sun, Moon, Mercury in Gemini
*September 8–26, 1978: Sun, Mercury, Venus, Saturn in Virgo
**November 23–December 22, 1978: Sun, Mercury, Mars, Neptune, Moon (11/30–12/2) in Sagittarius
*December 27–29, 1978: Moon, Mercury, Neptune in Sagittarius
*January 8, 1979: Mercury, Venus, Neptune in Sagittarius

*February 27–March 3, 1979: Sun, Moon, Mercury, Mars in Pisces

May 27, 1979: Sun, Moon, Mercury in Gemini

*August 25–September 21, 1979: Sun, Mercury, Venus, Saturn, Moon (8/25 and 9/19–21) in Virgo

During the latter half of 1979, and into 1980, there will be major Mutable stelliums in effect, as well as minor ones. The following is a list of these dual Mutable stellium dates. If danger lurks, these are particularly ominous dates:

**November 20, 1979–March 11, 1980: Mars, Jupiter, Saturn in Virgo

Overlapping with:

*November 23–28, 1979: Sun, Venus, Neptune in Sagittarius

*December 13–22, 1979: Sun, Mercury, Neptune, Moon (12/18–19) in Sagittarius

Then, out of the span of the first formation of that stellium of Mars, Jupiter, and Saturn in Virgo, will fall the following:

March 15–17, 1980: Sun, Moon, Mercury in Pisces; then the Virgo stellium will reform:

**May 5–July 10, 1980: Mars, Jupiter, Saturn in Virgo

Overlapping with:

June 11–13, 1980: Sun, Moon, Venus in Gemini

*August 23–September 22, 1980: Sun, Mercury, Jupiter, Saturn, Moon (9/8–10), in Virgo

*December 6–21, 1980: Sun, Mercury, Venus, Neptune, Moon (12/6–8) in Sagittarius.

Every one of the above dates has a heavier-than-average Mutable configuration or combination of planets among the four signs of the Mutable quality. In other words, there will be more than the three together in one sign that would constitute a stellium—there will be four or more planets in Mutables on these dates. Asterisks denote the presence within the stellium of a so-called "malefic" planet—Mars, Saturn, Uranus, Neptune, or Pluto. The more asterisks there are, the more dangerous the interval.

The months beginning with the 1976 and 1978 anniversaries of the JFK assassination seem particularly afflicted, as does the two-month period in 1980 when the Mars-Jupiter-Saturn combination in Virgo re-forms. But no time seems more critical for the Kennedys than the month-long period, again, in a macabre way connected to the original assassination, beginning at the time of the sixteenth anniversary of JFK's murder in 1979 and extending into 1980 and possibly beyond. At that time, stelliums will form with Neptune in Sagittarius and Mars and Saturn in Virgo, involving both lights and all the inner planets up to and including Jupiter.

No symbol or planet in astrology can stand as sole representative of a certain matter. There are, astrology teaches us, many paths to the same destination. Also, the reading of a certain matter couched in a particular symbol is not an absolute. That is to say, if Saturn arise seems to predetermine one's thinness of personal appearance (the rising house is how you look; Saturn, among other things, rules bones, including prominence of, and sparsity), it only continues to represent thinness throughout the native's life insofar as he or she *accepts* the condition. Saturn rising can also predispose a person to be somewhat fatalistic, or slow to grasp matters firmly. It is a planet that *can* symbolize the laziness of one who cannot stick to a (weight-gain) diet.

While a person can conquer a condition that seems predestined, as in the case above, he or she will always manifest Saturn rising in some manner: perhaps he will always choose to wear dark colors, or he will assume a life role full of responsibility, or he will always have a serious expression. A negative form of the symbol is as possible as a positive one, when a person seeks to overcome such an obstacle. Saturn rising can give great stick-to-itiveness, but also great self-pity. Instead of an eventual successful attempt at gaining weight, a person could compound his woes by remaining thin *and* constantly bemoaning the fact, or simply becoming a totally antisocial type. These are *transcendences,* or remanifestations of a symbol in the chart. Usually, it is assumed that *transcend* implies *evolve;* but, as I have shown, it could also be a retrogressive *involution.*

In any event, each of us—born with the same number of signs and symbols in our natal charts, although each is arranged in a distinctly personal pattern—has the opportunity to transcend those matters in a positive, evolutionary way if we simply look to the alternative matters represented by the symbols in question. Each planet and each sign can be seen related to an almost endless string of matters that grows along with our awareness as sentient beings. Thus, if a person with Saturn rising was so dedicated, he or she could gradually shape his or her life into a role of great and trust-laden authority, and mold an essential position in the community. Perhaps in the process of sticking to the regimens prerequisite to obtaining such a position, weight-gain dieting will just fall into place naturally.

The symbols that repeat themselves most often in the Kennedy composite are no different than those that appear in individual charts, although they probably represent developments that occur over a longer period of time. By investigating what areas, other than those already familiar to the family, these predominant indicators encroach on, we can see ways out for the Kennedys.

If the "curse," as we've defined and labeled it, lies primarily in a conditioned course of behavior passed on from Old Joe to his sons, then it is time they leave that path. But one cannot suddenly become what one is not. The person with Saturn rising cannot suddenly become the optimistic speculator that Jupiter rising would be. The planet Neptune and the eighth house and eighth-house sign, Scorpio, can only transcend one state of manifestation in a person's life to become in another, *related* state.

Neptune of the great charisma (which the Kennedy men are overtly known for), of the romantic escapism, of deluding mystiques and beliefs, can be transcended to mean, for instance, involvement with health matters, with socialism and medicine. In fact, we already know of Ted Kennedy's great efforts in these directions. Politically, Neptune is also connected to citizens' rights to privacy, the unions, and the disclosures of truth. There is a likelihood that, if the senator stays active in politics, these interests will come to consume a great deal of his time someday. In a nonpolitical framework, into directions the younger Kennedys may chose to head in—it is the planet of romanticism (but this is an area that has held too much fascination for Kennedy males, especially coupled with the matters of the eighth house and Scorpio, as you will soon see) and the abstract. It has to do with religion, all depth of expression in the fine arts. Some of its dangers lie in the escapist tendencies of those with the planet highly focused, which has lead to alcoholic leanings in the older generations and will probably cause drug problems in the current one.

The eighth house and Scorpio give substance to the charisma; it lends great magnetism, makes the appeal highly sexual, stimulates every sort of romantic, passionate illusion, and—because it is the psychoanalysis house—compulsion, both within the family and among those who are attracted to it. It is a house of revenge, which it is assumed killed the three boys: Joe, Jr. avenged his own heartbreak and loveless, though sexually sated, life in a Neptunian mushy moment. Neptune, remember, is of Pisces the self-sacrificer. Like one of his father's corny movie heroes, he threw away his life, an act we can see as a repudiation of all his father's expectations, perhaps vengeance for all the years he was forced to shoulder the burdens of those expectations. Both JFK and RFK seemed to have been murdered out of some sense of vengeance. And it is well known that much of Old Joe's striving for power was based on a compulsion to punish his old enemies—to wreak vengeance on all those who would not allow him into their WASP society in Boston when he was an up-and-comer. Being a fated area, it brought a life of vengefulness back home.

The procreative instinct is strong among those with concentrations in Scorpio or the eighth. But this is an easily heeded impulse, and can be responded to in higher ways. The tenacity of Scorpio makes her a greater mother force than the nurturing sign, Cancer, for Scorpio will do *anything* to protect its brood; the survival-related nature of this sign can be dedicated to the survival of others—again, something that Ted Kennedy has been relating to in serious ways over the last few years, especially in regard to refugee problems, tax breaks for the poor, and welfare programs. It will be likely that other of the young, politically minded Kennedys will become involved in these areas.

The eighth and Scorpio are also places of death and regeneration. We know too well the role death has played. Each family member will have to come to grips alone, eventually, with what the deaths of their most brilliant kin have come to mean. At the risk of seeming callous, life is for the living. An interest in the plight of those who don't even have the physical means—let alone the idealistic raison d'être embodied in famous and glamorous fathers, uncles, and grandfathers—will take them out of the grim rut a lot of death-consciousness can put them in. Regeneration is a moral and spiritual process, as well as a physical one.

Physically, regeneration is the process we have come to study so closely under the broad subject heading of ecology. The environment is currently in desperate need of vast processes of regeneration. Ted Kennedy has lent his voice, but the few who have tried to keep the issue alive are dwindling and the whole matter seems to be lost on the public. This cannot be allowed to happen, and maybe the Kennedy family will become the vanguard in protecting future generations against neglecting the environment. A poisoned earth is an image of the negative combination of Neptune and Scorpio. A consciousness that brings us to see ourselves as inextricably connected with every cell of every leaf can be seen as an image, or manifestation, of the positive combination of this planet and sign.

At the end of this book is a section on the matters, people, and things ruled by Neptune and Scorpio/the eighth house. I could speculate endlessly on how the family, in general, will evolve in the coming years, how they might transcend this or that symbol in this or that way. Instead, I have chosen to look at the possibilities inherent in the charts of the current generation of young Kennedys. I have taken each chart individually and have made comments on the directions it is likely that each will take. To determine the main areas, or even which of the specific areas, that will occupy the attention of the family as a whole, I have left up to the reader. It may be that without such influences as Old Joe around to goad them on, they will remain divided into distinct family units, with no mandatory unity of purpose. Readers may look into the lists for the planets and signs in the back of the book and decide for themselves the areas best suited to the family's talents. Here are advisory predictions for the sixteen young Kennedys of the current generation:

The Children of John Kennedy

Caroline Bouvier Kennedy (nineteen): She could become involved in politics, in fact, may have the best political chances of the whole group. She can choose whether to be right up front or to direct things from behind the scenes. She has all the luck, charisma, and family name she needs to accomplish a lot in these arenas. She would also find university life appealing and may even eventually pursue the literary career her father gave up. She could be a teacher, probably on the college level, or a celebrated traveler or political/economic theorist, and probably take off radically from her predecessors in the latter areas. She could also find herself a place in the sciences and technologies.

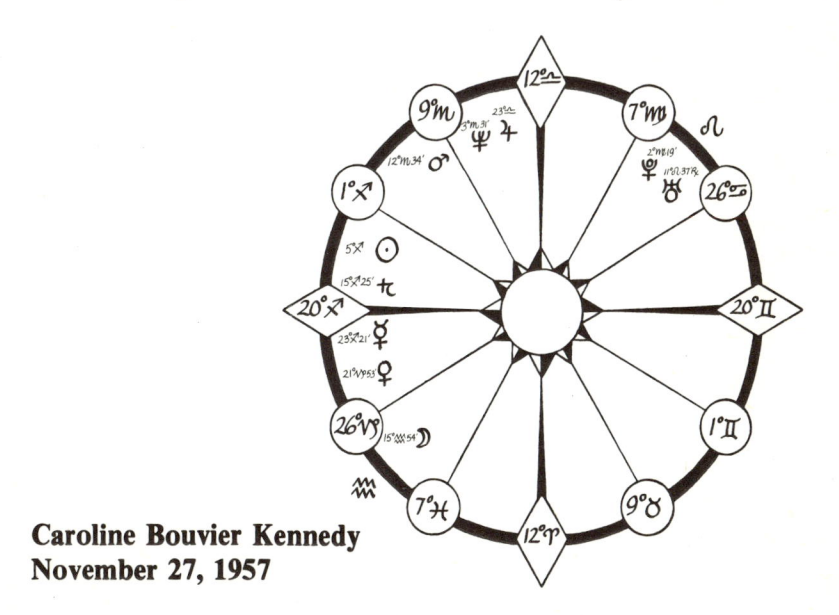

Caroline Bouvier Kennedy
November 27, 1957

182 THE KENNEDY CURSE

John Fitzgerald Kennedy, Jr. (sixteen): Not unlike his father, this young man is quite a bit to handle. Throughout the years of his early development, matters of control and self-control will be paramount. His mother will find it necessary to occasionally relinquish control to others. Everyone needs a break. Others who might help her in controlling him include "shrinks" of every variety and persuasion. Yet, once this boy comes into his own he may be quite a powerful social force to contend with. As you watch his career develop, remember how much the word *control* will mean to him. Conversely, "John-John" needs equally challenging outer obstacles to tackle. He must learn, as earlier generations did not, that this drive needn't end up in brash instances of simply putting life and health on the line. He can be up to greater challenges than those that are merely physical. Any undertaking that takes determination, great force, and exertion of one or another form of superhuman power, every sort of big business and real estate are potentials in his chart. His career, whatever it may be, will probably be at least multifaceted.

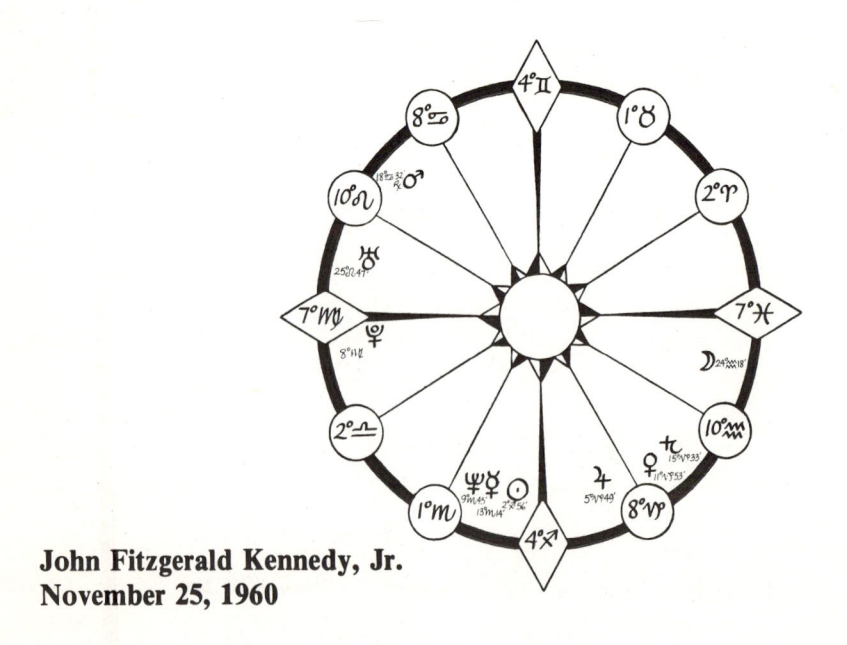

**John Fitzgerald Kennedy, Jr.
November 25, 1960**

The Children of Robert Kennedy

Kathleen Harrington Kennedy (twenty-five): Like those who went before her, her chart reflects deep involvement both in traditional politics and in family matters, so it wouldn't be unlikely for her to either run for elected office herself or marry a politician and have a large family. The latter possibility should be seriously considered first, as her somewhat difficult chart can give her a martyr complex and propensity for escapism.

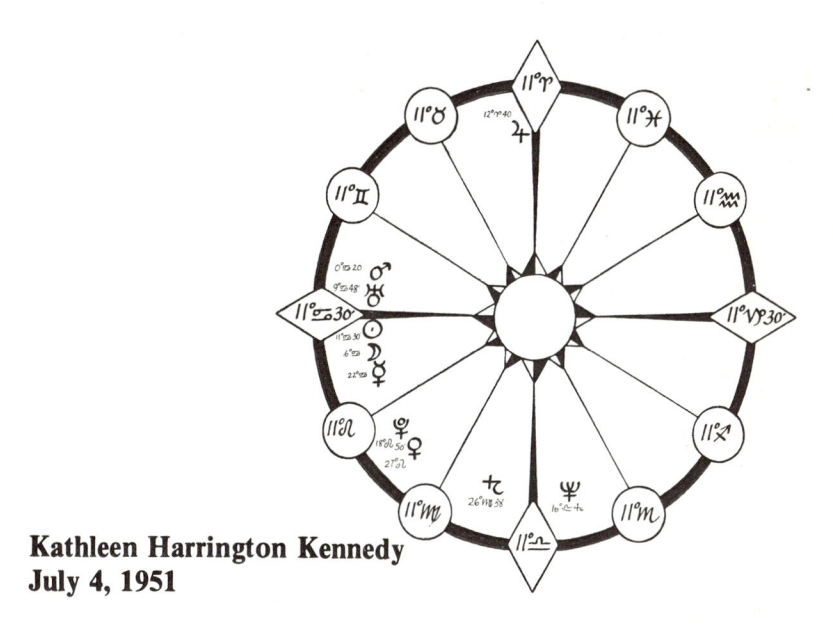

**Kathleen Harrington Kennedy
July 4, 1951**

Joseph Patrick Kennedy III (twenty-four): He can interact well with popular forces and learn ways to express himself via their common tongue, perhaps be a spokesman for special groups. He would excel in almost any field of the arts, especially in performance. He has to nurture his emotional development and not tyrannize himself, as his spontaneous excesses can often seem like liabilities. He needn't break his neck to check these, but instead find logical ways to harness this impulsiveness. He must also guard against a certain accident-prone side to his nature, and must come to grips with modern issues and these modern times.

Joseph Patrick Kennedy
September 24, 1952

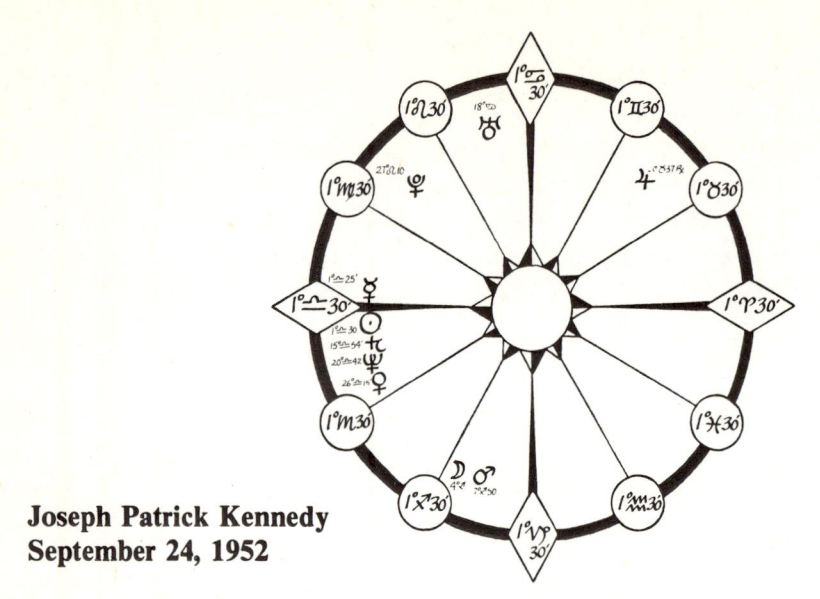

Robert Francis Kennedy, Jr. (twenty-two): May be a late developer, seemingly too tied up in family matters. Yet, he learns from this slow process. He may push himself or be too driven by others during his young years. He needs time to solve problems on his own. He has inbred abilities that would make him an excellent researcher-writer as well as a potentially successful politician. There will be nervousness in public as a young man, but he will come to handle large audiences well in future years.

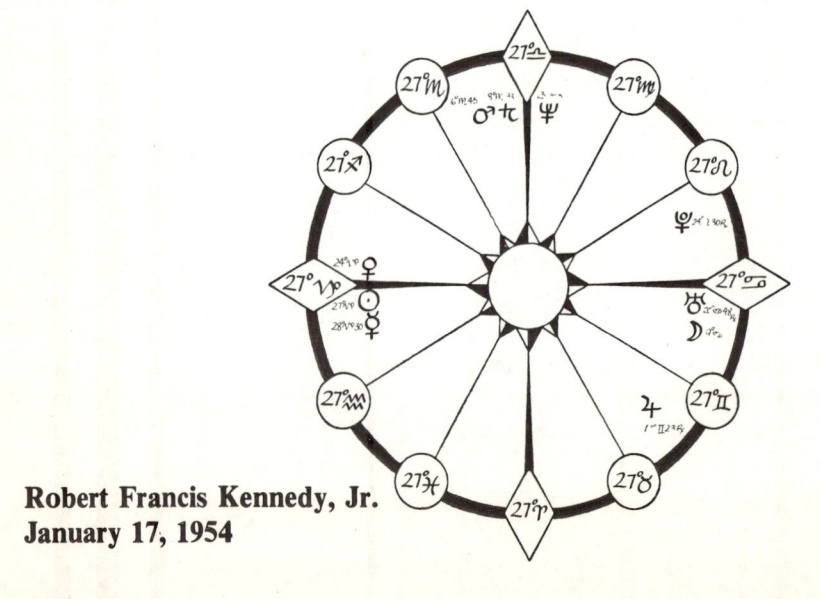

Robert Francis Kennedy, Jr.
January 17, 1954

David Anthony Kennedy (twenty-one): He may end up in one of the top political positions of the nation, but he won't make his way up through the ranks of politics. He seems more naturally bent to nitty-gritty involvements directly with the community. He can become an excellent businessman. He has multifaceted directions to shine in. He could be an artist, writer, or anything of the like; whatever he does, he will strive to be, and will probably succeed in becoming, tops in his field.

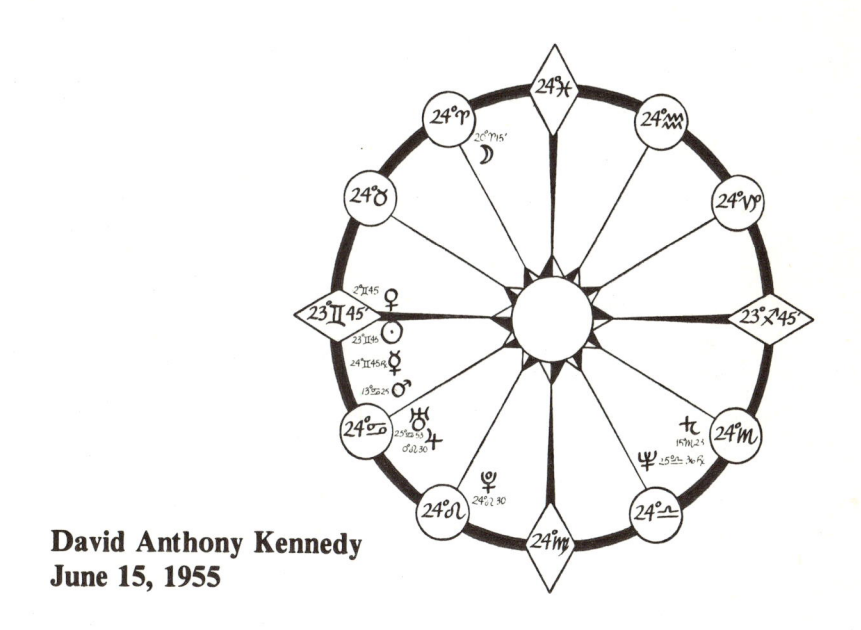

**David Anthony Kennedy
June 15, 1955**

Mary Courtney Kennedy (twenty): She is in need of a good deal of guidance, or, at least, seems to have needed it in the formative part of her development. But the resulting fruits of such labors of love can be a unique world view. She can develop a highly personalized feminist form to apply to her work and life-style. She can do much for children in her lifetime, as well as leave a valuable legacy.

**Mary Courtney Kennedy
September 9, 1956**

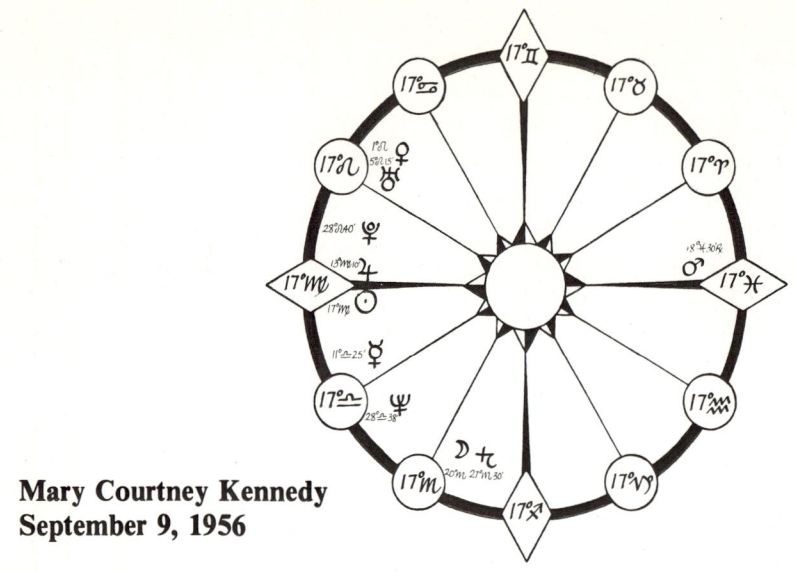

Michael LeMoyne Kennedy (eighteen): His is another very complex chart. I see family insecurities hounding his development, taking on morbid meanings he must learn to transcend. He may be drawn to a religious life, or life in total subservience or service to others. This stage may be preceded by a phase of bizarre indulgences, escapism, and self-endangerments. He has untapped psychic depths that may someday surface to mix with his more mundane functions. Politically, he would do much work for the poor or the disenfranchised.

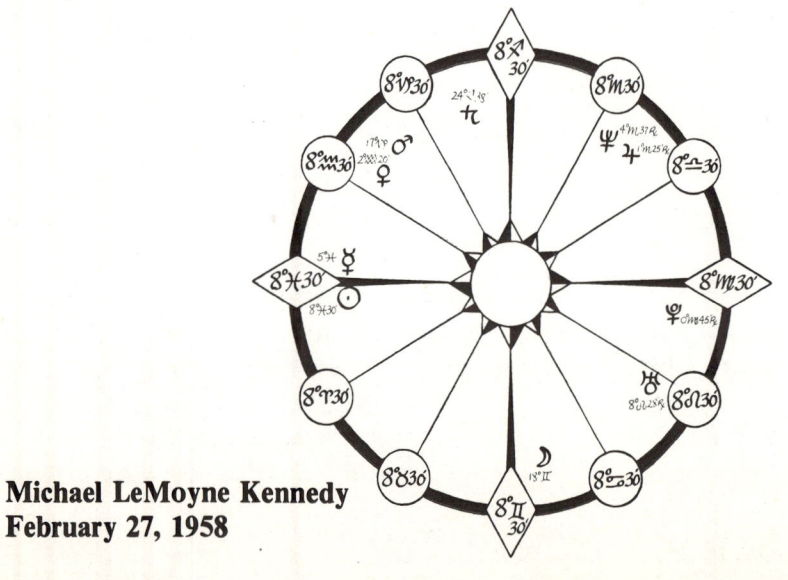

**Michael LeMoyne Kennedy
February 27, 1958**

Mary Kerry Kennedy (seventeen): She, too, may take a while to find herself, the easily entered province of the very rich. Leisure is important to Mary, however, since she insists too often on keeping busy. She is cut off from a good deal of life, but is extremely talented or involved in other areas. She will find a good bit of who she is in other people, once she learns to drop self-serving approaches to others and truly interacts. She, too, is a late achiever and has great potential to come into positions of great leadership later in life.

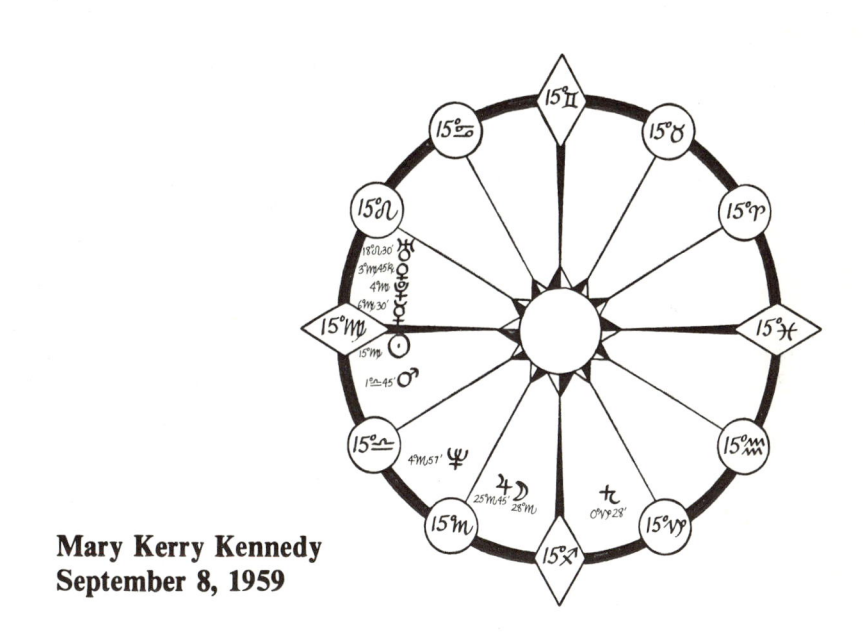

Mary Kerry Kennedy
September 8, 1959

Christopher George Kennedy (thirteen): Wants to make great contributions to America. He will probably succeed, and his methods are likely to be purely political, or by virtue of addressing himself to worthy public issues from other positions of power. He will find himself facing off *old* issues, rather than new ones. The longer issues have remained on the scene unsolved, the harder they tend to be to resolve. This young man will apply an innovative mind to every sort of new approach until he has been satisfied that he has the right approach; then he will be relentless until he has reached the goal.

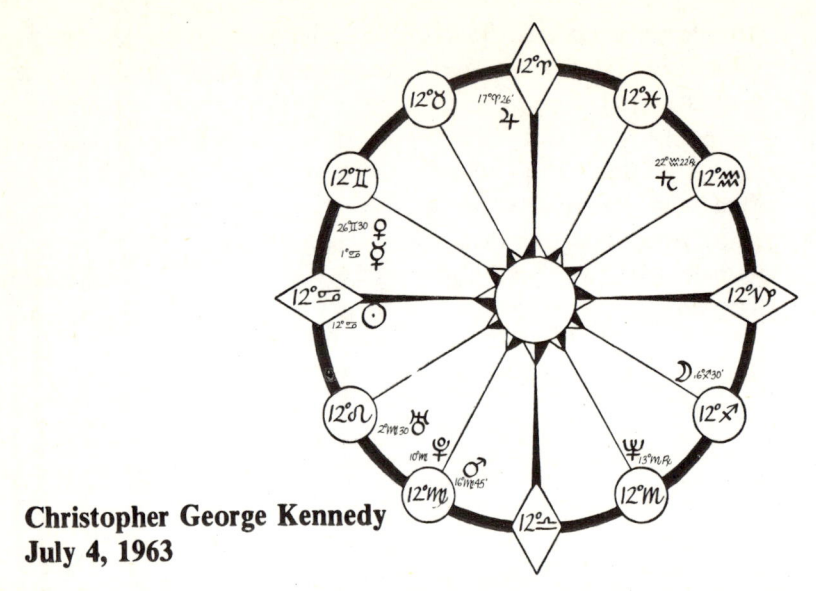

Christopher George Kennedy
July 4, 1963

Matthew Maxwell Taylor Kennedy (eleven): Another somewhat late developer. He is a practical, hard-working fellow, with a good deal of potential and talent as a teacher. He will discover that there is much to learn in foreign lands. His theoretical mind and work-ethic consciousness may lead him into theoretical back-alleys not entirely approved by the rest in his family, the least objectionable of which may be an expected affinity for new forms of democratic socialism.

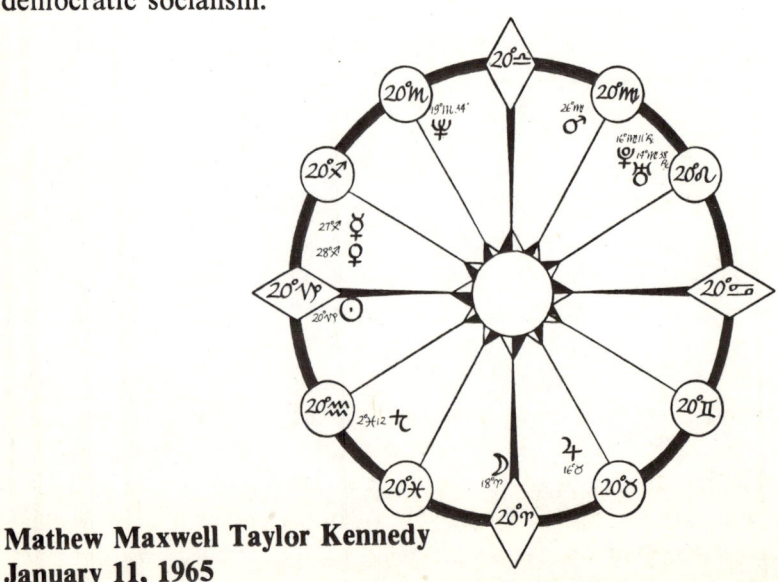

Mathew Maxwell Taylor Kennedy
January 11, 1965

Douglas Harriman Kennedy (nine): "If at first you don't succeed, try, try again" characterizes Douglas, an early starter, but a late developer. He will be noted not so much for thoughtful approaches, but for constantly maintaining a bright enthusiasm for trying just about anything once, anything worthwhile at *least* a few times more. He may soon become, though, one who will easily take on many unnecessary responsibilities and may have reasons to adopt an overly serious view of life. Work will be therapeutic. Sexual conflicts can plague his heels, but can be closely tied in to his strong and urgent creative drive.

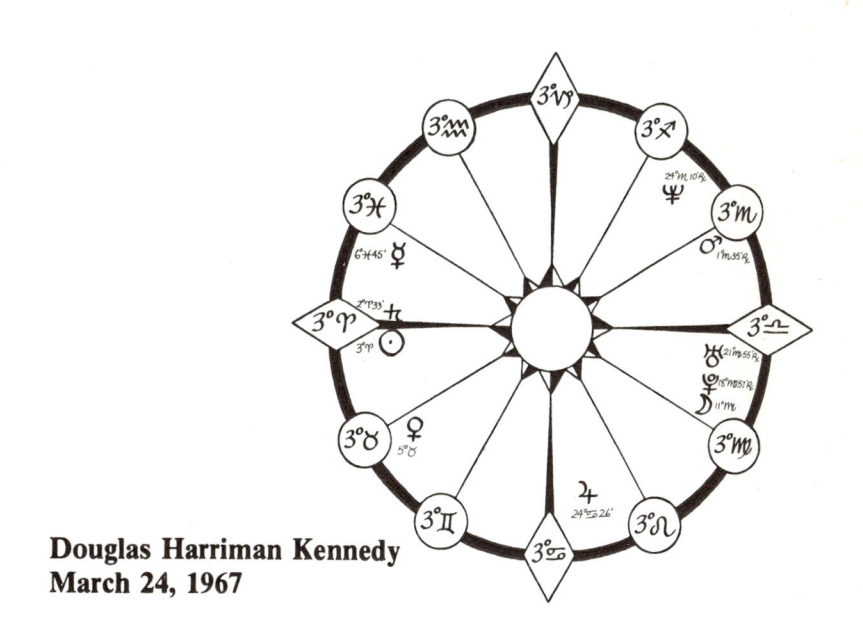

Douglas Harriman Kennedy
March 24, 1967

Rory Elizabeth Kennedy (eight): Another hardworking populist, politically attracted, probably internationalist offspring. She may play a major role in future eras of world cooperation, and will help re-shape traditions. She will prove to be one of the strongest-willed of her generation of Kennedys.

Rory Elizabeth Kennedy
December 12, 1968

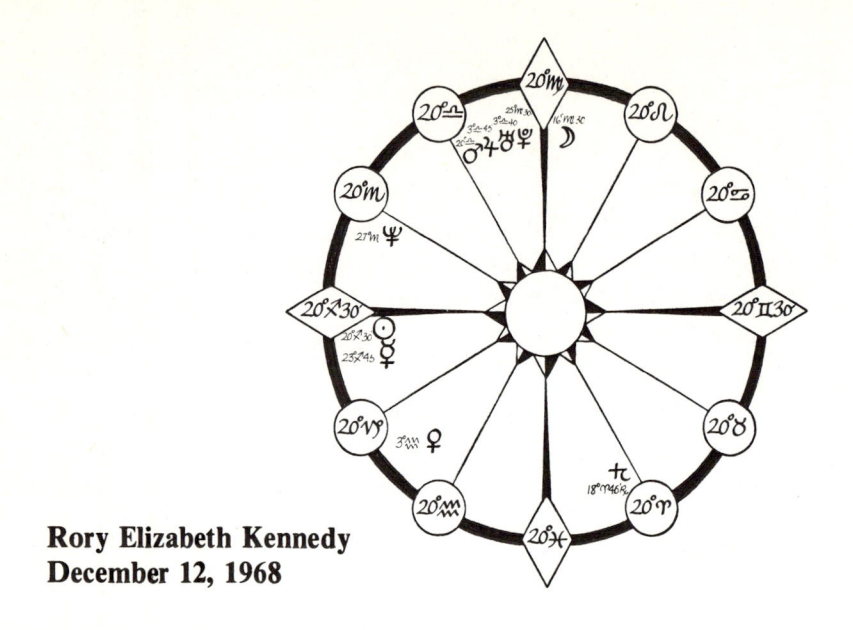

The children of Edward Kennedy

Kara Kennedy (sixteen): Is quite impulsive and in need of control and guidance as a young woman. She is seeking herself with possibly more urgency than her siblings and most of her cousins. Probably she is obsessed by a fear that she will not acknowledge and, until she is at least sure of her father's safety, she will be unable to operate independently of this specter. She may well try her own hand at politics one day, but more probably would enter politics for other than the standard Kennedy reasons for pursuit of power. She is a likely voice for the equal rights movement for women, but the cost of such extremes of involvement may be heavy for her. She, too, may eventually choose to enter a life of almost selfless service.

The Kennedy Curse Unmasked 191

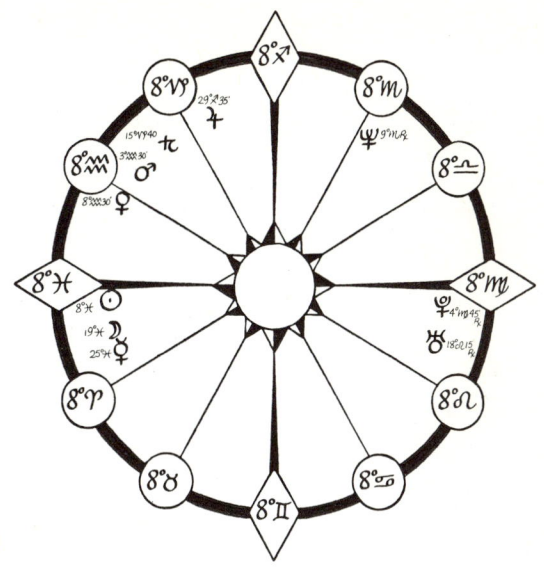

Kara Kennedy
February 27, 1960

Edward Moore Kennedy, Jr. (fifteen): Despite the handicap of amputation, this young man is destined to develop a personal dynamism that could make up for ten lost limbs. His even nature can be encouraged still to learn to separate the wheat from the chaff of life. It is in becoming a highly discerning person that his strengths lie. He can become a Svengali of a businessman and an excellent coordinator. He has talents in all the arts, especially in architecture and its expansion, city planning. A problem is his self-critical idealism—he must learn to become less difficult to please, for his loved ones' sake, while maintaining his high standards in other areas.

**Edward Kennedy, Jr.
September 26, 1961**

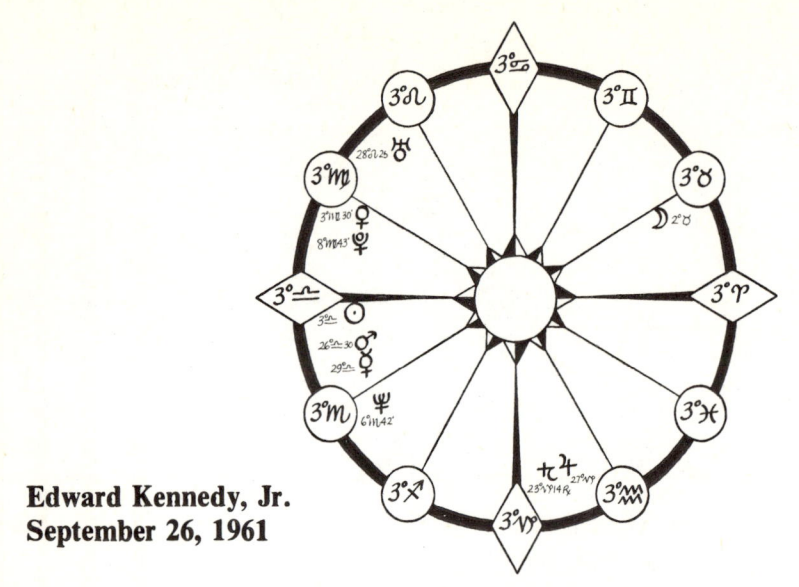

Patrick Kennedy (nine): This young man will probably be attracted to electoral politics at some time. He is a natural reformer, once he's learned the patience it takes to pursue the same goals relentlessly over the years until they've been cornered. All public-related work that takes such determination, and takes large amounts of time investing, will eventually hold fascination for him. Taking the cue from his father, he may turn out to be one of the staunchest of the young Kennedy environmentalists.

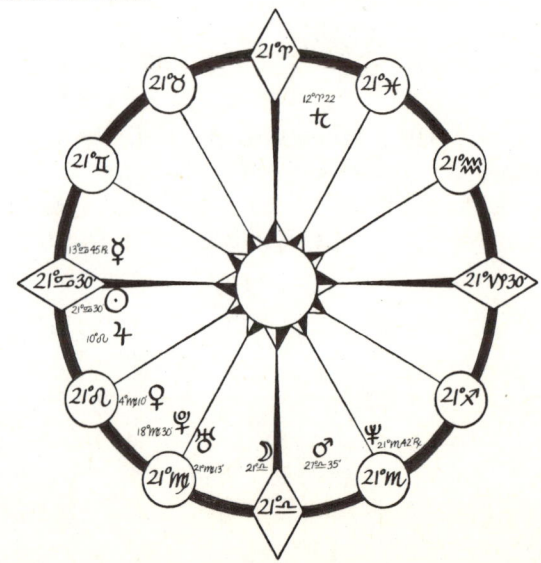

**Patrick Kennedy
July 14, 1967**

8

The Curse—Will Teddy Run Against It?

The 1976 Election

In comparing the chart drawn up for the first poll opening on Election Day (Hart's Location, New Hampshire, midnight, November 2, 1976) to that of the United States, it is clear that domestic issues will be paramount. The effects of "the depression that never was" are still very much with us, and this will be of prime interest and motivation to each person stepping into the voting booth. Secondarily, if not more vociferously, is the issue of the extent to which secret governmental agencies fall under the control of representatives chosen by the electorate. And, lastly, that even more heated issue that began all the questioning: whether there is official responsibility for the political assassinations of the past decade, both here and abroad.

The strength of liberalizing forces is evident in the fact that Jupiter sits at the zenith of the chart. A four-planet grouping, including the Sun in Scorpio, would also indicate the serious interests of the disenfranchised, the poor, undernourished, the old, the unemployed, and those bled dry by taxes. The dissatisfaction of the public is evident: we are not buying promises so easily these days.

On the other hand, dark forces can be seen to be gathering in

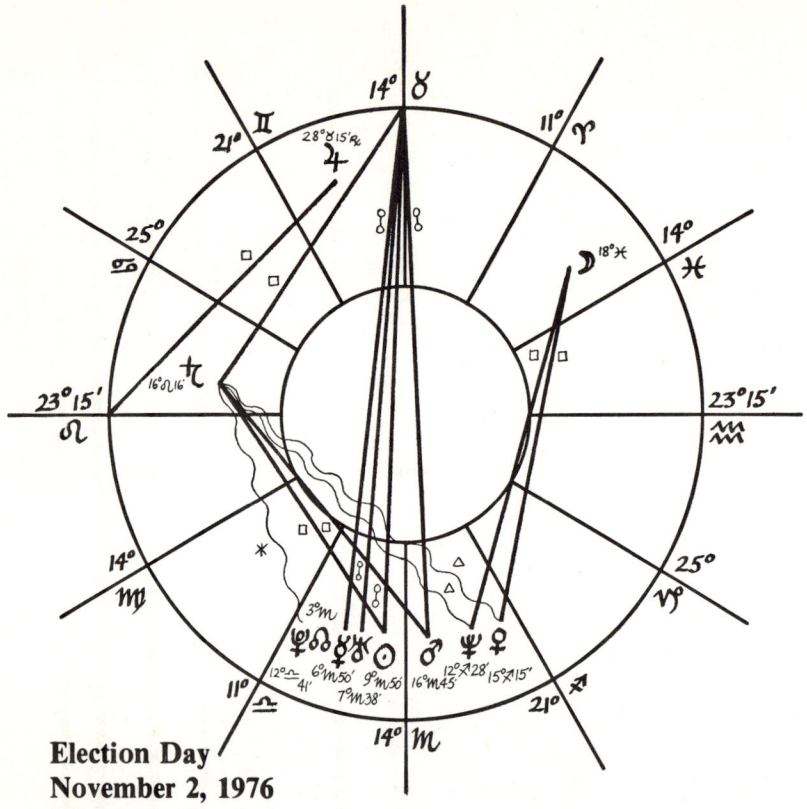

Election Day
November 2, 1976
Midnight: Hart's Location, New Hampshire

this tightly configured chart. All that Scorpio activity afflicting the Zenith, or Midheaven, of the chart can mean that secretive powers are at play to alter the results, or force them in a certain direction. Saturn highly afflicted in the twelfth house, and central to the most important aspects of the day, indicates behind-the-scenes intransigency of an authority not easily dislodged. The Moon in secretive Pisces, squaring Venus/Neptune—the latter ruling, the former exalted, in Pisces—reiterate a third time that this is all too possible. A rule of thumb in astrology is: if one aspect suggests, two makes something possible, and the third makes it probable. An activated and wary public may be able to prevent most of the dirty dealings, and Jupiter on high, squaring the Ascendant, may represent a fore-

The Curse—Will Teddy Run Against It?

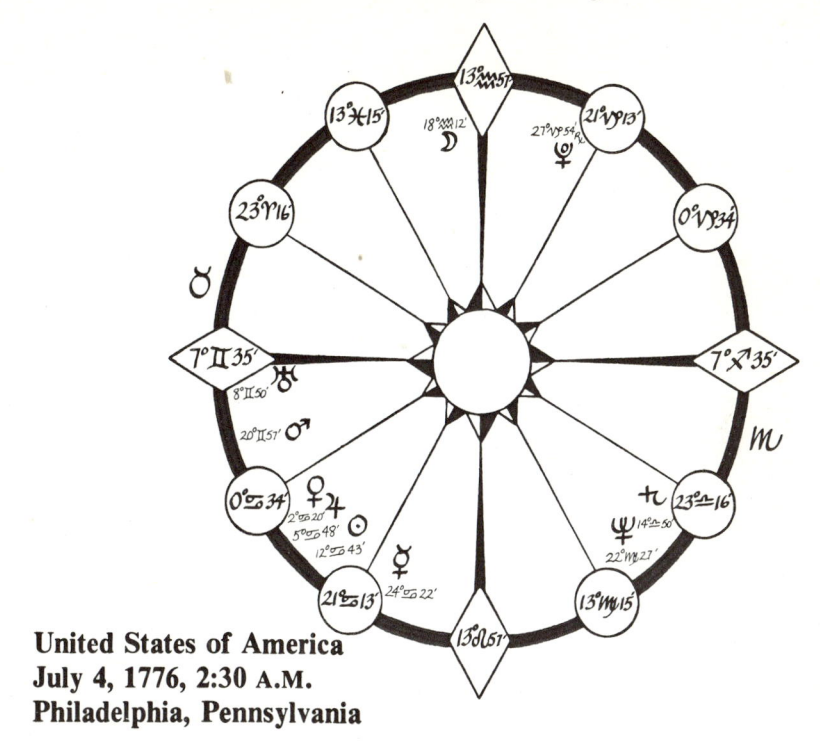

**United States of America
July 4, 1776, 2:30 A.M.
Philadelphia, Pennsylvania**

warned judiciary, both federal and local. This latter part of our Constitutional system of checks and balances could well be the only force, as disorganized as it may be relative to the executive or legislative branches. Quick action by federal, state, or local jurors could conceivably prevent an election from being stolen. Because of the concentration of planets in the third house, that of votes and voters, it is probable that there will be a record turnout at the polls.

Weather may be a factor in certain parts of the country, and citizen groups in areas considered hostile to the infamous military-industrial complex might be wise to be wary of "unauthorized" flights that may be seeding their clouds.

While the chart of an election cannot name the successful candidate, it is possible to further compare it to each candidate in turn, to determine which receives the most beneficial of its aspects. From this, an educated choice can be made. The chart of an election is a chart of that nationwide choice. It describes the four-year course of the nation that follows. Labor and welfare problems, as I've pointed out, are paramount. It is a difficult time, and the first two years of the presidency that begins on Inauguration Day, 1977, will be difficult ones. It will take a strong man to come through in one piece. This, suggest many acquaintances in astrology, may not be Teddy Kennedy's year. It'll be too hard, they warn; a president elected in 1976 may resign or, for many reasons, not be re-elected. The following, however, assumes the candidacy of two of the three charts looked at. I am not looking into the myriad candidacies among the Democrats. We are interested here in a possible Ted Kennedy candidacy, and I am assuming, for the purposes of this study, that if he throws his hat in the ring the Democrats will flock to him en masse. Gerald Ford's chart and that of Nelson Rockefeller are also considered. Despite Rockefeller's seeming disavowal of presidential ambitions, he cannot be ruled out as a possible Republican candidate.

Gerald Ford
At first glance, Jupiter on the day of the election rising in the president's natal chart would indicate that the normal run of fortune would be in his favor. However, the part of fortune drawn up for the moment the first poll opens puts another kind of fortune in his opponent's house (the seventh), which, combined with a four-planet solar stellium in Scorpio, opposes Ford's ascendant and roughly opposes transiting Jupiter ascending through his natal chart. Popular causes may be too strong for him, may find him lacking in too many ways to give him the nod for four more years.

In fact, the entire shaping of the election-day chart—the way it sits in the president's natal chart—bodes him ill. All of the planets of the day, when superimposed over Ford's chart, sit in the hemisphere of his opponent, all on the right, or "setting" side of the chart.

Venus and Neptune, representing a strong charisma, sit in the president's eighth house, indicating qualities possessed by his opponent. Mars sits in the seventh, assuring him of tough and active opposition. The Sun, Uranus, Mercury, and Pluto all sit in Ford's sixth house, indicating that his greatest opponents are in

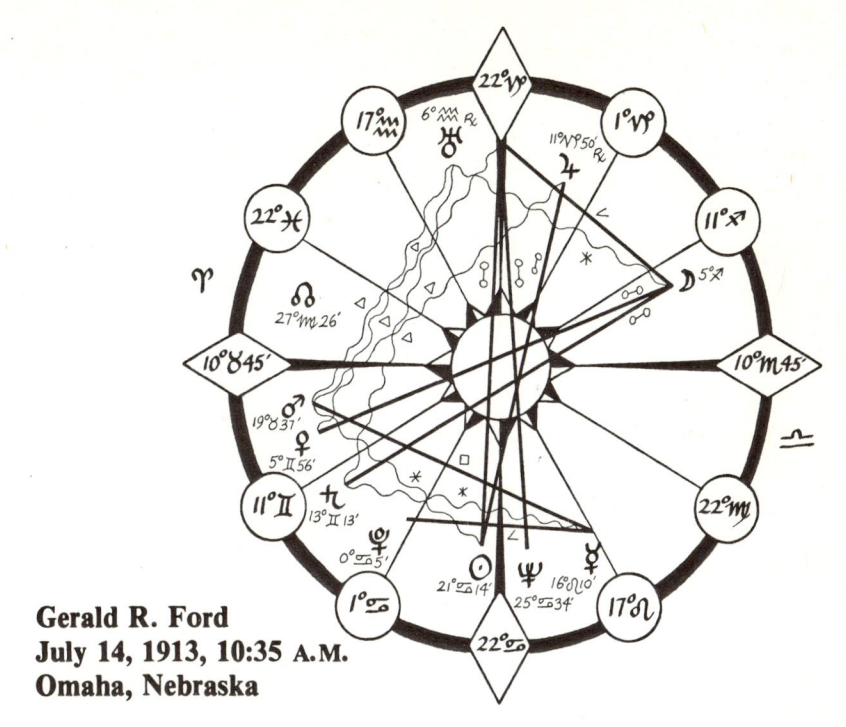

Gerald R. Ford
July 14, 1913, 10:35 A.M.
Omaha, Nebraska

the ranks of labor, the Scorpio positions of all but Pluto (yet Pluto is a co-ruler of Scorpio), all indicating the joined ranks of labor, the unemployed, overtaxed, poor, old, and any in need of vital, life-sustaining services.

Mercury, the planet of news, is tightly semisquare Ford's Pluto at birth. Pluto sits on his third house cusp, indicating unpleasant news when the square aspect between Ford's natal Mars rising and Mercury is adversely aspected. Because the third house and its ruler, Mercury, also represent votes and voters, we would look to these placements to see what outcome a given date would produce. On election day, 1976, transiting Saturn will be exactly conjunct Ford's natal Mercury and square his rising Mars—a symbol of both great struggle and bad news, or unfavorable votes.

The Moon is in Ford's eleventh house, having just squared his natal Moon and natal Saturn. The Moon's aspects to a natal chart are quite significant, as it is thought to rule the day of any chart drawn up for an event; it also represents the role of the public in any matter. While it poorly aspects Ford's Moon and Saturn, it approaches the trine of the Sun and Neptune. One might say that it could go either way, except for the following consideration. Usually, after a presidential election, the loser will behave in the following manner: If he is a challenger, he will take a two- or three-week vacation; if he is the incumbent, he will also take a vacation, but it will usually only last a few days, as he will remain in the office for ten more weeks. Winners rarely take vacations, being unable to escape from the press for very long. It is because of this that I feel it is very possible that Ford will lose. Before the end of the day, the Moon will enter Ford's twelfth house, that of exile, indicating that he will seclude himself from the public for approximately five days—crying in his beer at Camp David, perhaps?

A final look shows that Ford has the very sudden planet, Uranus, on high in his tenth house of career. This is squared by all the Scorpio planets, including transiting Uranus, on election day, 1976. It is a harbinger of a sudden fall from favor. Also, Saturn is about to leave Ford's fourth house and enter the most anonymous phase of its cycle through his chart. During these times, a person seems to disappear from the public eye. This may very well be the case with our unelected president-by-default.

Of course, there are other, more sinister ways to look at this chart. Death is strongly indicated by the strength of the death/regeneration sign Scorpio; Saturn rises (in the Election Day chart itself) in the twelfth house of endings, while the natural sign of the twelfth, Pisces, is the sign of the Moon, which is squared by Pisces' ruler, Neptune, which is conjunct the planet that is exalted in Pisces, Venus, also square the Moon. As I mentioned, this may indicate the dark forces, secretive, tyrannical, detectives at work at the time, but it may very well indicate the means by which they achieve their ends as well.

In Ford's chart, these placements are all on the side of the opponent (right-setting) which, because *he* is the president and fair-haired boy of the defense lobbyists, may mean that this is the way that opponents will be dealt with. While that may seem a somewhat extreme charge, remember that Ford was invited into the presidency by a man whose two most likely, formidable opponents—

RFK in 1968 and George Wallace in 1974—were shot under questionable circumstances. Ford has also been called "the CIA's biggest friend." If we suspect secret agencies of past murders, might we not be on our guard against future ones?

In other words, it's unlikely that the forces of death will, via the hand of men, be directed against Ford. That is, unless he disowns some of his more powerful "old friends." However, it is possible that great misfortune will strike the president, in any event.

Transiting Saturn is perched on the cusp of his fifth house of children, sitting on his natal Mercury, planet of young people. While this may easily stand for all the new voters aligned against him and his party, it could also have to do with serious matters connected with his children.

The heaviness of all that Scorpio and Pluto in Libra in his sixth house indicates a possible time of physical crisis for Ford. Power-play watchers have, in fact, sworn that Ford is only looking for the right opportunity to give up the reigns of government. Chances for reelection, unless something drastic or fatal afflicts his opponent, are poor.

Nelson Rockefeller

All of those Scorpio planets seem to be on the vice-president's side; they surround and bolster his rising Moon in Scorpio, sitting both in the second house and first, or rising house; this powerful solar stellium trines his natal solar stellium in Cancer in the ninth house, right at his midheaven, or highest career point. If there are serious underground goings on around the time of the election in 1976, chances are very good that Nelson will know about them and have control, to some extent, over them.

I am not of the opinion that the ills of a nation can be traced to one man. As an astrologer, I know that no one man, or small group of men, can be that powerful. The celestial trends that signal adverse developments among the great and near-great also signal those developments among all of us. Thus, I refuse to imagine Nelson Rockefeller as all-seeing and evil, as some of my friends see him. He is vulnerable in his own way. I would say that, were he a candidate in a moment charged with the danger of

**Nelson Rockefeller
July 8, 1908**

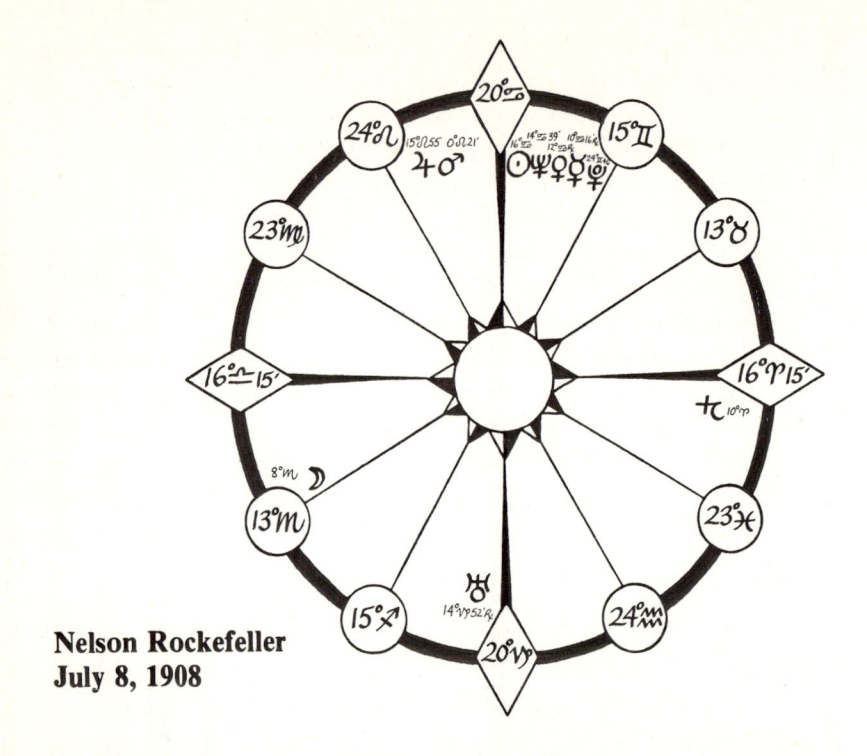

death, the danger might point to him as well as to a more liberal opponent. Being a realist, however, I don't imagine that percentage to be more than 20. In other words, if danger—or even just illegal controls exerted on returns—is a true watchout this next presidential election, it would be four to one that the opponent of Nelson Rockefeller was the target. While it would be most probable that any death threats would occur *before* the election, the importance of Saturn in the November 2 chart indicates that it could occur shortly after, or even some time later.

I must reiterate that there is within this potential for the operation of dark forces two primary distinctions: first (and they both can manifest) and possibly most strongly, the dark of the forces can easily be those kept in the dark suddenly demanding light. These are the poor, the despairing, the hungry, the ignorant. The stronger their presence in this election, the weaker, perhaps, the presence of the secret police forces; however, should these forces become overmilitant, or allow themselves to be permeated by agents-provocateurs, overt, as well as secret, police forces are likely to grow at an alarming rate. Secondly, there may be some of the more salient aspects of the sign Scorpio and its natural field, the eighth house, present during the campaign and during the early months of the new presidency. Death is only one of the extremes the sign can be seen to represent. And this death needn't be threatened by an unseen "they."

Nelson Rockefeller will be facing very heavy aspects at that time. He has four planets, including the Sun in Cancer conjunct a Cancer Midheaven, representing all he and his family have accomplished in and "in the name of" the United States. Yet, all this Cancer is in the ninth house, or that of foreign lands. Thus, his most karmic (water signs, like Cancer, are most soul oriented, thus very karmic) configuration involves him irrevocably with the affairs of foreign nations. Yet, right now, the people are most interested in *preventing* the government and its spy agencies from mixing dangerously and irresponsibly in the affairs of foreign nations. The truths of the past year, revealed in congressional committees regarding clandestine CIA activities at home and, especially, abroad, *had* to be revealed. The Rockefeller Commission, like most presidential commissions, probably was interested in concealing certain facts, and this will probably need to be answered for some day. But what about the chart before us?

Rocky's rising natal Moon, the very important angular planet that rules all that karmic Cancer happening at the top of the chart, is *surrounded* by afflicting planets. While the Sun conjunct Moon of this chart happens every year—perhaps indicating how the people often go against his higher interests (adverse aspects from Moon to tenth house) at election time, while providing him with enough foreign freedom of movement to "do his thing," if not domestically, then at least abroad (trines to ninth house)—the conjunction with his Moon of both Uranus and Mars is dangerously rare.

From the point of view of fated moments, rather than that of conspiracy, being the guiding hand of our nation's destiny of late, Nelson Rockefeller may prove too fragile to continue plodding

202   THE KENNEDY CURSE

toward the White House, to continue wielding such titanic power without buckling under its sheer karmic weight.

If the phenomenon of Jupiter/Saturn conjunctions (discussed elsewhere) signals the danger of presidential mortality, we might also worry about the conjunction of transiting Saturn (the heavy) with a president's natal Jupiter. I say *might* most advisedly: there's nothing but a combination of symbol and tentative logic behind that assumption. It has never been tested, as far as I know. The only thing we can be sure of is professional crises of some kind. In the fact that transiting Saturn, on election day 1976, is on Rocky's natal Jupiter means danger should he then become president, then the same goes for Ted Kennedy, exactly two Jupiter cycles (orbits) younger. Transiting Saturn is on *his* natal Jupiter as well. However, Nelson Rockefeller has this serious conjunction in his tenth house of career. Saturn brings endings. Can some unconquerable force be preparing to end Nelson Rockefeller's career? Saturn is in adversity in the sign of Leo, for it is the ruler of the spine and—perhaps more important for someone as old as Rocky, taking on as much labor and karma as he is—that of the heart muscle itself.

Jupiter, symbolizing the state of a person's health, sits significantly in the vice-president's tenth house: It is both his vast wealth and robust health. Which aspects will Saturn be coming to limit? Meanwhile, transiting Jupiter sits in the house of his opponent's possessions, giving them the success of the moment.

It may well be that the Democrats take the election due to a conspiracy by Providence. The Republican candidates can all call in sick. Or, it will be an intense campaign and one in which gut issues are strongest since the thirties—perhaps one that will bring out in deadly ways all the venomous lengths to which paramilitary and antidemocratic elements within our society will go to keep from surrendering power. But Rockefeller's health, either before or after the election, may be in serious question. It is possible that, if by some chance he should be nominated, he could win and later resign; but he would have to go a long way to beat his Democratic opponent, especially if it's Ted Kennedy, and the extent to which he would do anything to retain power could become embarrassingly evident. However, the square from the

Moon, in the house of young people (fifth) to Venus/Neptune on the third house cusp of his natal chart, would seem to bring him bad news about vote totals.

Edward M. Kennedy

The fact that election day falls at the same time each year means that the Sun will *always* be somewhere between the eighth and twelfth degrees of Scorpio, thus at the very top of Ted Kennedy's natal chart. This says something about his ability to win elections. However, this year the Sun is accompanied by Mercury, Mars, and Uranus, spotlighting a very important career phase. Uranus is exactly conjunct the senator's midheaven, signaling a drastic change of careers. While the chart for the United States may not be in very good shape for another few years, Ted Kennedy's may never again look so good. Maybe he's the man for hard times—or, then again, maybe he'll be the one to get the lion's share of blame for conditions just now *beginning* to get worse.

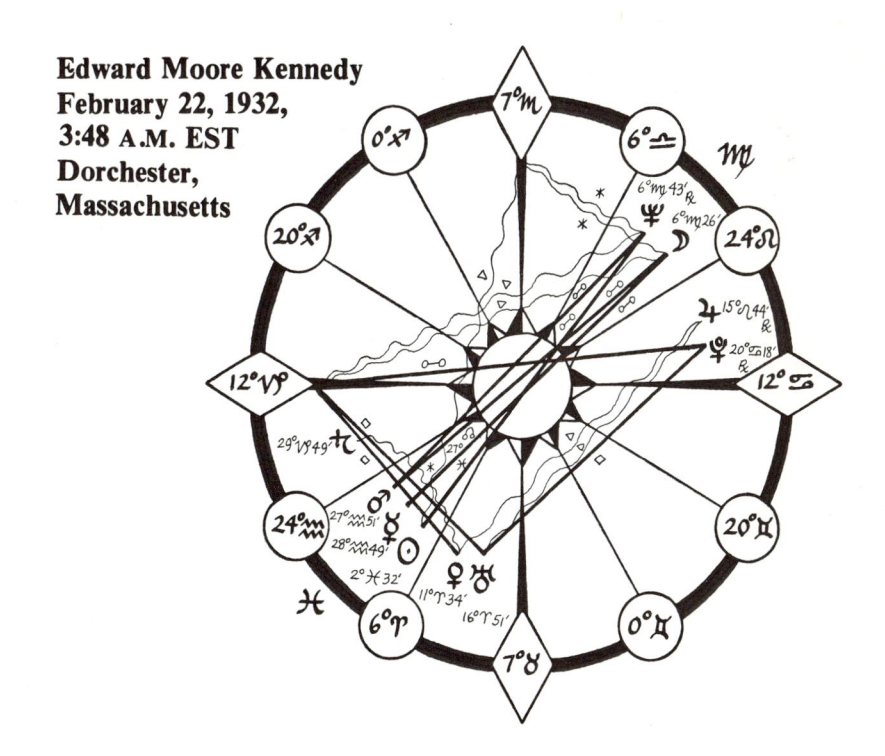

Edward Moore Kennedy
February 22, 1932,
3:48 A.M. EST
Dorchester,
Massachusetts

But it looks promising for him to take this election. Maybe those dark forces really *are* all our fellow citizens deprived for so long; and there they are, *with* Ted Kennedy all the way, at the top of his natal heaven. The Moon has just conjoined and passed over his natal Sun in Pisces, signaling emergence in a new form, and new beginnings. Benevolent Jupiter sits in Ted's fourth house, assuring him the support to win because of his family name, his domestic healing missions, his conservationist and spread-the-wealth legislative programs, and, yes, even his family image. Where does Chappaquiddick fit in? Perhaps the Moon of Election Day squaring Venus/Neptune represents not just the depleted image of Ted as a candidate, but the great expenses poured into campaigns to counter public uncertainty regarding circumstances surrounding the tragic drowning of Mary Jo Kopechne.

As for the potentially dangerous aspect that Teddy shares with Rockefeller, the transiting Saturn conjunct natal Jupiter: this occurs in the senator's seventh house, or that of his opponent. In other words, if this conjunction only indicates political crisis, both Teddy and the vice-president could share or even meet head-to-head in the conflict. Perhaps such a development would be another debate, such as the famous one between JFK and Nixon back in 1960; in any case, it would seem that Teddy would be the victorious one. Teddy would seem to be the one to survive and, perhaps, win the election against an ailing Republican candidate, should a Jupiter/Saturn conjunction be fatal to U.S. chief executives; however, it may become configured.

However—barring an election win by health default—the fact that Teddy would seem the better off in any political crisis (symbolized in the Jupiter/Saturn conjunction) does not automatically lead to the conclusion that he will certainly win the election. Rockefeller's chart is a tough one and used to a lot of tough going; he could prevail. But it wouldn't be in a totally above-board way. If this election is truly an expression of popular sentiment and nothing more, it's Ted Kennedy's, if he runs. However, *unless he gets out of politics altogether*, I don't see what other choice he'll have, with so many career-area planets compelling him, and with a nation so in need and so thoroughly convinced that the name Kennedy is synonymous with savior.

Ted in 1980?

There may not be an election in 1980 (*see* Chapter 9). The chief characteristic of the 1980 Election Day chart that makes me fear that something might prevent an election then is the heavy concentration of planetary forces in the sign Libra. Generally speaking, concentrations in Libra speak well for the chances of popular forces; however, the great imbalance caused by such a large grouping threatens, in my opinion, the two-sided, or multiple-choice, situation existing at election time. It may be that we go into an election with a foregone conclusion at that time; the danger, therefore, also exists that someone will be deciding the choice for us.

Election Day
November 4, 1980
Midnight: Hart's Location, New Hampshire

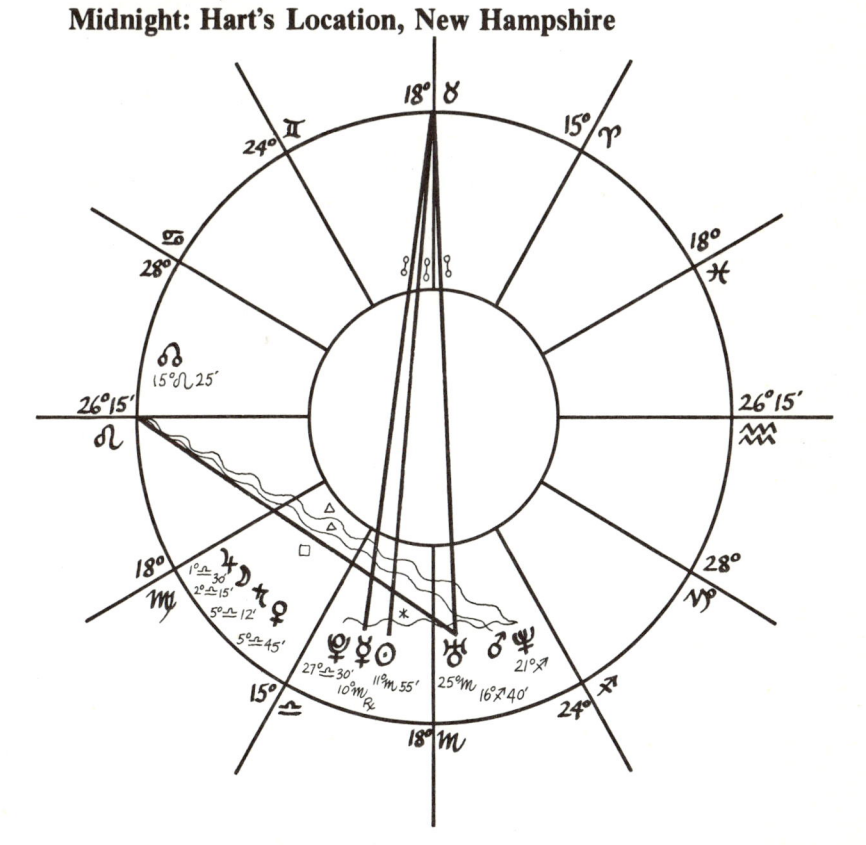

There are other possibilities as well, though. As I indicated, it may be a time of a great popular ground swell. Ted Kennedy may fit very nicely into such a picture, as he seems to be the only candidate at this time capable of pulling off so great a landslide. The sign Libra represents women in general, so, in many respects, this may be seen as a time when Ted's great appeal with women can pay off for him in a big way. If the male vote splits between Kennedy and his opponent in 1980, it is almost certain that Kennedy's ground swell of female votes would overwhelm any and all opposition.

The other great possibility is that 1980 will be the first year a woman runs as presidential candidate of a major party. And it looks as if, should she run, she will certainly win. If it is difficult to imagine a woman beating a man in a United States presidential race—especially as soundly as the chart seems to indicate—we may go further to interpret what we see in the way of great and overwhelming feminine struggle to mean that both major parties will have women in one of the two front-running positions. Certainly, should Ted Kennedy choose a woman as a running mate in 1980, the chart for the beginning of that election has his, and her, name written all over it.

9

Is There a Curse on the American Presidency?

The Strange American Twenty-Year Cycle

When the ninth president of the United States died one month after his inauguration, early in 1841, there was little metaphysical speculation mixed with the mourning the nation indulged in. William Henry Harrison was succeeded by John Tyler, and his well-hyped glory—the semivictory over the Shawnee Indians at Tippecanoe—faded along with whatever invulnerability the American presidency may have once seemed to have.

But then, everybody dies. Twenty-five years later, after a traumatic war that knocked the spirit of expansion from the young nation, that pitted neighbor against neighbor and brother against brother, the assassination of the sixteenth president of the United States, Abraham Lincoln, seemed just another cruel irony causally connected to the long bloodletting.

No one connected the twenty-year interval to the deaths of two American chief executives—perhaps because it wasn't yet clear that this was the case. Why would anyone suspect that the as-yet-unclear relationship between the two earliest presidential deaths had stemmed from the fact that both were elected in years ending in *zero*? (Because of the four-year interval between presidential elections, such zero election years occur every *twenty years*, i.e., *not* in 1830, 1850, 1870, 1890, 1910, 1930, 1950, 1970, 1990, etc.). No one paid the two deaths any attention in this respect . . . until the others began to fall in place.

James Garfield, elected in 1880, was assassinated in 1881. William McKinley was re-elected in 1900, and he, too, was assassinated. Shortly after the infamous Teapot Dome scandal had undermined once and for all the already weak administration of Warren Harding, the man who promised us a "return to normalcy" passed into a more and more forgetful and merciful history. Harding had been elected in 1920 and died in 1923. The unexplainable 20-year death cycle continued unbroken.

By this time, astrologers had figured out what was happening. After all, who was better equipped to decipher cycles? Of course, few paid any attention to their warnings. And, although he was said to have had a few excellent astrologers on his staff, FDR was one of those to refuse to heed the warning. Had he been satisfied with a normal run of just two terms instead of seeking an unprecedented third, Roosevelt might have lived a while longer. Instead, he was reelected in 19*40*, and—shortly after his unheard-of fourth election, in 1944—he, too, died in office. John F. Kennedy, a chief subject of all written here, brought the fatal cycle up to present times.

Of course, he, like half of those who died in office before him, might have died a natural death. There would have been no popular myth about a phenomenon known as "the Kennedy Curse" if JFK had not been assassinated. There are, therefore, valid reasons to investigate such things as an unbroken string of bad luck in the family, albeit the cycle being discussed here seemed to make it inevitable that John Fitzgerald Kennedy would die in office.

What celestial reoccurrence was the culprit? Astrologers discovered, soon after Garfield's death, that the twenty-year cycle involved was one of the conjunction of the planets Jupiter and Saturn. Of the ten bodies of the astrologer's study, these two, more than any others, represent the many facets of authority in society, and the highest of authorities. The two seem to go hand-

Is There a Curse on the American Presidency? 209

in-hand in most matters of high accomplishment: Saturn is determination, while Jupiter is success; Saturn is concentration, while Jupiter is expansion and exploration; Jupiter is magnanimity and the fellowship of all people on the planet, while Saturn is conservation and the aloofness of reigning power. All those in authority have one or both of these giants of the Solar System in a significant place in their natal horoscopes, if not in actual aspect. The *conjunction* of these two at birth will indicate a long and often painful political maturation process. Natives of a chart with this configuration at birth often are accused of fascist tendencies, while seeing themselves as crusaders for right. In any such configuration, there is serious interaction with the concepts of law and order, as well as with the most important of the laws of the land.

The conjunction of these two in the skies, however (a *transiting,* or *mutual* conjunction) will herald serious times for young lands. It is an aspect that is difficult to face when one's diplomacy and internal legal structures are unused to great trials and have not withstood many tests of time. Saturn rules the perfection one achieves in old age and does not yield favorable trends when conjoining Jupiter until certain lessons have been ingrained into the popular or political psyche. Once the Saturnian connection every twenty years has *set in,* has told us something about the permanence of power, as it seems—then perhaps the more favorable of the Jupiterian vibes will be experienced.

Jupiter in our nation's Sun sign no doubt signifies something about the health and good will generated toward our leaders. Saturn brings severe restriction. It brings endings. In purely political terms, it is a serious clash between conservatism and reaction (Saturn) and liberalism and permissiveness (Jupiter). In the deaths of Lincoln, Roosevelt, and Kennedy, at least, it would seem that the Saturn forces had the upper hand—or wrested it violently. This is in keeping with the above-stated nature of the two planets and reflects the rulership of Saturn over the conjunction until a level of maturity as a people has been reached.

Not only are presidential deaths indicated by these conjunctions, but—because they relate as well to all political matters—they usually correspond with critical times in the politics or economics of the nation as well. The "Debt Repudiation Depression" corresponded to the death of the first of these American presidents, William Henry Harrison, in 1841, in the midst of the depression that lasted from 1840 to 1844. The War Between the States corresponded to Lincoln's assassination, as well as to the Secession Depression of 1865-66. The Secondary Post-War Depression preceded Garfield's election in 1880. While the conjunction of 1900 was accompanied by prosperous times (other cycles may supersede the Jupiter/Saturn cycle), the period within the 1920-22 stretch was scarred by the Primary Post-War Depression. We entered World War II shortly after the 1940 election and, finally, were engaged in one of the hottest periods of the Cold War around 1960, having been surpassed in the space and missile race by the Russians and hoodwinked by the Cubans, who, after their revolution, invited a strong Russian military presence into our hemisphere for the first time since our purchase of Alaska from them in the mid-1800s.

The last of the conjunctions, the one corresponding to the assassination of JFK, also marked the hardly noticed intensification of American involvement in Indo-China, as well as the growth of vast security agencies within our borders and a corresponding buildup of centralized and often unresponsive government—three developments that may have proven to be more a threat to our democracy than any communist menace ever could.

Since 1842, the conjunctions of Jupiter and Saturn have recurred at an approximate, or average, regularity of every 19.853 years, and have all occurred in Earth signs:

January 26, 1842: in 8 degrees, 54 minutes of Capricorn
October 21, 1861: in 18 degrees, 23 minutes of Virgo
April 18, 1881: in 1 degree, 36 minutes of Taurus
November 28, 1901: in 13 degrees, 59 minutes Capricorn
September 10, 1921: in 26 degrees, 39 minutes of Virgo
August 8, 1940: in 14 degrees, 27 minutes of Taurus }
February 15, 1941: in 9 degrees, 6 minutes of Taurus }
February 19, 1961: in 25 degrees, 21 minutes of Capricorn

Both planets, Jupiter and Saturn, belong to the entire solar system, to all mankind, not just to the United States. Following their progress, astrologers from ancient until recent times have been able to successfully chart the course of worldwide political affairs by noting their aspects through the heavens. So why should the United States be the only nation afflicted?

Two answers suggest themselves: The first is that the greatest manifestation of these aspects occurs in lands that hold the greatest sway in the leadership of the world community. This may be a somewhat weak contention when we take into account the earlier years, especially those before we demonstrated our young herculean strength during the First World War. Were we among the most powerful of the world's leading nations as early as 1840? There are many who say we were, that great potential had always waited to be tapped, that we lacked only the international arena in which to demonstrate this. We had beaten Great Britain twice; didn't this alone qualify us?

The Jupiter/Saturn conjunction was also tied to this nation through simple planetary identification: at birth, we had the vital Jupiter conjunct our natal Sun in Cancer; however, we were also born with the severe Saturn in Libra, tightly squaring the birth Sun, and Jupiter. No other powerful nation, then or now, shares this particular planetary-cycle karma with us. This alone gives us the right to say, in matters of economics and politics and world-shattering events, that as the United States goes, so goes the world.

The Jupiter/Saturn Cycle hits this country hardest, then, because it is a particularly American cycle. The question in everyone's mind remains, What will happen to the president elected or reelected in 1980? And the more strident question for many of those reading these words is, can we wait until it happens to find out? Or can we take steps to head off the more disastrous possibilities? Will Little Brother Kennedy run in 1976, and then again in perilous 1980? Or—would we be content with a one-term presidency for Teddy Kennedy?

The awareness of this cycle—rather than enlightening, as astrology is meant to do—has thrown thousands into despair. We are all more concerned than we've ever been about effective and responsive national leadership than with charisma; TV has apprised us of the endlessness of the politically superficial or evasive. We, as a people, are beginning to actively seek or nurture such leadership, when a seemingly divergent reality enters in. What *about* the Jupiter/Saturn thing? Do we ask effective government to wait in the car as some silent, unexplainable cycle wreaks its havoc?

The American Cycle: A Whimper or a Bang?

Things happen to cycles. They themselves fall under the sway of other cycles that may be extraneous, as the case of prevalent prosperity cycles overriding the effects of Jupiter/Saturn in 1900.

Effecting the Jupiter/Saturn Cycle is what is called the Great Mutation Cycle, which, as impressive as it may sound, is only the turn-of-the-century astrological label, given the fact that, when these conjunctions of Jupiter and Saturn occur, they happen in signs of one element for a period of approximately 160 years. This is a product, or side product, of each planet's orbit and its relative speed; Jupiter makes more than two revolutions about the Sun for every one of Saturn's.

A Great Mutation is when these regular twenty-year conjunctions stop happening in signs of one element and switch to signs of another element. This is one very significant thing that can happen to cycles. It could, in fact, *end* certain aspects of the American Cycle.

Thomas Jefferson was the first United States president elected during one of these Jupiter/Saturn conjunctions; however, Jefferson did not die in office. James Monroe followed along in the 1820 election and also lived out his term. The telling difference between these two and the rest, however, is that their Jupiter/Saturn conjunction occurred in the element Fire—Jefferson's 1800 conjunction having occurred in Leo and Monroe's in Aries. It seems it is only when the conjunction occurs in Earth signs that U.S. presidents die. Or, to be more accurate: U.S. presidents seem to be immune to any fatal effects of the Jupiter/Saturn Cycle when it occurs in Fire but seem to fall victim to it when it occurs in Earth. We have yet to experience what would occur during the Great Mutations in Air and Water.

At this point, and most importantly, because of the *coming* Great Mutation into Air—astrologers are speculating that the coming conjunction of Jupiter and Saturn in 1980 (which occurs in the Air sign, Libra) will end the earth-related subcycle of American presidential deaths.

Actually, the full 160 years of the Great Mutation in Earth won't be over until the year 2000, for in that fateful and final year of the Earth sojourn Jupiter and Saturn will conjoin in Earth for a final time before a 480-year exile from that element (160 years each in Air, Water, and Fire, in that order). The out-of-step conjunction in Air in 1980 is quite natural from our normally geocentric astrological point of view. Since such long cycles as that of the planet Pluto take, very often, as many as six years longer simply to go through a sign than it takes for Jupiter and Saturn to conjoin, we experience the same phenomenon at certain times when the planet crosses a cusp from one sign into another. The phenomenon of retrograde, explained elsewhere in this book, often causes a reversal in orbit, so that two years after Pluto had first entered its current sign of transit, Libra, it was to be found in the previous sign, Virgo. So it is that the Jupiter-Saturn conjunctions are sometimes found to occur in an element that is out of an otherwise normal sequence.

The great significance here is that the fatal nature of the conjunction is not likely to repeat until 2000—24 years from now. It would then seem that Ted Kennedy is "safe."

Or is he? Do we know anything at all about the conjunction's occurrence in Air?

Earth houses and signs in the zodiac are those of 1) wealth, possessions, land, luxurious living, finances (Taurus—second house); 2) service, armed forces, health matters, routine, forces of labor, bureaucracy, and, esoterically, magicians (Virgo—sixth house); and 3) authority, control, long-sought-after goals, and overall development in the eyes of the world community (Capricorn—tenth house). On the other hand, the Air signs and houses are involved in matters of 1) travel, media communication, neighborhoods, votes, short distances, brothers, sisters, neighbors, thinking, business, and commerce (Gemini—third house); 2) partnerships, alliances, enemies, war, liberties, law, and the arts (Libra—seventh house); and 3) innovation, shared information, genius available to all, machines, and advancements in technologies and science, the machinery of media, the electorate, democracy (Aquarius—eleventh house).

The chief house and sign of the so-called Earth *triplicity* is the *Cardinal* sign and angle of Capricorn, for it represents the leadership of the nation that was so afflicted by the series of conjunctions. This is symbolically so, as it was the president who died, not the head of a bank or a great general. Taurean-second house problems about economics and/or sovereignty may have accompanied the great occurrences and—as in the case of the sovereignty squabble that began the tragic American Civil War or World War II—may have been far more tragic than the presidential death. And Virgoan-sixth house matters may have been present as well, armed forces being swallowed up in the wars and labor forces in the depressions. We tend to identify the death of a chief executive as the single-most important death of the cycle, even if he was as inefficient and corrupt as a Warren Harding. With the problem entering the Air element, what can we expect?

To begin with, we can expect assaults on our freedoms to step up considerably. In fact (see the section on the 1976 and 1980 elections) we might even see the first of what may be *many* elections *disallowed* by authoritarian forces. Notice, if you will, that thought, association, communication, etc., are the fiber of Air. Presidents, if they become more and more dictatorial, can make themselves virtually invulnerable. *We're* the ones who are most vulnerable; our rights are hard to defend against totalitarian technologies. As Saturn seems to still control (with its most negative manifestations) the way these times turn out, we can expect—or should begin now to defend against—the growth of totalitarian technologies.

A president can probably die outside of the cycle. There seems to be no hard-and-fast rules in astrology that can be expected to operate from every perspective. Just because these cycles seem to cause certain events, they don't imply necessarily that the cycles are the only things that can bring on events of that nature. Thus, a liberal

Is There a Curse on the American Presidency? 215

president elected in 1976 could conceivably be replaced (by whatever means) by the same sorts of underhanded forces that snatched Jack Kennedy from us. And "they" might deny us a chance to vote his successor out of office in 1980, or find some way to give us no choice. But maybe that return to Earth of the American Cycle in the year 2000 will rectify *that* situation. Who knows? All is speculation beyond certain points.

When the Jupiter/Saturn Cycle is firmly established in Air, whatever the most dire manifestations are, we may have a better chance to learn our great political lessons as a people. Earth can often be the element of the ploddingly slow in development and change, whereas Air is fast and represents intellect. What I've said may serve to further perpetuate the myth that Saturn is evil or even an undesirable astrological quantity. This is not so. Saturn is cold reality, and—natally—this country has difficulties, for some reason, in facing up to that. This may be a carry-over from the human characteristic of a similar nature in the Cancer-born—this preference for hiding from painful truths. As we must have faith in all people's ability to develop, we must also have the daily patience to wait for the slow development of the Cancer nature. Maybe because we're so heavily a Cancer nation from birth, we prefer to live through the Jupiter-conjunct-Sun magnanimity and optimism (Jupiter is in its sign of exaltation when in Cancer) and not at all listen to the urgent demands of Saturn, also in *its* exaltation in Libra, not heed the demands of outer (foreign?) realities and the cold hard facts of life (poverty, slavery, injustice?).

Saturn gives us only what we deserve; maybe that's why he's so hated. The lessons we learn when the Jupiter/Saturn conjunction occurs, in four short years in Libra, is likely to be *most* significant: This is the sign Saturn was in at our birth. Also, we can't help recalling the golden state of the American Presidency and the American Condition prior to the Great Mutation into Earth, in the days of the Federalists. Why was that?

The best answer seems to be within this explanation: in their rulerships and co-rulerships of the signs of the Zodiac, Saturn rules Capricorn and co-rules Aquarius, but Jupiter rules Sagittarius and co-rules Pisces. These signs happen to be of all four elements: Capricorn is Earth, Aquarius is Air, Sagittarius is Fire, and Pisces is Water. So, it seems, the reason we were so relatively well-off between George Washington and Andrew Jackson was because the Jupiter/Saturn conjunction occurred then in the element Fire—the Jupiter, or more benevolent element. Earth has always been the realm of the more gloomy Saturn influence—as will be the case with the element Air, perhaps more so for the United States, as we have Saturn in Air at birth.

In other words, we may have just begun to learn political lessons! None of us will be around to experience the Golden Age that awaits us (if we're still around as a nation) in 2160, when the Great Mutation is into Water—the natal element of both the United States, Jupiter, *and* its Sun, Venus, and Mercury. It won't matter unless we safeguard ourselves. The cycle's occurrence in Air is the most challenging yet, although, because of modern health and protection technologies, we may not see another death of a president while in office again until 2000—and then, possibly never again. What we may see die however, could be a lot more priceless than the life of one elected leader.

As for Teddy's chances for electoral success—I evaluated them in the previous chapter. How the American cycle of presidential deaths will affect him if he's elected or reelected in 1980, I cannot be sure. What I'm least certain of is whether the so-called "powers that be" will *let* us vote for him or anyone.

APPENDIXES

Astrological Basics

The Signs	The Dates	Their Symbols	Human Functional Keywords
ARIES	(March 21–April 20)		"I Am"
TAURUS	(April 21–May 20)		"I Have"
GEMINI	(May 21–June 21)		"I Think"
CANCER	(June 22-July 22)		"I Feel"
LEO	(July 23-August 23)		"I Will"
VIRGO	(August 24-September 22)		"I Analyze"
LIBRA	(September 23-October 22)		"I Balance"
SCORPIO	(October 23-November 22)		"I Desire"
SAGITTARIUS	(November 23-December 21)		"I See"
CAPRICORN	(December 22-January 20)		"I Use"
AQUARIUS	(January 21-February 19)		"I Know"
PISCES	(February 20-March 20)		"I Believe"

Some Matters of the Signs

ARIES: initiative, daring, pioneering instincts, aggressiveness, giving birth to, the immediate matters, urgency, the beginnings of things;

TAURUS: possessions, valuable things, wealth, important feelings, comfort, keen impressions, land, conservation, aesthetics;

GEMINI: communication and transport, and businesses connected with such matters; logical thought, intellect, brothers and sisters, self-expression in verbal areas;

CANCER: security, domestic considerations, root matters, parents, country, politics, children, nutrition;

LEO: Love and pride, one's children and their development, speculation, sports, creativity, passions, early schooling, loyalty, kings, rulers, sociability;

Some Matters of the Houses

I: the matter at hand, aggression and war, the self, one's perspective;

II: talents, financing, values, the rich;

III: neighborhood, familiar environments, writings and publications, media uses;

IV: one's base, home life, conditioning and prejudices;

V: lovers, creative projects, elementary schools and teachers, leadership, pleasurable activities;

Some Matters of the Rulers of the Signs

ARIES/MARS: soldiers, weaponry, cutting tools, blades, fire and its uses, surgeons, policemen, firemen, the male principle;

TAURUS/VENUS: artists, bankers, decorators or clothiers, luxuries, beauty, the female principle;

GEMINI/MERCURY: teachers, writers, publishers, messengers, messages, schedules, appointments, younger people, intellectual types, businessmen;

CANCER/MOON: children, mothers, women in general, growth, food, homes, family, the public, one's homeland, changes of mood, emotionalism, response;

LEO/SUN: initiative, purpose, confidence, creativity, rulers, celebrities, sportsmen and gamblers, rulers;

VIRGO: service, health, regimentation, routine, efficiency, work, forces of labor and the consumer, armed services, bureaucracy;

LIBRA: matchmaking, art appreciation, performance, balances and affinities, union, partnership, enmity, competition, diplomacy, populism, others;

SCORPIO: legacy, trust, secrecy, that which is gotten from a partner, that which is on the side of one's competitors, research, psychic and occult matters, vengeance, death, regeneration, poverty, survival;

SAGITTARIUS: higher-mind communication, long-distance travel, foreign trade, the exotic, the philosophical and strange, exploration, sports;

CAPRICORN: authority, career, status, reputation, limitations, tradition, older forces, political institutions;

VI: public service, businesses that serve the public exclusively, civil servants, health personnel, nurses;

VII: agreements, social contracts, the law of the land, courts, peacemakers, one's tasks in life shared with others;

VIII: investigators, secret agencies, deadly opponents, decay, conservation, sexual liaison;

IX: foreign lands, universities, published books and larger works, teachers, treaties, olympic sports, equestrian sports, culture, orthodoxies;

X: achievement, those in authority, life's ambitions, places of highest personal development;

VIRGO/MERCURY: assistants, servants, personnel, laborers, union people, consumers, health-conscious people, geniuses in limited areas, details people;

LIBRA/VENUS: artists on display, performers, marriage partners, diplomats, healers, arbitrators, ideals;

SCORPIO/MARS: guardians, doctors, surgeons, sexually active types, seducers;
SCORPIO/PLUTO: detectives, spies, coroners, researchers, occultists, account-keepers;

SAGITTARIUS/JUPITER: doctors, judges, professors, clergymen, wealthy people, orthodox types, philosophers, ambassadors;

CAPRICORN/SATURN: leaders, authorities, obstructors, time, the facts of life, high position, controllers, gradual change;

AQUARIUS: science and higher logic, technology, groups of common interest, religion, innovation, democracy, the people;

PISCES: abstracts, matters that are hard to pin down, that contain mysteries, religion, charities, universal sentiments, romanticism, deception, escapism, illusion;

XI: professional relationships, acquaintances, the new advancements one applies to life, perversities, license;

XII: self-undoing, hidden matters, exile and getting away from it all, dealings with one's own inner life, facing matters of depth and religious or cosmic mystery;

AQUARIUS/SATURN: dedicated researchers and practitioners of the sciences, logicians;
AQUARIUS/URANUS: scientific breakthroughs, scientific geniuses, technologists, civil libertarians, reformers, innovators;

PISCES/JUPITER: doctors, administrators of public services, clerics, theologians;
PISCES/NEPTUNE: medical researchers, gas, anesthetics, drugs, those dealing in any of the above, convicted criminals, prisoners, exiles, martyrs;

Elements and Qualities of the Signs

The four *elements* of the signs of the zodiac are:

Fire: *emotive* and outwardly directed
Earth: *sensory* and inner-directed
Air: *intellectual* and outer-directed
Water: *intuitive* and inner-directed

The three *qualities* of the signs of the zodiac are:
Cardinal: concerned with objective reality;
Fixed: concerned with subjective reality;
Mutable: a balancing of the objective and subjective perspectives.

The twelve signs of the zodiac are divided into groupings:

Aries: Cardinal Fire
Taurus: Fixed Earth
Gemini: Mutable Air
Cancer: Cardinal Water
Leo: Fixed Fire
Virgo: Mutable Earth

Libra: Cardinal Air
Scorpio: Fixed Water
Sagittarius: Mutable Fire
Capricorn: Cardinal Earth
Aquarius: Fixed Air
Pisces: Mutable Water

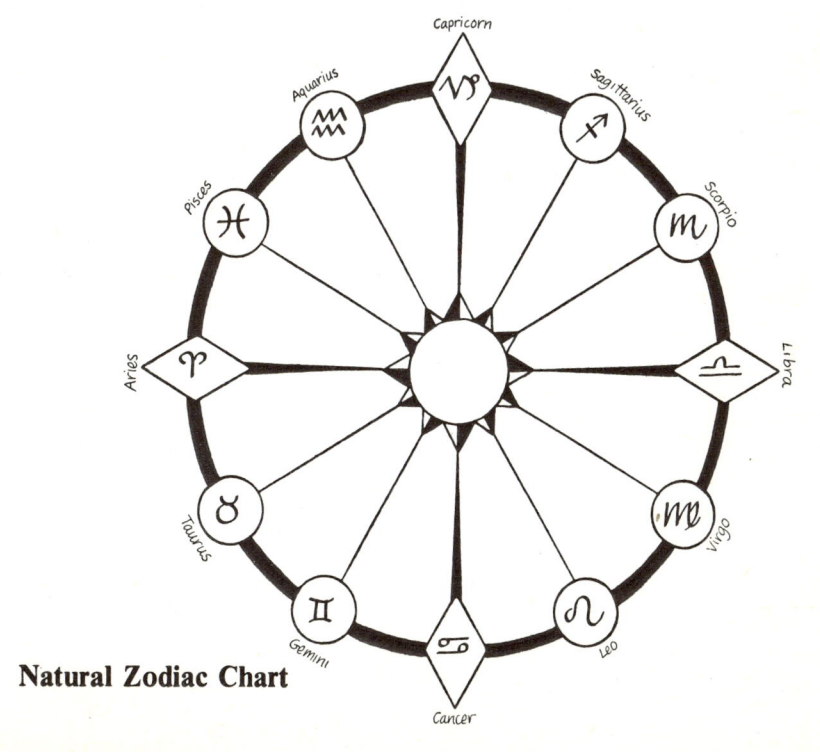

Natural Zodiac Chart

The Natural Zodiac

The chart above shows the sign and planetary rulerships given to the twelve houses of the zodiac, or what is referred to as the natural zodiac. In actuality, only about 1/12 of the population has Aries rising. To understand this, we must first come to understand what people mean when they say, "She's a double Taurus," or "double" anything. A popular misconception has it that the term refers to the Sun and the Moon in the same sign. This is not so. "Double" refers to a sunrise birth; when the sun is in any given sign, that sign rises with it, "pulling" the next sign in the zodiac behind it (on the cusp of the second house), and so on. Thus, if you were born at 6:20 A.M. on April 29 of any given year, you were born with the Sun in Taurus and the rising sign Taurus as well. Since it takes about two hours for a complete sign to ascend on the eastern horizon, if you were born at about 8:30 A.M., instead of 6:30, you would be a Taurus Sun, with the *next* sign in the zodiac rising, or Gemini. Carrying this along, those born at sun*set* on the same day would have Taurus' *opposite* sign—Scorpio, rising.

Planet/Sign Glossary

Affinity: relationships of signs, houses, and planets, and the matters connected with them, to similar signs, houses, planets, and matters connected; example: Aries affinity with Leo, via the Fire element; Jupiter and Venus have affinity in the field of health; the eighth and twelfth house have affinity in psychic matters; Neptune has affinity with the eighth house via the Water element and all hidden matters.

Affliction: stressful or difficult relationship within the natal chart, or from planets in the skies at any given moment. Usually necessary to growth, aspects from planets are considered afflictions when they are *squares, semisquares, quincunxes, oppositions,* and *conjunctions* with *"malefic"* planets. (See: Aspects)

Angles: those points in the chart that are exactly on the horizon (east or west) and those that are exactly perpendicular to the horizon (north or south). The houses these angles create are the first (ascendant), or rising house (east), the seventh (descendant), or setting house (west), the fourth house (nadir) or midnight house (north), and the tenth, or noonday house—also known as the midheaven, the M.C., and the zenith (south). Matters that are represented for a person in any of these houses usually are most clearly manifest in a person's life; example: Jupiter rising will indicate great wealth or weight.

Ascendant: the rising house in a chart, known as the native's "rising sign"; the first house of the chart (see Angles).

Aspects: angular relationships between planets, as well as between planets and angles or house cusps, within a 360-degree plane. The most used are:

conjunction: 0 degrees; *semisextile:* 30 degrees; *semisquare:* 45 degrees; *sextile:* 60 degrees; *square:* 90 degrees; *trine:* 120 degrees; *quincunx (or inconjunct):* 150 degrees; and *opposition:* 180 degrees. Of these, the semisextile, sextile, and trine are considered "easy," "benefic," or otherwise comfortable relationships, while the semisquare, square, quincunx, and opposition are considered "difficult," "hard," or "malefic." The conjunction is generally good, except when it combines a planet considered a malefic planet with another malefic, or a benefic.

Benefic: the easy aspects, but more generally used to mean the planets that give power, energy, and opportunity: the Sun, Venus, and Jupiter. Both the Moon and Mercury are neutral, reflecting the natures of the signs they are in, as well as the planets most closely associated with them in the chart.

Combust: a planet very close to the Sun in longitude, about 15 degrees either side, can have its power "burnt out" by such close proximity. Mars is the exception, seeming to grow in power with the combust location.

Culmination: as used here, means the point at which an aspect between two planets becomes exact (see also: Partile).

Cusp: either the beginning three days, or final three days, or degrees, of a sign. Also, the twelve-fold division of the chart; each line radiating from the center is a house cusp.

Direct: a planet moving foreward through the signs of the zodiac, i.e., from Aries toward Libra, etc., is "direct"; those, by apparency, that are moving in the opposite direction are considered moving "retrograde."

Double-Bodied Signs: signs that are associated with dual matters coexisting at the same time. The double-bodied signs are: Gemini, Sagittarius, and Pisces.

Elevation: the planet closest to the zenith of any chart, or highest in the skies at the moment the chart was drawn for, is elevated. This is what astrologers call an "accidental dignity," and it makes the planet more significant than planets lower on the horizon, in many cases.

Feminine Signs: signs that are otherwise called "negative," "magnetic," "responsive," and "passive." Every other sign of the zodiac is feminine, beginning with Taurus, Cancer, Virgo, etc. Another way to remember which they are is to note that all Earth and Water signs are feminine.

Intercepted Signs: signs that fall within a house, but not on its cusp. The house-cusp, twelvefold division is based on a perfect circle, whereas the planes of the ecliptic that it divides form a wavy ellipse. Occasionally, when dividing the latter by the former, the phenomenon of the intercepted sign occurs. The farther north one is born, the more intercepted signs he is likely to have in the houses of his chart. Intercepted signs, because they rule no cusps, hold hidden sway over the matters of the houses they are in.

Karma: a Hindi-Sanskrit word that has come into its own in modern Western thought. Two ideas prevail about karma; the first is based on beliefs of reincarnation, and says: To the extent that one was good or evil in a past life, he or she will reap the benefits or consequences in this life. The more worldly view is that *action* of every sort goes into the makeup of one's karma, and that what we do in this life, as well, will and must be answered for in one form or another. In the

Bible, an extension of this is found in areas of heredity: "The sins of the fathers shall be visited upon the sons, unto the fifth and sixth generations." Saint Paul, in the New Testament, reminds us that every jot and tittle of our lives will become known at the Last Judgment and must be cleansed away. In terms of modern parapsychological theory, karma may be seen as the accumulation of ideoforms, or thought forms, layered on the astral body, or soul, generated by one's every thought and deed. (*see* p.169)

Lights: when the Sun and Moon are not lumped together with the planets and called by that name (planet means wanderer, and even the Sun, from relationship of celestial apparencies based on earth perspective that is astrology, seems to wander across our skies every day), they are otherwise referred to as the lights.

Lord of the Horoscope: the planet that rules the rising sign in a chart.

Malefic: either a difficult relationship between planets, or between planets and angles or house cusps of the chart, or else the planets thought to be themselves the most stress-related: Mars, Saturn, Uranus, Neptune, and Pluto.

Masculine Signs: are signs that are otherwise called "positive," "electric," "assertive," or "aggressive." Every other sign, beginning with Aries, is masculine. All Fire and Air signs are masculine.

Maternal Signs: Cancer, Leo, and Virgo.

Orbs: as used here, the distances at which aspects between one planet and another will come into effect. The lights usually get greater orbs (as much as 15 degrees either side of exactness) than the planets; however, planets on major angles are often given wider orbs. Example: The Moon at 10 degrees of Aries is in orb of a trine aspect to Mercury at 14 degrees of Leo, for the two are 124 degrees apart, 120 being the exact orb of the trine.

Partile: an aspect is partile when it is exact. Partile aspects have greater meaning, for instance, than an aspect at the limits of its orb of effectiveness. (See also: Culmination)

Posited: placed or in position anywhere in the chart, or in the celestial zodiac.

Quadrants: four sections of the chart begun at each of the major angles (see: Angles). Aries to the beginning of Cancer is the first, Cancer to the beginning of Libra the second, Libra to the beginning of Capricorn the third, and Capricorn to the beginning of Aries the fourth. These are usually chart, and not zodiacal, distinctions, however, and represent the three-house groups in the circle from first-fourth, fourth-seventh, seventh-tenth, and tenth to first.

Retrograde: when a planet appears to move backward, against the order of the signs, it is considered to be "retrograde." This is purely a visual orbital phenomenon, as planets do not behave this way. However, since all of astrology is based upon the relationships viewed from a geocentric- or earth-perspective, it must be taken into account. It usually indicates that the matters the planet signifies will manifest in unusual or unexpected ways, experiencing delays in its functions.

Solar chart: when the time of birth is unknown, a solar chart is constructed to find not the *true* relationships of the planets (also in time charts), but the *symbolic* relationship of those planets to the houses of the chart. While this is not as accurate a picture as that formed by a time chart, it nevertheless tells a great deal about the native of the chart.

Station (or Stationary): at the point when a planet is turning retrograde or direct in its orbit, it seems to stand still for a brief period. The degrees posited by the planets at these points are strongly emphasized, and can have major effects on natal planets occupying the same or closely related degrees.

Stellium (or Satellitium): a grouping of three or more planets or lights within a sign. When five or more, including one of the lights, group together in the same sign, it is called a Grand Conjunction.

Transit: the movement of planets in the heavens over degrees occupied by or affecting planets of the natal chart.

Kennedy Keywords

General JFK-Assassination Keywords

Eighth House

autopsies
coroners
dead, the, and matters connected
death
death, the manner of one's
executioners, executions
government, end of existing
mortality
morticians
possessions of the deceased
slaughter, slaughterhouses
suicides
surgeons, surgery
tyranny triumphant over the state (mundane astrology)
undertakers

(Secondary)

overthrowing, overthrows
state, destruction of the, by the will of the people (mundane)

Scorpio

autopsies
butchers
dead, the, and matters connected with the dead
death
executioners, executions
funeral directors, funerals, funeral trains
genitals
hate
legacies
life after death
morgues
morticians
mortuaries
operations, surgical; operating rooms and objects used in them
organs, sex
resentment
scrota
sex, sex energy, sex force, sexuality
sexual intercourse; sexual relations, legitimate and extramarital
slaughter, slaughterhouses
surgeons, surgery
testicles, excretory vessels of the testicles
transformation
tyranny, tyrants
tyranny triumphant over the state (mundane)
undertakers
vermin, vermin-infested places

(Secondary)

gains from psychic experiences
psychic experiences and disturbances

psychic influences
psychic receptivity and faculties
psychics
psychism
psychometry and psychometric functions of the body

Neptune

ambiguities
ambushes
assassinations, assassins
beguilement, the beguiling
blind spots, one's own
cameras
camouflage
chaos
chicanery
clairsentience (forty percent of Americans interviewed in the sixties said: "I had the feeling something was going to happen to him"; or "I had the feeling they were going to kill him.")
clairvoyance, clairvoyants
clandestine associates, clandestineness
clues
collusion
confessions
crime, crimes, criminals
delusions, mass delusions
disappearances
disloyalty
dispersion
dissolution
dissolving
doubtful, the
drama
elusiveness
enigmas
escape
evasion

exaggerations
exposés
fakes
falsity
fantasy
fascination
fictitious names
films, filmdom
flimsiness
forebodings
forecasting, forecasts
fraud, frauds
gullibility
hidden forces
hidden and underhanded opposition, hidden places, hidden side of life
hoaxes
hospitalization, hospitals, hospital workers
hysteria
idealism, impractical
idealists
illicit undertakings
illusions
immeasurable, the
imprisonment
incomprehensible, the
indefiniteness
informers
insanity
instability
intrigues
intuition, intuitive intellect and receptivity
inundation
investigators, private
jailors, jails
leaking, leaks
lenses
liars

Appendix: Kennedy Keywords 233

manias
melodramas
misrepresentations
mob psychology, mobs
morbid, the
motion picture theaters and owners, motion picture producers, motion pictures
mysteries; the mysterious
nebulousness
nets
obsessing entities, obsession, obsessions
opposition, hidden and underhanded
paranoia
penitentiaries
plotting, plots against one
predictions
premonitions
prescience
prophecy, prophets
puzzles
scandal
schemers, schemes
secrets of every kind
sedition
seers
slander
sorrows
subterfuge
subversion, the subversive
transparency
treachery
underhandedness
vagueness
vehicles
viaducts
weakness, bodily; weaknesses (JFK's corset)
weird, that which is
x-ray processing rooms

234 THE KENNEDY CURSE

(Secondary)

movements (democratic, political, popular, social, and socialistic)
omissions
opinions, fluctuations of popular
perjury
political instability
presidents
prevarication
propaganda, political propaganda
sacrifice, sacrifices
secretive persons
stool pigeons
strategy
stretchers (they found a Connally bullet on the stretcher)
suicides
uncanny, the

JFK Assassination Clue Keywords

Eighth House

foreign persons, losses through
pallbearers
sex organs, male
sex, sex energy, sex force, sexuality

(Secondary)

organizations, financial

Scorpio

detection, detectives, espionage
embalmers, embalming
magic, magicians
organs, sex

pallbearers
penis
scrota
sex, sex energy, sex force, sexuality
sex intrigue, sexual intercourse, sexual relations
sorcerers, sorcery
testicles, excretory vessels of
witchcraft, witches

(Secondary)

investigators, private

Clue places

Algeria
Baltimore
Barbary
Bavaria
Catalonia
Dover, England
Fez, Morocco
Frankfurt
Ghent, Belgium
Halifax, Nova Scotia
Hull, England
Judea
Jutland
Korea
Liverpool
Messina, Sicily
Milwaukee
Morocco
New Orleans
Newcastle, England
Norway
Paraguay
Queensland, Australia

St. John's, Newfoundland
Stockport, England
Syria
Transvaal, South Africa
Worthington, England
Washington, D.C.

(Secondary)

Bolivia, eastern
Boston
Brazil
Cappadocia
China, Red
Cincinnati
Cleveland
East Indies
Glossop, England
Japan
Manchuria
North Carolina
North Dakota
Oklahoma
Philippines
Portland, Oregon
Prussia
Russia
San Francisco
Siberia
South Dakota
Tokyo
Turkey
Washington State

Appendix: Kennedy Keywords 237

JFK Assassination Keywords Clue

KEY
1 conspiracy-connected
2 motive suggested
3 Oswald-connected
4 CIA-Hoover-Hunt-Sturgis-
    Gonzalez-Martinez connected
5 name or occupation suggestions

Neptune

4,1	accomplices
5,1	actors, actresses
5,1	actors, character
2	addicts
5	admirals
4,3,1	aliases
4,1	alibis
4,3	aliens
4,1	alliances, covert
5,4	barkers
4	bays
4,2,1	betrayal
5	black magicians
4,1	bogus, bogus companies
4,1	brotherhoods
1	cabals
4,1	confidential positions, matters, and activities
5,4,1	con men
4,1	conspiracies
4,3,1	covert, the

3	crazy persons
1	debauchery
4,1	deceit, deceivers, deception
5,4	detection, detectives
4,1	disguises
2	drugs, in general
2	dangers of drugs; drug addiction; drugs, habit-forming; drugs which produce unconsciousness or sleep
3,1	dupes, duping
5,4,1	espionage
4,3,1	fictitious names
5	films, filmdom
5,4,1	foreign agents, confidential
4,1	forgers, forgery
4,1	genius, geniuses
2	graft, grafters
5,2	heroin
4,1	impersonation, impersonators
4,1	imposters
4,1	incognitos
1	lures, luring
5	magic, black
4,1	makeup, makeup artists
5	motion-picture producers
3,1	mysterious origin, persons of
5,2	narcotics
5,4,3	navies
5,2	oil, oil fields, oil-well operators, oil wells, oil workers, oil tanks
5,2	opiates
5,2	opium, opium trade
5,4,1	organizations, large
4,3,1	persecution, persecution by secret enemies
5,2	petroleum
2	poppies, opium
4,1	pretenders, pretending, pretense, pretexts

Appendix: Kennedy Keywords

5,4,1	pseudonyms, work conducted under
5	quack doctors
5	sea, the deep
4,1	secret societies
5	ships, shipping, shippers
5,4,2	smuggling
5	sorcerers, sorcery
5,4,1	spies
4,1	toupees (Sturgis?)
1	veils
5	voodoo (Nixon, Hunt)
5	witches, witchcraft
5	wizards
5	writers, occult
1	x-ray processing rooms

(Secondary)

2	candidates
5	colonels
4,3,2	communism
5	Congress, congresses, congressmen
1	kidnappers, kidnapping
4	officials, government (civic or state)
4	officials, public
4	plumbers, plumbing, plumbing lines, plumbing supplies (also Scorpio)
4,1	sects

Keywords for the Family and Teddy

Eighth House

sex, sex energy, sex force, sexuality

Scorpio

bogs

mud
procreative act, the; reproduction
quagmires

(Secondary)

brewers, breweries

Neptune

adultery
alcohol, alcoholism; alcoholic beverages
bartenders
beverages, intoxicating
bootlegging, bootleggers
clandestineness, clandestine associates
distillers, distilleries
drinks, drinking
heirs apparent
intoxication (karma: the men became intoxicated by other women)
liquors, liquor dealers
philanderers
places overflowed with water, especially from the sea or a lake (T)
swamps
water, occupations connected with water, water pursuits and those engaged in them, water tanks and pipes, water fowl and their breeding places, waterways and vehicles, water meters, places or houses near water, water in the body.
whiskey

(Secondary)

patriarchs

Critical Points in Suspects' Charts

Before analyzing the stress that existed between the natal charts of John Kennedy and each of the twenty-six real and control-group suspects, it was necessary to distinguish between those points in the suspects' charts that were inherently of potential malevolence and those that were rather easygoing parts of the person's nature. I have made a distinction between these more or less innocuous planets and points, and the critical-behavior group I call the *high-frequency malefics* (HFM).

Traditionally, the malefics in astrology are Mars, Saturn, Uranus, Neptune, and Pluto. My list also contains the Sun, ascendant, midheaven (MC), and Jupiter. The latter, chief among the benefics, might seem out of place among difficult planets; however, keep in mind that Jupiter represents one's beliefs and sense of the law. Conspirators of the type who would execute an American president will probably have an afflicted Jupiter in their charts in a good number of instances. Jupiter will delude them into thinking that what they do is for some general good, and

242   THE KENNEDY CURSE

their sense of the law will be something they pervert rather than honor by their actions. The midheaven, or MC, is one's goals, the ascendant one's image, and the Sun one's general purpose, all of which will be involved in the stew of murders that were committed. When any of these are in stressful circumstances at the native's birth, I have labeled them HFM, and judged aspects to and from them to be of higher significance than other aspects.

You will note that many of the names have, listed after them, five or possibly six HFMs, as opposed to the four that are the average for the others. Some charts are more afflicted at birth than others. In such instances, especially where that native is a powerful man, they deserve to be given more credit for the ruthless potential attributable to very powerful men.

I have also assigned HFM status to JFK's chart positions, allowing that eight of the twelve natal points were aspected in his final moment and should be seen as critical contact areas.

High-Frequency Malefics
Gen. Charles Cabell: Mars, Jupiter, Uranus, Neptune, Pluto
Fidel Castro: Ascendant, Saturn, Jupiter/Uranus, Neptune
Central Intelligence Agency: Sun, Mars, Jupiter, Saturn/Pluto, Uranus
John Connally: Sun/Mars, Jupiter, Uranus, Neptune
Thomas Dewey: Sun, Mars, Uranus, Neptune
Dwight Eisenhower: Mars, Jupiter, Saturn, Uranus
Barry Goldwater: MC, Saturn, Uranus, Neptune
Virgilio Gonzales: Sun, Jupiter, Saturn, Neptune, Pluto
Billy Graham: MC, Mars, Saturn, Uranus
J. Edgar Hoover: Sun, Mars, Saturn/MC, Neptune/Pluto
Howard Hughes: Ascendant, Mars/Saturn, Jupiter, Uranus, Neptune, Pluto
E. Howard Hunt: Sun, Mars, Jupiter, Saturn, Uranus
Lyndon Baines Johnson: Mars, Saturn, Uranus, Neptune
John F. Kennedy: Ascendant, Sun, Moon, Mars, Venus, Uranus, Saturn/Neptune
Nikita Khrushchev: Ascendant, Sun, Mars, Saturn, Uranus

Appendix: Critical Points in Suspects' Charts

G. Gordon Liddy: Sun, Jupiter, Saturn, Uranus
Mao Tse-tung: Sun, Mars, Jupiter, Uranus, Neptune
Eugenio Martinez: Sun/Pluto, Mars, Jupiter, Saturn
Richard Nixon: Sun, Mars, Saturn, Neptune, Pluto
Aristotle Onassis: Sun, Mars, Saturn, Uranus, Pluto
Lee Harvey Oswald: Sun, Mars, Saturn, Pluto
Ronald Reagan: Sun, Mars, Uranus, Neptune
Nelson Rockefeller: Sun, Mars, Saturn, Jupiter, Uranus, Neptune
Jack Ruby: Mars, Saturn, Uranus, Pluto
Adlai Stevenson: Mars, Saturn, Uranus, Neptune
Frank Sturgis: Sun, Mars/Uranus, Neptune, Pluto
George Wallace: Jupiter, Saturn, Uranus, Pluto

Technical Approach to Synastry/Motive Analysis

In analyzing the aspects between the charts of JFK and each suspect, I studied the major ptolemaic aspects—conjunctions, oppositions, squares, trines, and sextiles; since it is adversity that I was looking for, I also noted the quincunx, or 150-degree aspect between planets, which indicates subtle yet all-pervasive strain.

Orbs

For those unfamiliar with the term when applied to measurement, astrologers mean by *orb* the range of effectiveness of a particular aspect. That is to say, if an aspect between two planets, say Mars and Jupiter, has an orb of eight degrees, then the aspect would be, in effect, eight degrees before becoming exact, as well as eight degrees after culmination. What determines orb is the strength or relative weakness of the type of aspect and the planets or lights involved. Thus:

Aspect	Involving	Orb
conjunction, opposition, square, trine	Sun, Moon, Ascendant or MC	12°
conjunction, opposition, square, trine	all other planets	8°
sextile, quincunx	Sun, Moon, Ascendant or Mc	4°
sextile, quincunx	all other planets	3°

Using these orbs, I set up the synastry, or chart comparison, between each of the twenty-five suspects and the murdered President's chart. When each chart had been gone over with a fine-toothed comb, I listed the aspects and assigned to each a numerical score of from one to ten, based on the strength of the aspect and the exactness of the orb, as follows:

10: partile (exact) conjunction

9: partile opposition, trine or square; first ¼ orb of conjunction (1½°–3° or 1½°–2°)

8: first ¼ of orb of opposition, trine or square (1½°–3° or 1½°–2°)

7: second ¼ of orb of conjunction (3°–6° or 2°–4°)

6: second ¼ of orb of opposition, trine or square (3°–6° or 2°–4°)

5: partile sextile or quincunx

4: third ¼ orb of conjunction (6°–9° or 4°–6°)

3: third ¼ orb of opposition, trine or square (6°–9° or 4°–6°); final ½ orb of sextile or quincunx (1½°–4° or 1½°–3°)

2: final ¼ orb of conjunction (9°–12° or 6°–8°)

1: final ¼ orb of opposition, trine or square (9°–12° or 6°–8°)

It should be noted here that these values were assigned to both negative and positive aspects, collected in two separate columns. I then needed to differentiate between critical and

Appendix: Technical Approach to Synastry/Motive Analysis

noncritical planets involved in the aspects I had collected. Certainly, a partile conjunction of Mercury and Venus would be worth far less in this evaluation of stress than would be a partile conjunction between a suspect's Mars, especially if that Mars happened also to be designated HFM—and JFK's Sun.

To distinguish between critical and noncritical aspects then, I devised or assigned four differentiating multipliers, assigned to aspects as follows:

Contact between two non-HFMs:	×1
Contact between suspect HFM and JFK non-HFM:	×1½
Contact between suspect non-HFM and JFK HFM:	×2
Contact between two HFMs:	×4

Having circled all the HFMs on my lists of aspects, it was easy to pick them out and multiply their orb value by the differentiating multipliers above. Once these final values were arrived at, I subtracted the total of positive aspects from the total of negative aspects and arrived at my synastry ratings. Only in two cases, those of Dewey and Goldwater, did I have to subtract the negative total from the larger positive total. Everyone, it seemed, had at least something against Kennedy. Percentile ratings were arrived at using a curve in which the highest stress score in relation to JFK's chart was assigned a "motive value" of 94 percent. These final tallies can be found on page 133-34.

Synastry: Motive Analysis

Suspect List	Resistant/Negative	Adversity toward JFK
John Connally	−378.00	94.50%
Mao Tse-tung	−342.50	85.62%
Frank (Fiorini) Sturgis	−262.50	65.62%
J. Edgar Hoover	−248.50	62.13%
Virgilio Gonzales	−244.00	61.00%
Nikita Khrushchev	−209.50	52.37%
Howard Hughes	−207.00	51.75%
Central Intelligence Agency	−186.00	46.50%
G. Gordon Liddy	−176.00	44.00%
Billy Graham	−164.50	41.12%

Richard Nixon	−163.50	40.87%
Lee Harvey Oswald	−126.00	31.50%
Gen. Charles Cabell	−112.75	27.50%
Adlai Stevenson	−67.00	18.75%
Dwight D. Eisenhower	−62.00	17.50%
E. Howard Hunt	−54.00	13.50%
George Wallace	−45.00	11.50%
Ronald Reagan	−43.50	11.13%
Eugenio Martinez	−42.50	10.63%
Jack Ruby	−40.50	10.13%
Lyndon B. Johnson	−40.50	10.13%
Nelson Rockefeller	−29.00	4.50%
Aristotle Onassis	−18.00	4.00%
Fidel Castro	−15.00	3.75%

Supportive/Positive

Thomas Dewey	+60.50	−20.00%
Barry Goldwater	+146.00	−35.00%

Technical Approach to the Moment of JFK's Execution: Stressful Aspect Analysis

In studying the relationship between the chart of each of the twenty-six suspects and the events in Dallas on November 22, 1963, I drew up a chart for the moment of the president's execution that appears on page 132.

Practically every point in this chart received a major stressful aspect; however, the only ones chosen as absolutely essential are those that received the major stress of the moment: This is practically the whole chart, save Jupiter and Pluto. Certainly, Pluto, old ruler of death itself, was ever-present in Dallas at the fatal moment; yet it is connected to Uranus, which was the *real* significance of that death—an internal American Revolution. Uranus, conjunct Pluto in a major angle (that of opposition— here, deadly and powerful opponents), is partile square Mercury holding the midheaven; Neptune, slightly above in the ninth house, is squared by the ascendant (appearances), the Moon (the public), and Saturn (sacrifice; lies). The Moon conjunct Saturn is great public deception, and Neptune is doubtlessly the coverup, but, still, Neptune, Mercury, and Uranus are bit players.

Appendix: Technical Approach to Synastry/Motive Analysis 249

The major critical points are the personal ones: Sun, Moon, and ascendant, as well as the conjunction in the tenth house of Mars and Venus and that in the twelfth house and rising of the Moon conjoined Saturn. The ascendant is the matter at hand—quite a serious one; the Sun is the power behind the moment—a dark, treacherous, and deadly force perched in the final minutes of the sign Scorpio, fourteen degrees ahead of Neptune in the ninth house, squaring the ascendant and thus appalling the world. The Moon in mundane astrology is the body of the executive, the man whose form, like the Moon through the weeks, changes every four years. It is also the public. Here it is a mournful public, in the twelfth house of endings, conjunct the planet of endings, squaring the sorrow-laden natural ruler of that twelfth house, Neptune, co-ruler of the rising house (Neptune's Pisces is *intercepted* in the first house).

When Saturn is in adverse relationship to Neptune, martyrdom is in the air. The Moon in the chart for the United States, July 4, 1776, is in Aquarius, as was the Moon on November 22, 1963, almost on the same degree. This is the body of the president, as I said; this was your martyr.

Though the square between Mercury holding the midheaven and Uranus conjunct Pluto in the seventh house is partile and cause for electric nerves and other things, it is by no means the most significant aspect, for it cannot actually characterize what the other aspects have thus far only suggested. A less exact, nevertheless potent, aspect occurs where things happen that characterize moments—in the tenth house. The less than one-degree conjunction of Venus and Mars is the actual violence that sent us down the paths we now find ourselves on. These two are of the exceedingly human group of planets, the kind we experience every day; however, every couple of years or so they become conjunct. They create classic friction prior to romance, but they do this best in other aspects; when they are together—watch out! As passionate as love and love quarrels can be, so equally real was the sight of supposedly the most important man in America, if not the world, being executed in broad daylight as though the people who were keeping him alive were suddenly tired of doing so.

For the reasons outlined, I chose to look at the aspects in two categories—those from the minor factors—Mercury, Uranus, and Neptune—and those from the heavier indicators of the moment: Ascendant, Sun, Venus/Mars, Moon/Saturn (the latter being intimately involved with all matters of responsibility and plotting). To the minor group I assigned a multiplier number of 1 and to the other, more powerful, indicators, the value of 2. These were meant to multiply the values of the following classifications of aspects and orbs:

Aspect	Value
partile conjunct an HFM of suspect	5
conjunct HFM; partile conjunct suspect's personal points (Sun Moon ascendant, MC)	4
partile opposite HFM; conjunct personal point	3
partile opposite personal point; opposition HFM; partile square HFM	2
square HFM	1

(Partile trines of HFMs eliminates partile squares of same.)

Percentile ratings were derived from a curve in which the suspect with the highest stress rating for the moment of the execution was computed as the top. This may seem a rather haphazard way of applying percentages in this case, but it would also be erroneous to assume too much from these findings. While the synastry analysis would serve as a reasonably valid evaluation of each suspect's real or potential relationship with Kennedy, the

Appendix: Technical Approach to Synastry/Motive Analysis 251

second analysis of *stress* at the moment of the execution must not be taken to imply murderous activity—only the potential for it. Therefore, purposely lowering my curve in this manner gives us composite totals, once all three analysis systems have been combined, a lower percentile total. A lower percentile range will still accomplish the purpose of demonstrating *relative* potential guilt, especially in the case of Oswald, and prevent the casual scanner from coming away from this book with the notion in mind that so-and-so probably murdered Kennedy because his percentile rating read 80 percent.

Death-Moment Stress Analysis

Suspect List	**Stress count***
Virgilio Gonzales	77
Nikita Khrushchev	56
Central Intelligence Agency	55
Howard Hughes	48
Adlai Stevenson	46
John Connally	43
Frank (Fiorini) Sturgis	40
Gen. Charles Cabell	37
E. Howard Hunt	36
Fidel Castro	33
Billy Graham	33
Richard Nixon	31
Mao Tse-tung	28
George Wallace	27
G. Gordon Liddy	21
J. Edgar Hoover	20
Ronald Reagan	20
Lee Harvey Oswald	18
Lyndon B. Johnson	16
Eugenio Martinez	15

Jack Ruby	12
Aristotle Onassis	12
Dwight D. Eisenhower	9
Thomas Dewey	5
Nelson Rockefeller	0
Barry Goldwater	0

*Based on possible 100

Bibliography

Books

The Circle Book of Charts. Circle Books, 1972.
Clinch, Nancy Gager. *The Kennedy Neurosis.* New York: Grosset & Dunlap, 1973.
Glass, Justine. *They Foresaw the Future.* New York: Berkeley Publishing Corp., 1970.
Kennedy, Rose. *Times to Remember.* New York: Doubleday & Co., Inc., 1975.
Koskoff, David E. *Joseph P. Kennedy, A Life and Times.* Englewood Cliffs, N.J.: Prentice-Hall, 1975.
Laing, Margaret. *The Next Kennedy.* New York: Coward, McCann & Geoghegan, Inc., 1968.
Moore, Marcia, and Douglas, Mark. *Astrology in Action.* Arcane Books, 1970.
Noyes, Peter. *Legacy of Doubt.* New York: Pinnacle Books, 1973.
O'Toole, George. *The Assassination Tapes.* Penthouse Press, 1975.
Penfield, Marc. *An Astrological Who's Who.* Arcane Books, 1972.
In the Shadow of Dallas—anthology/collection. Palo Alto, Calif.: Ramparts Press, Inc., 1967.
Whalen, Richard J. *The Founding Father.* New York: New American Library, 1964.
Wilson, Earl. *Show Business Laid Bare.* New York: G. P. Putnam's Sons, 1974.

Newspaper and Magazine Articles

"America's Long Vigil" (special publication). *TV Guide,* January 1964.

Anson, Robert Sam. "The Greatest Cover-Up of All." *New York Times Magazine,* April 18, 1975.

"Assassination of a President." Viking Press (*New York Times* reprints, November 23–28, 1963).

Boyle, Richard. "The Strange Death of Clay Shaw." *True Magazine,* April 1975.

Branch, Taylor, and Crile, George III. "The Kennedy Vendetta." *Harper's Magazine,* August 1975.

Dallas Morning News (Jack Ruby obituary), January 4, 1967.

Everywoman's Daily Horoscope Magazine (Kennedy children data), November 1967.

Kaiser, Robert Blair. "The JFK Assassination: Why Congress Should Reopen the Investigation." *Rolling Stone,* April 24, 1975.

Meskill, Paul. "Secrets of the CIA." *New York Daily News,* April 1975.

O'Toole, George. "Lee Harvey Oswald Was Innocent." *Penthouse,* March 1975.

Richler, Mordecai. "It's a Plot!" *Playboy,* July 1975.

Smith, Daniel. "The Strange American Twenty-Year Cycle." *Astrology Guide Magazine,* October 1958.

Sparks, Fred. "Those Wild, Wild Kennedy Boys." *National Star,* September–October 1974.

Sturgis, Frank. *New York Times* (UPI), September 16, 1963, p. 39.

Vidal, Gore (interview). *Penthouse,* August 1975.

"The Whole Earth Conspiracy Catalogue." *Crawdaddy Magazine,* August 1975.

"The World's Number One Assassin Talks." *Male Magazine,* July 1975.

Index

A

Advertisements, 18-19
AFA. *See* American Federation of Astrologers
Affinity, 223
Affliction, 223
Air (element), 48, 106, 107, 213-14, 221, 226
Airplane crashes (Kennedys), 35, 36, 37-38
Alcoholism, 72-73, 169-70, 171, 179
Alexander, William, 152
Alexander the Great, 4-5
Allende, Salvador, 168
All the President's Men, 149
American Federation of Astrologers (AFA), xiii
Anderson, Jack, 127, 139
Angles, 27, 224
Anti-Castro groups, 127, 129, 138, 147, 149
Aquarius, 217, 220, 221
   element, 48, 214
   quality, 107
Arbenz, Jacobo, 147
Aries, 217, 218, 221
   element, 48
   quality, 107
Ascendent, 222, 224, 242
Aspects, 131-32, 224. *See also types of aspects as* Square.
   orbs, 245-46
   repetition in Kennedy family, 108-14, *graph*, 112
   synastry analysis technique, 245-47, 250
Assassination (JFK), x, 36, 37, 58, 59-60, 102, 112, 208, 210, 248-49, *chart*, 132. *See also* Oswald, Lee Harvey; Suspects; Warren Commission
   keywords: eighth house, 229-30, 234, Neptune, 231-34, 237-39, place names, 235-36, Scorpio, 230-31, 234-35
   mysteries, 115-36: autopsy, 124, disappearance of brain, 121, magic bullet, 122-23, 126, rifle, 123-24, tramp photos, 119-20, 144, 145-46, witnesses, 36, 124-26, Zapruder film, 120-21
Association for Research and Enlightenment, 21
Asteroids, 60
Astrology as a profession, xiii-xiv, 24
Astrology in Action, 40, 116
Augustus, 2-3

B

Bancroft, Peggy Bedford, Duchess d'Uzesn, 92
Barrett, Robert, 153
Battle Abbey, 6-7
Bay of Pigs, 127, 144, 147, 149, 150-51
Bell and McQuiston research team, 117
Benefic, 224
Bhagavid-Gita, 12

255

Index

Bottos, Alex, 150
Bowers, Lee, 125-26
Bremmer, Arthur, 148
Browne, Sir Anthony, 6-8
Brussell, Mae, 142
Bullet, magic, 122-23, 126
Burden, Amanda, 96

C

Cabell, Charles: synastry/horary suspect analysis, 134, 136, 138, 154, 156, 158, 242, 248, 251, *chart,* 161
Caesar, Julius, 1-2
Cancer, 64, 217, 218, 221, 226
   element, 48
   Kennedy family and, 104, 105, Joe, Jr., 82, 85
   quality, 107
Capricorn, 34, 217, 219, 221
   element, 48, 213
   John Kennedy and, 171
   quality, 107
Cardinal signs, 107-8, 172, 221
Cassini, Igor, 89
Cassini, Oleg, 89
Castro, Fidel
   CIA assassination attempts, 117, 138, 140, 147, 149
   synastry/horary suspect analysis, 127-28, 134, 136, 154, 242, 248, 251, *chart,* 164
Cayce, Edgar, 20-21, 23
Central Intelligence Agency (CIA)
   assassination of foreign statesmen, 116-17, 144-45, 168
   Cabell and, 138
   Cuban operations, 127-28, 129, 140, 147, 149, 150
   Hughes and, 140
   Hunt and, 129, 147
   Lake Pontchartrain training camp, 145
   Mafia connections, 116-17
   Martinez and, 138
   Oswald and, 127, 142
   Rockefeller committee investigation, 115
   Ruby and, 129
   synastry/horary suspect analysis, 134, 136, 143-45, 154, 156, 158, 242, 247, 251, *chart,* 155
Centroverts, 107, 108
Chain letters, 18
Chappaquiddick, 36, 38, 44, 95, 168, 174, 204
Chile: CIA and, 117, 168
CIA and the Cult of Intelligence, 144
Colson, Chuck, 148
Combust, 224
Commercials, 18-19
Common signs. *See* Mutable signs
Conjunction, 223, 224
Connally, John
   bullet wound, 120, 122, 123, 126-27
   synastry/horary suspect analysis, 133, 136-38, 154, 156, 158, 242, 247, 251, *chart,* 159
Conservative politicians, horoscope of, 50
Cowdray, House of, 6-8
Cuban Revolutionary Committee, 147
Cubela, Rolando, 147
Culmination, 224
Curry, Jesse, 143
Curse, 5-6, 12-18
   famous historical curses, 6-11
   hereditary factor, 13
   legislation governing, 12
Cusp, 225

D

Davis, Rennie, xi
Degrees: significance of numbers, 27
Depression, economic, 210
Desloge, Diure Malcom, 91
Destiny heredity, 22
Dewey, Thomas: synastry/horary suspect analysis, 134, 136, 137, 156, 242, 248, 252, *chart,* 164
Direct planet, 225
Double, 222
Double-bodied signs, 225
Douglas, Mark, 40, 116

Dulles, Allen, 152
Duvalier, "Papa Doc," 117

E

Earth (element), 48, 106, 107, 213, 221, 225
    Jupiter/Saturn Cycle in, 212
Egan, Arthur, 96
Eighth house, 178, 180
    Kennedy family and, 96, 101-3, 104, 166-67, 168, 169-70, 179-80: Joe, Jr., 179, Joe, Sr., 73, John, 54, 55, 56, 57, 58, Robert, 51, 102-3, 105, 166-67, Ted, 44, 167-68, 180
    key words, 170, 229-30, 234, 239
Eisenhower, Dwight D.
    Cuba and, 147
    synastry/horary suspect analysis, 134, 136, 137, 156, 242, 248, 252, *chart*, 162
Elections, presidential
    1976, 193-94, 195-96, 214, *chart*, 194
    1980, 205-6, 211, 214, *chart*, 205
    twenty-year cycle, 207-16
Elements, 48, 106-7, 221. *See also* Air; Earth; Fire; Water
Elevation, 225
Eleventh house, 34
Ellsberg, Daniel, 149
Extrasensory perception (ESP), 13, 14, 17
Extroverts, 107, 108

F

Fain, John, 152-53
Fair Play for Cuba Committee, 129, 147
Family relationships, 21. *See also* Heredity, *subhead* destiny
Fatalism, 24
Federal Bureau of Investigation (FBI), 142. *See also* Hoover, J. Edgar
Feminine signs, 225

Ferrie, David, 128, 145
Fifth house, 46-47
    Kennedy family and, 101, 108: Robert, 46-47, Rose, 65
Fire (element), 30, 48, 106, 107, 221, 226
First house, 224
Fitzgerald, John F. "Honey Fitz," 64, 67, 68, 72
    solarscope, 79-82, *chart*, 80: Neptune/Saturn, 81, Pluto, 81, T-squares, 79-80
Fixed signs, 107-8, 172, 221
Ford, Gerald
    1976 election, 196-99, *chart*, 197
    Warren Commission, 120
Fourth house, 27, 59, 224
Free Cuba Committee, 129

G

Garbo, Greta, 89
Garfield, James, 208, 210
Garrison, Jim, 128-29, 145
Gaynor, Janet, 89
Gemini, 217, 218, 221, 225
    element, 48, 214
    John Kennedy and, 55
    quality, 107
Give Us This Day, 147
Glomar Explorer, 140
Goldwater, Barry: synastry/horary suspect analysis, 134, 136, 137, 156, 242, 248, 252, *chart*, 164
Gonzales, Virgilio: synastry/horary suspect analysis, 133, 135, 137, 154, 156, 242, 247, 251, *chart*, 157
Graham, Billy: synastry/horary suspect analysis, 134, 136, 137, 154, 156, 242, 247, 251, *chart*, 161
Grand conjunction, 227
Great Mutation Cycle, 212-16
Gregory, Dick, 145
Grimm, Jacob, 32-34, *chart*, 33
Grimm, Wilhelm, 32-34, *chart*, 33

H

Harding, Warren, 214

258 *Index*

Harlow, Jean, 89
Harrison, William Henry, 207, 210
Hartington, Kathleen Kennedy. *See* Kennedy, Kathleen
Hayden, Tom, xi
Hepburn, Katharine, 90
Heredity, 13
  destiny, 22, 23, 25, 26
HFM. *See* High-frequency malefic
Hi and Ho, 5
High-frequency malefic (HFM), 135, 241, 242-43
Hoover, J. Edgar
  Hoover memo, 142
  memorial service for, 149
  synastry/horary suspect analysis, 122-23, 133, 136, 151-53, 154, 156, 158, 242, 247, 251, *chart*, 160
Hope Diamond, 16
Horary analysis, 134-37, 153, 158, *chart*, 132. *See also* Suspects
Horizon, above and below the, 105
Horoscope, 39, 99
  comparison, *See* Synastry
Hosty, James, 152
House of Cowdray, 6-8
Houses, 105, 224. *See also names of houses as* Eighth house
  Kennedy family composite, 99-103, *chart*, 100
Hughes, Howard: synastry/horary suspect analysis, 134, 136, 140-41, 154, 156, 242, 247, 251, *chart*, 160
Hunt, E. Howard
  CIA operations, 129, 147
  Nixon and, 139-40, 147, 148, 168
  synastry/horary suspect analysis, 134, 136, 139-40, 144, 145-48, 148-49, 154, 156, 158, 242, 248, 251, *chart*, 162
  Uranus Half-Cycle, 146-47
  wife, 147

I

Intercepted signs, 225

Introverts, 107-8
Involution, 178

J

Jefferson, Thomas, 212
Jesus Christ, 1-2, 3-4
Johnson, Lyndon Baines
  Castro and, 127, 147
  synastry/horary suspect analysis, 134, 136, 137, 154, 156, 158, 242, 248, 251, *chart*, 163
John the Baptist, 19
Jupiter, 34, 65, 178, 224, 241-42
  Kennedy family and, 111: Joe, Jr., 73-74, 78, 85, PJ, 78, Rose, 64-65, Ted, 42
  /Saturn cycle, 207-16: in Air, 213, 215, in Earth, 212
  Wright brothers and, 31

K

Karma, 86, 169, 171-72, 225-26
Kelly, Grace, 92
Kennedy (family), 35-38, 180-81
  airplane crashes, 35, 36, 37-38
  enemies, 104, 113, 166
  house activity, 99-103, 168, *chart*, 100: eighth house, 96, 101-3, 104, 166-67, 168, 169-70, 179-80, 239
  keywords, 239-40
  liquor business, 72-73, 101, 169-70
  marriages, 87-89, 104
  Mutable stelliums, 172-77: dangerous periods, 175-76
  palm reading, 23-24
  planet aspects, 108-14, *graph*, 112
  planet/element distribution, 107, 108
  planet/sign activity, 103-14, *chart*, 103, 106: Neptune, 96, 101, 104, 107-9, 112, 113, 114, 166, 169-70, 240, Pluto, 81, 108, 112, 113, 169, Scorpio, 96, 101-3, 104, 105, 114, 179-80, 239-40
  sign/quality distribution, 107, 108
  tragedy chronology, 37-38

Index 259

Kennedy, Caroline Bouvier, 181, *chart*, 181
Kennedy, Christopher George, 187, *chart*, 188
Kennedy, David Anthony, 185, *chart*, 185
Kennedy, Douglas Harriman, 189, *chart*, 189
Kennedy, Edward Moore
  airplane crash, 38
  Chappaquiddick, 36, 38, 44, 95, 168, 174, 204
  children, 38, 190-92
  horoscope, 40-46, *chart*, 41: eighth house, 44, 167-68, 180, Jupiter, 42, Libra, 206, Mutable stelliums, 174-75, Neptune, 44, 168, 178-79, opposite polarity, 41-44, Pisces, 43, Saturn, 41, 45, Sun/Moon, 42-43, T-square, 45-46
  presidential candidacy: (1976) 44-45, 69, 114, 166, 168, 193-96, 203-6, 211, 216, *chart*, 203, (1980) 205-6, 211, 216, *chart*, 205
  women, 95-96
Kennedy, Edward Moore, Jr., 38, 191, *chart*, 192
Kennedy, Ethel, 37, 49
Kennedy, Eunice, *chart*, 63
Kennedy, Jacqueline. *See* Onassis, Jacqueline Kennedy
Kennedy, Jean Ann, *chart*, 64
Kennedy, John F., x, 85. *See also* Assassination
  career, 55-56, 105-6
  children, 181-82
  health, 111, 112, 171
  horoscope, 53-61, *chart*, 53: Air element, 107, Capricorn, 171, eighth house, 54, 55, 56, 57, 58, 102-3, 166-67, fourth house, 59, Gemini, 55, Leo, 171, Mars, 58, Mutable stelliums, 173-74, Saturn/Neptune, 57-58, Uranus, 58-59, Venus, 53-54, 55

Kennedy, Mary Kerry, 187, *chart*, 187
Kennedy, Mary Courtney, 185, *chart*, 186
Kennedy, Matthew Maxwell Taylor, 188, *chart*, 188
Kennedy, Michael Le Moyne, 186, *chart*, 186
Kennedy, Patricia, 94-95, *chart*, 63
Kennedy, Patrick, 192, *chart*, 192
Kennedy, Patrick Joseph, (PJ), 75, 76
  solarscope, 75-79, *chart*, 75: Pluto/Jupiter, 78, Saturn, 76, 79, T-squares, 76-77, Uranus/Neptune, 77, Venus, 77
  presidency, 35-36, 56, 57: Bay of Pigs, 127, 144, 147, 149, 150-51
  women, 90-94
Kennedy, John F., Jr., 182, *chart*, 182
Kennedy, Joseph Patrick, Sr., 35, 36, 38, 83, 86-87, 169, 171-72
  enemies, 60, 73-74
  extramarital affairs, 88, 89-90, 91
  horoscope, 70-74, 173, *chart*, 71: Earth element, 71, Jupiter/eighth house, 73, Mars/Jupiter, 73-74, Mutable stelliums, 172-73, Neptune, 101, 171-72, Neptune/Pluto, 71, 73, 74, Saturn, 74, sixth house, 72, 73, tenth house, 101, Venus/Pluto, 74, Virgo, 72
  liquor business and wealth, 72-73, 89, 171
Kennedy, Joseph Patrick, Jr., 35, 36, 37, 55, 85-86
  solarscope, 82-87, *chart*, 83: Cancer, 82, 85, eighth house, 179, Jupiter, 85, Mutable stelliums, 174, Neptune, 84, tenth house, 168, twelfth house, 84-85
  women, 90
Kennedy, Joseph Patrick III, 183, *chart*, 184
Kennedy, Kara, 190, *chart*, 191
Kennedy, Kathleen, 37, *chart*, 62
Kennedy, Kathleen Harrington, 183, *chart*, 183

Kennedy, Robert F., 48, 50, 57
  assassination, xv, 36, 37, 38, 52-53, 102, 112
  children, 183-90
  horoscope, 46-53, *chart*, 47: eighth house, 51, 102-3, 105, 166-67, fifth house, 46-47, Mercury, 51, Mutable stelliums, 174, Neptune, 46-48, 48-49, 49-50, Pluto, 51-53, Saturn, 48, Scorpio, 51, 105, Venus, 46
  Marilyn Monroe and, 94-95
Kennedy, Robert F. Jr., 184, *chart*, 184
Kennedy, Rory Elizabeth, 189, *chart*, 190
Kennedy, Rose, 39-40, 66, 67-68, 70, 81, 89
  horoscope, 60-70, *chart*, 61: fifth house, 65, Jupiter, 64-65, Neptune/Pluto, 66, 70, ninth house, 66, Saturn/Virgo, 68, twelfth house, 70, Venus/Saturn, 65
Kennedy, Rosemary, 37, *chart*, 62
Keywords
  assassination: eighth house, 229-30, 234, Neptune, 231-34, 237-39, place names, 235-36, Scorpio, 230-31, 234-35
  Kennedy family: eighth house, 239, Neptune, 240, Scorpio, 239-40
  signs, 217
Khrushchev, Nikita: synastry/horary suspect analysis, 134, 136, 150-51, 154, 156, 242, 247, 251, *chart*, 159
Kilgallen, Dorothy, 125
King, Martin Luther, Jr., 149
Kissinger, Henry, 88
Kopechne, Mary Jo, 36, 38, 44, 168, 174, 204

L

Lane, Mark, 136
Lawford, Pat and Peter, 94-95

Leo, 217, 218, 221, 226
  element, 48
  Kennedy family and, 104, 105: John, 171
  quality, 107
Libra, 64, 217, 219, 221
  element, 48, 214
  Kennedy family and, 104: Ted, 206
  quality, 107
Liddy, G. Gordon: synastry/horary suspect analysis, 134, 136, 138-39, 154, 156, 243, 247, 251, *chart*, 160
Lie detector, 117-18, 151
Lights, 226
Lincoln, Abraham, 207, 209, 210
Lineage, shared, 21
Lord of the Horoscope, 226

M

McCarthy, Joe, 50
McKenzie, Francis Humbertson, 10
McKenzie, Kenneth, Earl of Seaforth, 8-11
McKenzie, Kenneth, Warlock of the Glen, 8-11
McKinley, William, 208
Mafia, 116-17, 140, 149
Magic bullet theory, 122-23, 126
Malefic aspects, 223, 226
  Kennedy family, 113
Malefic planets, 113, 226, 241
Manchurian Candidate, The, 150
Mannlicher-Carcano rifle, 122, 123-24, 143
Mao Tse-tung: synastry/horary suspect analysis, 133, 136, 137, 154, 156, 243, 247, 251, *chart*, 160
Marchetti, Victor, 144
Markham, Dean, 38
Mars, 32, 224, 226, 241
  Kennedy family and, 110-11, 113: Joe, Sr., 73-74, John, 58
Martinez, Eugenio: synastry/horary suspect analysis, 134, 136, 138, 156, 243, 248, 251, *chart*, 163
Masculine signs, 226

Maternal signs, 226
MC, 224, 242
Mental retardation, 37
Mercer, Julia, 129
Mercury, 48, 51
   Kennedy family and, 109-10: Robert, 51
Mexico City, Mexico, 142
Midheaven, 224, 242
Midnight house. *See* Fourth house
Midpoint calculation, 59
Mills, Hayley, 25-28, *chart*, 26
Mills, John, 25-28, *chart*, 25
Monroe, Marilyn, 93-95
Montague, Viscount, 8
Moon, 26-27, 42-43, 109, 226
   Kennedy family and, 109, 110: Ted, 42-43, 44
Moore, Marcia, 40, 116
Morton, Charles V., 146
Motive analysis, 133-34, 247-48
Mummy's Tomb, 16
Mutable, or Common, signs, 31-32, 107-8, 172, 221
Mutable stellium, 172-77
   Kennedy danger periods, 175-76

N

Names, personal, 21-22
National Archives, 121
National Council for Geocosmic Research, xii-xiv
Natural zodiac, 222, *chart*, 221
Nectanebo, 4-5
Neptune, 50, 178, 226, 241
   Kennedy family and, 96, 101, 104, 107-9, 112, 113, 114, 169-70: Honey Fitz, 81, Joe, Jr., 84, Joe, Sr., 71, 73, 74, 101, 171-72, John, 57-58, PJ, 77, Robert, 46-48, 48-49, 49-50, Rose, 66, 70, Ted, 44, 168, 178-79
   keywords, 170, 231-34, 237-39, 240
Neutron Activation Analysis, 122-23
Newark, New Jersey, xi
New Left, ix-x, xi
New Times magazine, 124, 126

New York: legislation on curses, 12
New York Daily News, 140, 149-50
New York Review of Books, 147-48
Ngo Dinh Diem, 117, 148
Nigidius Figulus, 2
Ninth house, 66
Nix, Orville: film, 125-26
Nixon, Richard Milhous, 35, 139
   Hunt and, 139-40, 147, 148, 168
   synastry/horary suspect analysis, 134, 136, 139-40, 154, 156, 158, 243, 248, 251, *chart*, 161
Noonday house. *See* Tenth house
Nostradamus, 23
Numerology, 21-22

O

Octavius, 2-3
Oedipus, 20
Onassis, Aristotle: synastry/horary suspect analysis, 134, 136, 137, 156, 243, 248, 252, *chart*, 164
Onassis, Jacqueline Kennedy, 92, *chart*, 54
Opal, 16-17
Opposition, 223, 224
Orbs, 226, 245-48
Oswald, Lee Harvey
   Cuban activities, 127, 129, 147
   FBI and, 152
   Ferrie and, 145
   guilt or innocence, x, xv, 115-16, 117, 120, 121, 128, 142, 143, 148, 153
   other Oswald theory, 141-42, 153
   PSE test, 118, 151
   rifle used, 123-24, 143
   Russian defection, 150-51
   synastry/horary analysis, 134, 136, 141-43, 154, 156, 158, 243, 248, 251, *chart*, 116, 130, 155
O'Toole, George, 117, 118, 141

P

Palmistry, 22-24
Partile, 226

Penthouse magazine, 115, 117
Philip, King of Macedonia, 4
Pisces, 34, 217, 220, 221, 225
   element, 48
   quality, 107
   Ted Kennedy and, 43
Planets in elements: Kennedy family, 107
Planets in signs: Kennedy family, 103-14, *chart*, 103, 106
Pleaides, 59, 66
Pluto, 27, 226, 241
   Kennedy family and, 81, 107-9, 112, 113-14, 169, Honey Fitz, 81, Joe, Sr., 71, 73, 74, 78, PJ, 78, Robert, 51-53, Rose, 66, 70
Polygraph, 117-18, 151
Pontchartrain, Lake, 145
Posited, 227
Prayer, power of, 13, 14, 18
Presidential deaths, 207-12, 214
Presidential elections
   1976, 193-94, 195-96, 214, *chart*, 194
   1980, 205-6, 211, 214, *chart*, 205
   twenty-year cycle, 207-16
Progressions, 116
Pronouncements of doom, 12
Prophecies, 19-20
Psychological Stress Evaluator (PSE), 117-18, 141, 151
Pyramids, 17

Q

Quadrants, 227
Qualities of signs, 106, 107-8, 172. *See also* Cardinal; Fixed; Mutable
Quincunx, 223, 224

R

Radziwill, Princess Lee, 92
Reagan, Ronald: synastry/horary suspect analysis, 134, 136, 137, 156, 243, 248, 251, *chart*, 169
Reincarnation, 20-21
Retrograde, 225, 227

Retrogressive involution, 178
Reynolds, Warren, 143
Rising house. *See* First house
Rising sign. *See* Ascendent
Rockefeller, Nelson, 115
   1976 election, 199-203, 204, *chart*, 200
   synastry/horary suspect analysis, 134, 136, 137, 156, 243, 252, *chart*, 163
Rolling Stone magazine, 145, 148
Roosevelt, Franklin Delano, 208, 209
   Joe Kennedy and, 89, 171-72
Roselli, John (Don Giovanni), 140
Rubirosa, Porfirio, 89
Ruby, Jack
   CIA and, 129
   Oswald murder, 119, 128, 153
   synastry/horary suspect analysis, 128-30, 134, 136, 154, 156, 158, 248, 252, *chart*, 163

S

Sagittarius, 217, 219, 221, 225
   element, 48
   quality, 107
Saturn, 30, 146-47, 177-78, 226, 241
   /Jupiter Cycle, 207-16: in Air, 213, 215, in Earth, 212
   Kennedy family and, 110-11, 113: Honey Fitz, 81, Joe, Sr., 74, John, 57-58, PJ, 76, 79, Robert, 48, Rose, 65, Ted, 41, 45
   Wynn family and, 29-30
Scorpio, 26-27, 178, 180, 217, 219, 221
   element, 48
   Kennedy family and, 96, 101-3, 104, 105, 114, 179-80: Robert, 51, 105
   keywords, 230-31, 234-35, 239-40
   quality, 107
   rulers, 27
SDS. *See* Students for a Democratic Society
Seers, 19-20
Self-fulfilling prophecies, 12-13, 15-16, 69-70
Semisextile, 224

Semisquare, 223, 224
Setting house. *See* Seventh house
Seven Sisters. *See* Pleaides
Seventh house, 56, 101, 224
Sextile, 132, 224
Shared lineage, 21
Shaw, Clay, 128
Shearer, Norma, 89
Shriver, Eunice. *See* Kennedy, Eunice
Sibyl, 3
Signs, 217-22
    Kennedy family activity, 103-14, *chart*, 103, 106
Sinatra, Frank, 95
Sirhan, Sirhan B., xv, 52, 53, 148
Sixth house, 72, 73
Skakel, George, Jr., 37, 38
Skakel, Mr. and Mrs. George, 37
Smith, Harry, 18
Smith, Joe, 124
Solarscope, or solar chart, 39, 99-100, 227
Soviet Electrotechnical Institute, 150
Square, 131, 223, 224
Station, or Stationary, 227
Stellium, 172, 227
Stevenson, Adlai: synastry/horary suspect analysis, 134, 136, 137, 154, 156, 243, 248, 251
Stork Club, 91
Stressful moment analysis, 134-37, 158, 241-43, 248-52
Students for a Democratic Society (SDS), xi
Sturgis, Frank
    CIA and, 140
    synastry/horary suspect analysis, 133, 136, 138, 144, 145, 148-50, 154, 156, 158, 243, 247, 251, *chart*, 157
Sun, 224, 226, 242
    Kennedy family and, 42-43, 109, 110, 111, 112, 113
Suspects, synastry and horary analysis of
    circumstantial evidence, 138-41
    clues, 141-54

    critical moment stressful aspect, 134-37, 158, 241-43, 248-52
    involvement potential, 154-58
    motive potential, 133-34, 247-48
    no evidence, 137
    techniques, 131-33, 135, 153-54, 245-52
Swank magazine, 93
Swanson, Gloria, 89
Synastry analysis, 131-33, 153-54, 156, 245-52. *See also* Suspects
Szulc, Tad, 147

T

Taurus, 217, 218, 221
    element, 48, 213
    quality, 107
Tenth house, 101, 168, 224
Third house, 53
Time, Inc., 120
Time chart, 99, 227
Time magazine, 116
Tippit, Officer, 118, 143
Tombs, 16, 17
Tramps photos, 119-20, 144, 145-46, 148-49
Transcendences, 177-78
Transits, 116, 227
Trine, 132, 224
Trujillo, Rafael, 117
T-squares, 45-46, 76
Tunney, John V., 96
Tutankhamen's Tomb, 16
Twelfth house, 70, 84-85
Twenty-year cycle, 207-16

U

United States
    horoscope, 104, *chart*, 195
    presidents. *See* Presidential deaths; Presidential elections
    twenty-year cycle, 207-16
Uranus, 30, 59, 146-47, 226, 241
    Half-Cycle, 146-47
    Kennedy family and, 108, 111, 113-14: John, 58-59, PJ, 77
    Wright brothers and, 31

V

Ventura, Charles, 91
Venus, 30, 65, 224
    Kennedy family and, 109-10, John, 53-54, 55, Joe, Sr., 74, PJ, 77, Robert, 46, Rose, 65
Vestricius Spurinna, 1, 2
Vidal, Gore, 148
Virgo, 72, 217, 219, 221, 226
    element, 48, 213
    Kennedy family and, 105, 108, Joe, Sr., 72, Rose, 68
    quality, 107
    rulership, 60

W

Wallace, George
    assassination attempt, 148
    synastry/horary suspect analysis, 134, 136, 137, 156, 243, 248, 251, *chart*, 162
Warren Commission, 102, 116, 120, 122, 123, 136
Water (element), 31, 48, 106, 107, 221, 225
Watergate, 139-40, 147, 148
Wilson, Earl, 93
Wright, Orville, 30-32, *chart*, 31
Wright, Wilbur, 30-32, *chart*, 30
Wynn, Ed, 28-30, *chart*, 28
Wynn, Keenan, 28-30, *chart*, 29

Y

Yao, Emperor, 5

Z

Zapruder, Abraham, 125
    film, 116, 120-21, 122, 125
Zenith, 224
Zodiac, natural, 222, *chart*, 221